The
CHURCH
EPISTLES
Romans to
Thessalonians

The
CHURCH EPISTLES
Romans to Thessalonians

E.W. BULLINGER

COSIMOCLASSICS

NEW YORK

THE CHURCH EPISTLES: Romans to Thessalonians
Cover © 2007 Cosimo, Inc.

For information, address:

Cosimo, P.O. Box 416
Old Chelsea Station
New York, NY 10113-0416

or visit our website at:
www.cosimobooks.com

THE CHURCH EPISTLES: Romans to Thessalonians was originally
published in 1905.

Cover design by www.kerndesign.net

ISBN: 978-1-60206-047-0

The words of Christ, and the words of Paul are equal in weight and importance, inasmuch as both are recorded and given to us by the same holy Spirit; and are therefore equal in authority.

—from "The Seven Church Epistles"

CONTENTS

APPENDIXES—

Introduction

When the Apostle Paul preached the good news concerning Christ and His Church, at Ephesus, his ministry continued in Asia for the space of two years (Acts xix, 10). We read that the Word of God grew mightily and prevailed, and that **"all they which dwelt in Asia heard the word of the Lord Jesus."** And yet, at the close of his ministry, and of his life, he writes his last Epistle to Timothy, when he says " I am now ready to be offered, and the time of my departure is at hand" (2 Tim, i. 15): **"This thou knowest that all they that be in Asia have turned away from me."**

We are told, on every hand, to-day, that we must go back to the first three centuries to find the purity of faith and worship of the primitive church!

But it is clear from this comparison of Acts xix. 10 and 2 Tim. i. 15, that we cannot go back to the first century. No, not even to the apostle's own life-time!

This turning away could not have been merely personal; but must have included his teaching also. For in chap. ii. 18, he speaks of those "who concerning **the truth** have erred." In chap. iii. 8, he speaks of those who "resist the truth" In chap. iv. 4, he speaks of those who "turn away their ears from **the truth**" and are "turned unto fables."

It was Pauline truth and teaching from which all had "turned away."

It was this turning away from the truth as taught by the Holy Spirit through Paul, especially as contained in the epistles to the Ephesians, that led necessarily

(1) To the loss of the teaching concerning the Mystery; that truth concerning the one Body of Christ. The effect of this was at once to put everything wrong ecclesiastically, and to make room for all the various and different "Bodies," so-called, with all the

1

consequent divisions and schisms of the church.

Instead of recognising "the One Body" which God had had made, men set about making their own "Bodies" and Sects! and with this ecclesiastical confusion came the loss of the truth as to the Christian's perfect standing in Christ as having died and risen in Him.

2. Next, after this, went the truth of the Lord's promised return from heaven; and of resurrection, as the one great and blessed hope of the church. Other hopes, or rather fears, came in their place, and "death and judgment" took the place of those lost hopes. Having lost the truth of what God had made Christ to be unto us, and the joy as to our standing thus given, in looking for that blessed hope, preparation for death and judgment was the necessary result, and therefore

3. The next thing to go was the truth as to what God had made us to be in Christ; and "justification by faith" and by grace was lost. The way was now open for the full tide of error to come in: and it came in, like a flood, with all the corruption and superstition which ended in centuries which have the significant description "the dark ages."

Everyone is familiar with the term, and with the fact. But what were the dark ages? How did they come? They were not brought on suddenly by some untoward event. There must have been some cause, something that made them possible. The corruption is historical. The eastern churches to-day are in similar darkness. And the Western churches, where the Reformation has not removed it, are in the same darkness.

The reformation itself—what was it, but the beginning of a recovery of these great truths? The remarkable fact is that the recovery of these truths has taken place *in the inverse order* to that in which they were lost.

Justification by grace through faith was the first great truth recovered at the Reformation. This was the truth over which that great battle was fought and won, though the victory was far from complete. For not until the nineteenth century had well begun did the Lord's return from heaven begin to become again the blessed hope of His church. In later years the subject has become more and more precious to increasing numbers. But this great and "blessed hope" is not yet really learned, because it ought to be the natural outcome of truth received and held, instead of being treated as an independent subject artificially produced. It must come from the heart into the life, and not be merely held and retained in the head, if it is to be productive of the blessed results seen in the Thessalonian church. It must be learned experimentally as a vital and essential part of our standing as Christians, and not be studied as if it were an extra subject, in order to produce Thessalonian fruit. Hence, it is that we more often see prophecy taken up as a study, rather than as the result of waiting for God's Son from heaven.

The last of three truths to be recovered is the truth taught in Ephesians; and it is only in our own day that we see any real sense of the loss, with any real effort to recover it.

The truth of the Mystery, as it was the first to go, so, it seems, is the last to be recovered.

It is with the hope of doing something to recover this truth that these papers have been written on the Church Epistles. May the Lord use them to bring back vital truths to their proper place, that their power may be felt in the hearts and seen in the lives of an increasing number of the members of the Body of Christ.

The cause of all the confusion around is that thousands of those who profess to be Christians know little or nothing of these Church Epistles. There is no other profession which they could enter without being able to pass a satisfactory examination in the text-books set forth for that purpose. There is no position in life that any one could apply for without being asked how much one knew of its duties and responsibilities. But the Christian "profession" is treated in quite a different manner, and as quite a different matter. Anyone may undertake that, and all the while be totally ignorant of these Church Epistles:—"The Creed, the Lord's Prayer and the Ten Commandments," are considered as *sufficient* for Christian position and profession. Hence the almost total neglect of these Epistles. The four Gospels and the Sermon on the Mount are taken as the essence of Christianity, instead of the Epistles specially addressed to Churches. Hence the great ignorance of Christians as to all that God has made Christ to be unto His people, and all that He has made them to be in Him. Not knowing their standing in Christ, and their completeness and perfection in Him, they are easily led into error concerning their *state* and their *walk*. Many, who know they are justified by grace, yet seek to be sanctified by works.

Nothing but full knowledge of what is revealed for our instruction in these Church Epistles will effectually deliver us from all the new doctrines and schools of thought which find an entrance into our midst.

May the great Head of the Body the Church, own this effort, and use it and bless it to the deliverance of many from all the variable winds of doctrine, and build them up in their most holy faith.

The Seven Church Epistles.
THE IMPORTANCE OF THEIR ORDER.

It is a serious blow to Inspiration when the importance of one part of Scripture is exalted above another. To do this is to reduce the Bible to the position of any other book, and practically to deny that the whole is made up of "the words which the Holy Ghost teacheth."

This is done in the present day when, according to the new Ritschlian School, *The Teaching of Jesus* us exalted above the Teachings of the Holy Spirit by Paul, as though they were a rivalry between the two.

The words of Christ, and the words of Paul are equal in weight and importance, inasmuch as both are recorded and given to us by the same Holy Spirit; and are therefore equal in authority. That authority is Divine: and no difference can be made between them without jeopardising the very essence of Inspiration.

That there is a difference is clear. But this difference arises from failing to rightly divide the word of Truth as to the various Dispensations of which it treats.

What He said on earth is necessarily of the highest importance to us dispensationally as showing how, through His rejection by His people Israel, "the salvation of God has been sent to the Gentiles" (Acts xxviii. 28). But that teaching was given to special persons under special circumstances, and it must be interpreted and applied accordingly. It was not designed as a compendium of instruction for the Church of God, for the Church was not then being formed, and, as a matter of fact, the churches to whom the epistles were addressed did not at that time possess the four Gospels as we have them. On the contrary Christ expressly said, "I have yet many things to say unto you, but ye cannot bear them now. Howbeit when He, the Spirit of truth, is come, He will guide you into all truth (R.V., 'all the truth'): For He shall not speak of (or from) Himself;

5

but whatsoever He shall hear, that shall He speak; and He will show you things to come. He shall glorify Me: for He shall receive of Mine, and shall show it unto you. All things that the Father hath are Mine: therefore said I that He shall take of Mine, and shall show it unto you" (John xvi. 12-15).

May we not ask How, When and Where this promise and prophecy was fulfilled? Does this promise refer to use only as individuals, and to a subjective personal communication of the Holy Spirit to each individually? Or, Are we to look for some formal and special realisation of the Lord's words?[1]

What is meant by "all truths," or, as the Revised Version has it, "all the truth," into which the Holy Spirit was to guide the Church? Where are "the things of Christ" which He was to show unto us? Does it mean that the Holy Spirit shows one truth to one person and another to another person, and these are so different that those who receive them proceed to quarrel as to which is the truth? It cannot be!

Where are we to look then for this specially promised teaching and guidance?

Surely, when we take these words of Christ, in connection with His last seven-times repeated injunction from the glory, we are to look for some specific fulfilment of such a definite promise as this.

All those parts of the promise, "He shall guide . . . He shall

---

1. If this guidance is not individual can it be collective, or find its fulfillment in the Church of God as a whole. A mistaken view of these words has led mere ecclesiastics to see in these words the figment called "the inspiration of the Church" (see an article in *The Expository Times,* for Oct., 1898, in which this is affirmed). The difficulty with regard to the Church of Rome is at once raised, and is evaded by maintaining that "moral inspiration" must precede and be the foundation of the "doctrinal inspiration," and this "moral inspiration" is seen "in all that greater care for the poor, in all that wider sympathy for suffering, in all that deeper horror of bloodshed, in all that greater purity of life, in all the profounder sense of sin, in all that true love of simply, unaffected goodness," &c., &c.

And this is the popular theology of the present day substituted for Christianity by which "the Christian faith" (instead of being the revelation of the Holy Spirit in these seven epistles) has for its striking feature the "power of assimilating itself to the advancing knowledge of the human race"!

speak . . . He shall show you . . ." etc., are very precise, and must surely have a specific performance in some definite teaching of the Spirit specially addressed to "the churches" as such, and not merely to the experiences of individuals.

Where are we then to look for this, if not in the epistles addressed to churches, as such, by the Holy Spirit?

How many churches were so addressed? How many Bible students are there who can say at once how many there are? We have not yet found one who could do so! What a solemn comment this fact is as to the universal disregard of the Lord's last injuction!

Seven churches were addressed as such by the Holy Spirit. *Seven* being the number of spiritual perfection.[2]

Is it not remarkable that the Holy Spirit addressed seven churches and no more: exactly the same number as the Lord Himself addressed later from the glory?

The seven epistles of the Holy Spirit by Paul had already been written and read, and neglected and practically forsaken, when Christ sent His own seven to those seven churches in Rev. ii. and iii. This is evident when we compare Acts xix. 10 with 2 Tim. i. 15. See the Introduction, page 1. Some would tell us to go back to the first three centuries to find primitive Christianity in its purity. But these Scriptures show that we cannot even go back to the first century. The only successors the Apostle knew of were likened to "grievous wolves" (Acts xx. 29).

The seven churches to which the Holy Spirit addressed His epistles by Paul are Romans, Corinthians, Galatians, Ephesians, Philippians, Colossians, and Thessalonians.[3]

In these epistles we have the perfect embodiment of the Spirit's teaching for the churches. These contain the "all truth," into which

---

2. There were nine epistles altogether so addressed, two being addressed to the Church at Corinth, and two to "the Church of the Thessalonians." And *nine* is the square (or completeness) of Divine perfection: *three* times *three* (3 X 3).

3. The other epistles are "General" (John), or are addressed to "Hebrews," or "to the Twelve Tribes" (James), or to "the Dispersion" (Peter), or to individuals (Timothy, Titus, Philemon and 2 John).

the Spirit of Truth was to "guide" us. Where are we to look for this "all truth," if not here? These contain the things which Christ could not speak on earth, for the time for such teaching was not then. These contain the "things to come," which the spirit was to show. These "glorify" Christ. These contain the "things of Christ" which the Spirit was to receive and show unto us. Where else are we to look for the fulfilment of the Spirit's mission as the great Teacher, if not here?

Not only is the *number* of these epistles perfect, but their *order* is perfect also.

The order in which they come to us is no more to be questioned than their contents. But what is that order?

Is it chronological? No! Man is fond of arranging them according to the times when he thinks they were written, but God has not so arranged them. Indeed, He seems to have specially disposed of that for all times, and to have forbidden all attempts to arrange them thus, by placing the Epistles to the Thessalonians last of all, though they were written first.

This question, therefore, is settled for us at the outset, and so decisively as to bid us look for some other reason or the order in which the Holy Spirit has presented them for our learning.

In all the hundred of Greek manuscripts of the New Testament, the order of these seven epistles addressed to churches is exactly the same.

We have examined the five most ancient in existence, *viz.*, the Codex Vaticanus (Cent. IV.), the Codex Sinaiticus (Cent. IV.), the Codex Alexandrinus (Cent. V.), the Codex Ephraemi (Cent. V.), and the Codex Bezae (Cent. V. or VI.).

The general order of the books of the New Testament takes the form of groups, *viz.* (1) the Four Gospels, (2) the Acts, (3) the General Epistles, (4) the Pauline Epistles, and (5) the Apocalypse.

But while the order of these five groups varies in some of the MSS.: and the Pauline Epistles vary in their position with respect to the other four groups: and while the Pauline Epistles themselves vary in their order (*e.g.*, Hebrews in some cases following Thessalonians), yet *the order of these seven addressed to churches never varies.*

8

And, further though the four Gospels vary in their order (even in the five most ancient MSS.), these seven epistles are *never given in any other order* than that in which they have come down to us, an are given in our English Bibles.

That order therefore must present to use the line of study marked out for the churches by the Holy Spirit: a complete course which shall begin and finish the education of the Christian: a curriculum which contains everything necessary for the Christian's standing and his walk: the "all truth" into which the Spirit guides him. If he is ignorant of this, he must necessarily err, and be an easy prey for every new teacher who may rise up. He has no foundation on which he may securely rest: no anchorage on which he may depend. He is at the mercy of every "wind of doctrine" against which he has no protection. He will be carried away by any new "views" or teaching that may be put forth from time to time, for he has no standard by which to try them!

How can it be otherwise, if a Christian does not give earnest heed to what has been specially written for his instruction? Every word of Scripture is *for* him and for his learning, but every word is not *about* him. But these epistles are all about him and about the special position in which he finds himself placed with reference to the Jew and the Gentile; the old creation and the new; the flesh and the spirit, and all the various phenomena which he finds in his experience.

But now let us seek, in connection with the order in which these seven epistles come to us, for their division into *three* and *four*: for such division there must be.

We find it in the fact that three of these epistles stand out distinct from all the others as being *treatises* rather than epistles; and as containing so much more *doctrinal* matter as compared with that which is *epistolary*. This will be clearly seen when we come later on to notice the structure, which exhibits the contents of each.

These *three* epistles are Romans, Ephesians, and Thessalonnians.

And the *four* are placed between these three in two pairs each pair containing respectively "reproof" and "Correction" in contrast to the other three, which contain "Doctrine and Instruction"

9

(according to 2 Tim. iii. 16):

A | ROMANS (Doctrine and Instruction).
    B| CORINTHIANS (Reproof).
        C | GALATIANS (Correction).
  A | EPHESIANS (Doctrine and Instruction).
    B | PHILIPPIANS (Reproof).
        C| COLOSSIANS (Correction).
  A| THESSALONIANS (Doctrine and Instruction).[4]

We must leave the inter-relation of these epistles for our next chapter, and then having looked at them as a whole, and in relation and contrast to each other, we propose to consider each of them in the light of the whole, and in detail, as that detail is suggested and brought out by the special relation of each to the whole.

One fact, however, we may notice here, and that is the reason why *Thessalonians*, which was written before all the others, is put last of all. We may be certain that the order is perfect, and that the reason is divine. Is it not this?

The epistles to "the Church of the Thessalonians" are the epistles in which the special revelation is given concerning the coming again of the Lord Jesus. If we have "ears to hear," this fact

---

4. There is a further and different division of the seven into *four* and *three*. One within the other. We believe that the one we have given above is the true one and the one for our instruction. But there is another more technical, which interlaces it and enhances its perfection.

Four of the seven churches were in what became the *Western* half of the Roman Empire (now called Europe): and three were in what became the eastern half (now called Asia).

And each one answers to the other, West to West and east to East, as follows:—

West	ROMANS.	
	CORINTHIANS *West.*	
	GALATIANS	*East*
East	EPHESIANS.	
	PHILIPPIANS *West.*	
	COLOSSIANS	*East.*
West	THESSALONIANS.	

speaks to us, and it says"— (Listen!)

It is useless to teach Christians the truths learned connected with the Lord's coming, until they have learned the truths in the other epistles!

Until they know and understand what God has made them to be in Christ, and what He has made Christ to be unto them, they have no place for the truths concerning His return from heaven!

Until they have learnt what is taught concerning their *standing* and their walk, they will be occupied with themselves, and have no use for the truths connected with the Lord's coming again!

How important, then, that we should set ourselves to give heed to "what the Spirit saith unto the churches," and thank God for the opened ear, while we pray that, the eyes of our understanding being enlightened, we may see what has been thus written and given and sent to us for our learning.

The Seven Church-Epistles as a Whole: Their Inter-Relation.

We come now to consider the seven Epistles as a whole, and their inter-relation with each other.

We have seen that their *order*, like their *number*, is spiritually perfect.

We have referred to their division into *three* and four.

Let us first look at and compare the three—Romans, Ephesians, and Thessalonians.

They are treatises rather than letters,[5] and, taken together, they contain the whole revelation of the Spirit concerning Christian standing and state, both individually and collectively: the "all truth" into which He was to "guide" them (John xvi. 12).

Romans stands first, as containing the A B C of Christian education. Until its great lesson is learnt we know nothing. If we are wrong here, we must be wrong altogether. The Spirit has placed it first because it lies at the threshold of church-teaching.

It begins, "Paul, a servant of Jesus Christ, by Divine calling an apostle, *separated unto God's Gospel*, which . . ." and then he proceeds to unfold and reveal the gospel of God's grace. Man is shown to be utterly ruined and helpless, and ungodly sinners of the Gentiles and Jewish transgressors are alike made to know themselves as lost, and how they are justified by God. The doctrinal portion , consisting of the first eight chapters, shows what God has done with "sins" and with "sin," and how the saved sinner has died with Christ, and is risen with Christ—made a son and heir of God in Him.

---

5. Lightfoot (*Biblical Essays*, p.388) says (comparing Romans and Ephesians), "Both alike partake of the character rather of a formal treatise than of a familiar letter."

This is where EPHESIANS starts from! It begins, not with man, but with God. It approaches its great subject, not from man's necessities, but from God's purposes. It is occupied not so much with what the saved sinner is made in Christ, but with what Christ is made to be unto him.

It is God's point of view rather than man's. Notice how it begins (after the salutation), "Blessed be the God and Father of our Lord Jesus Christ, who hath blessed us with all spiritual blessings in the heavenlies in Christ," and Christ is shown to be the Head of all things, the Head of His Body, the church.

It is not so much the knowledge of ourselves which is the subject here, but the knowledge of God and of His purposes in Christ. Its first great prayer is "that the God of our Lord Jesus Christ, the Glorious Father, may give unto you the spirit of wisdom and revelation in the knowledge of HIM: the eyes of your understanding being enlightened, that ye may know what is the hope of HIS calling, and what the glorious riches (or the rich glory) of HIS inheritance in the saints. And what the exceeding greatness of HIS power to usward who believe" (i. 17-19).

In Romans we have the Gospel: in Ephesians the Mystery.

In Romans it is Jew and Gentile sinners individually: in Ephesians it is the Jew and Gentile collectively, made "one new man"—in Christ (ii. 15).

In Romans the saved sinner is shown as *dead* and *risen* with Christ: in Ephesians as *seated* in the heavenlies in Christ; while in Thessalonians he is seen for ever in glory with Christ.

Romans takes up the sinner in his lowest depths of degradation: and Thessalonians leaves him on "the throne of glory" for ever with the Lord: while, midway between, Ephesians views us now by faith as already seated with Him there. Our feet have been taken out of the mire and clay (Romans i.); they are now set upon the rock (Eph. i.); and resently we shall be upon the throne (1 Thess. iv.).

This is the relation which these three Epistles bear to each other. Viewed together, they form the A B C of the Christian faith, as distinct from all else in the whole Bible—nothing like it is found elsewhere. All the rest is written *for* us, for our learning. But this is all *about* us. The course of instruction is complete, and it is perfect. It commences at the lowest point and leaves us at the highest. We cannot proceed further in either direction. It begins with us on "the dunghill," and ends with us on "the throne of glory." It begins with us as "beggars," and ends with us among "princes." It finds us "poor," and makes us "rich." And having brought us "low," it "lifteth us up" to the highest heaven, caught up to meet the Lord in the air, "for ever with the Lord." The Lord's dealings are thus stated in 1 Sam. ii. 6-8, but how they were to be manifested in the Gospel of His grace is revealed only in these Epistles.

And now, having seen the mutual relation of these *three* Epistles, let us look at the other four.

Where are they placed? In our previous chapter we saw that they are placed in two pairs, the first pair coming after Romans, and the second pair after Ephesians. So that there are two Epistles arranged between the three.

Now the question is, Why are they so placed? There must be some design in this order; and it is not far to seek.

The first pair (Corinthians and Galatians) follow Romans because they exhibit departure from its special teaching.

The second pair (Philippians and Colossians) follow Ephesians because they exhibit departure from its special teaching.

So that we have the whole course of church teaching; the complete curriculum of Christian education, set before us as a whole, positively and negatively.

In the *three* (Rom., Eph., and Thess.), we have "doctrine" and "instruction." In the *four* (Cor., Gal., Phil., and Col.), we have "reproof" and "correction." Here is seen how "profitable" these Epistles are for the perfection (i.e., the complete education) of "the man of God," fitting him out for every duty and every emergency.

But there is a further correspondence between these *four* Epistles.

The first of each pair (Cor. And Phi.) Exhibits *practical* departure, while the second of each pair (Gal. and Col.) exhibits *doctrinal* departure. That is to say, in Corinthians we have *practical* failure as to the teaching of Romans, while in Philippians we have a failure to exhibit in *practical* life the teaching of Ephesians as to the unity of the members of Christ's Body. (We

14

shall show this more completely when we come to look at these Epistles separately).

On the other hand, in Galatians we have *doctrinal* failure as to the teaching of Romans. This is why Gal. and Rom. are so much alike, as everyone knows; though, all that most can see in this likeness is that they were "written about the same time"! The real difference is that what is stated as "doctrine" in Romans is repeated as "correction" in Galatians. Romans begins, "I marvel that ye are so soon removed from Him that called you into the grace of God unto another (or different) Gospel."

So in Colossians we have *doctrinal* failure as to the teaching of Ephesian truth.[6] In Ephesians, Christ is revealed and set forth as "the head of the Body." In Col. we have the doctrinal evils which come from "not holding the Head" (Col. ii. 19).

We may thus exhibit the structure of

THE SEVEN EPISTLES TO THE CHURCHES.

A | ROMANS. "Doctrine and Instruction." The Gospel of God: never hidden, but "promised afore." God's justification of Jew and Gentile individually—dead and risen with Christ (i.-viii.). Their relation dispensationally (ix.-xi.). The subjective foundation of the mystery.

B | CORINTHIANS. "Reproof." *Practical* failure to exhibitthe teaching of Romans through not seeing their standing as having died and risen with Christ. "Leaven" in practice (1 Cor. v. 6).

C | GALATIANS. "Correction." *Doctrinal* failure as to the teaching of Romans. Beginning with the truth of the new nature ("spirit"), they were "soon removed" (i. 6), and sought to be made perfect in the old nature ("flesh") (iii. 3). "Leaven" in doctrine (v. 9).

---

6. Lightfoot says, "The Epistle to the Ephesians stands to the Epistle to the Colossians in very much the same relation as the Romans to the Galatians. (*Biblical Essays*, p. 395)

A | EPHESIANS. "Doctrine and Instruction." The Mystery of God, always hidden, never before revealed. Jews and Gentiles collectively made "one new man" in Christ. Seated in the heavenlies with Christ.

    B | PHILIPPIANS. "Reproof." *Practical* failure to exhibit the teaching of Ephesians in manifesting "the mind of Christ" as members of the one Body.

        C | COLOSSIANS. "Correction." *Doctrinal* failure as to the teaching of Ephesians. Wrong doctrines which come from "not holding the Head" (ii. 9), and not seeing their completeness and perfection in Christ (ii. 8-10).

A | THESSALONIANS. "Doctrine and Instruction." Not only "dead and risen with Christ" (as in Romans) not only seated in the heavenlies with Christ (as in Ephesians); but "caught up to meet the Lord in the air, so to be for ever with the Lord." In Rom., justified in Christ; in Eph., sanctified in Christ; in Thess., glorified with Christ. No "reproof." No "correction." All praise and thanksgiving. A typical Church.

And now we see another reason why Thessalonians comes last. There are no Epistles beyond this, because there is no higher truth to be taught. The consummation is reached. This is the highest Form in the school of grace, where the Holy Spirit is the great Divine Teacher. "All the truth" culminates here—the "all truth" into which He was to guide the Church of God. It is led from the depths of degradation (in Romans) to the heights of glory (in Thess), caught up to be for ever with the Lord, and left there in eternal blessing "in," and "with," Christ.

This completes the view of the Seven Church-Epistles as a whole. In our next chapters we will look at each Epistle separately. (1) Exhibiting its structure, (2) showing from that, its special scope and teaching, and (3) giving such details (by translation and comment on special passages) as may be necessary for the education of Christians in the school of grace, so that they may know their proper standing in Christ.

It is interesting to note that Lightfoot's classification (*Bib. Ess.*, page 222, &c.) is practically the same, even though he arranges the Epistles chronologically.

He puts Thessalonians by themselves, as standing alone and distinguished by their connection with "*the Tribunal.*"

He places Cor., Gal., and Rom. together, as being all three connected with "*the cross*": while he places Phil., Eph., and Col. together, as being all three connected by their subject-matter with "*the Throne.*"

It is something to have such testimony as this in a matter so important. It is not affected by the different chronological order. The grouping is exactly the same; we have the same two groups, with Thessalonians standing out alone. This agreement with so thoughtful and learned a teacher will commend what we have written above to the attention of all earnest Biblical students.

The Epistle to the Romans.
(1) INTRODUCTORY

We come now to look at the Epistles separately, as addressed to the Seven Churches by the Holy Spirit, and we must look at each in the light of the whole.

Romans has been placed first as containing the first principles of Gospel teaching: and until we have mastered its lessons we can know nothing as to our true Christian position; and cannot go forward or learn anything else to our real advantage. All other truth which we may learn will be out of proportion and out of place if it is not subordinated to and dominated by the essential and fundamental truths written in the Epistle to the Romans.

The design and scope of the Epistle is the first important point, because this governs everything in it, and gives us the key to its right interpretation.

Set forth in its briefest form, we may thus present

THE EPISTLE AS A WHOLE:

A| i. 1-6. The Gospel (revealed before, never hidden).
   B| 7-15. Epistolary (Salutation, &c.).
      C| a| i. 16-viii. 39. Dispensational.
         b| ix.-xi. Practical.
     C|a| xii. 1-xv. 7. Practical.
        b | 8-13. Dispensational.
   B|xv. 14-xvi. 24. Epistolary (Salutations, &c.).
A | 25-27. The Mystery (hidden before, now revealed).

In this simple form we see at a glance the perfection of the design as well as the scope of the whole epistle.

We are struck at the outset with what is set forth first of all. It is

"THE GOSPEL OF GOD,"

which is the great subject of its revelation: *i.e.*, God's Gospel.

This is what meets our eye first, after the rejection of Christ as recorded in the sad history written in the four Gospels (completing the Old Testament as well as commencing the New Testament); after the further rejection of Christ and of the Holy Spirit's own testimony concerning Him, as recorded in the Acts of the Apostles. After all this we open the Epistle to the Romans, and the first thing which the Holy Spirit has to say to the churches is concerning "the Gospel of God." The good news is that, in spite of all the sin and wickedness of man, of all the ungodliness, both of Jew and Gentile, God will deal with man in grace; and how—notwithstanding man's unrighteousness, God can be just and yet the Justifier of the lost and ruined sinner who believeth in Jesus.

Does not this commend itself to our spiritual instinct as being perfect as to its order? What could be more appropriate or more blessed?

Then we have, at the end of the Epistle, as put in contrast with this Gospel which was "promised afore," the Mystery which had been hidden and "kept secret since the world began but now is made manifest." Romans goes on to explain the Gospel (from i. 16-viii. 39), while Ephesians takes up the mystery with which Romans ends.

It will be noted also that the prominent feature of the epistle is the long doctrinal portion which forms one half of the whole by comparison. This tells us that doctrine is the most important point, and dominates the whole.

The first six verses introducing the great subject of God's Gospel are worthy of close attention. They are terse and full of meaning. The following may be taken as the most exact translation we can give:[7]

"Paul, a bond-servant of Jesus-Christ, by Divine calling an

---

7. In this, and in all subsequent translations, we propose to give the exact translation itself in thick type, and running parenthetic, paraphrastic explanatory comments intermingled with it, but in different type, so as to keep it clear to the eye, and make it clear to the mind.

apostle (Acts ix. 4-16), **separated** (Acts xiii. 2) **unto God's Gospel, which He announced in former times through His Prophets in Holy Scripture,** *viz.,* **concerning His Son, who was born of David's line according to his flesh, and was powerfully** (this appears to be the force of *ἐν δυνάμει* taken adverbially) **demonstrated to be God's Son with respect to His holy spiritual body** (Psa. xvi.; Psa. ii. 7: Acts xiii. 33, and Heb. i. 5) **by the fact of a rising again of the dead** (Matt. xxvii. 52, 53, also ix. 25. Luke vii. 14, 15, and compare John v. 21), **even Jesus Christ our Lord, through whom we have received apostolic grace** (*lit.*,grace—yes, and apostolic grace, too; for this is the force of the figure of *Hendiadys* here used), **with a view to faith-obedience among all the Gentiles** (chap. xvi. 26; Eph. iii. 9; 1 Tim. iii. 16), **for His glory** (*lit.*, for His Name's sake). **Among whom ye** (Gentile believers in Rome) **are yourselves also—the called of Jesus Christ.**"

Before we proceed further, let us pause and note that each separate member of the structure given above partakes of the perfection of the whole; and, down to the smallest member, each has its own special and peculiar structure.

For example, the two *Epistolary* portions, one at the beginning and the other at the end of this Epistle (i. 7-15 and xv. 12-xvi. 24), though separated by so large a space, yet correspond to each other down to the minutest particular:

THE TWO EPISTOLARY MEMBERS COMPARED.
B (i. 7-15 and B (xv. 14-xvi. 24)

```
B | c |  i. 7.    Salutation.
  |   d |  8-10.    Prayer and thanksgiving (his for them).
  |     e |  10-13.  His journey to them.
  |       f |  14, 15.  His ministry.
B |           f |  xv. 14-21.  His ministry.
  |         e |  22-29.   His journey to them.
  |       d |  30-33.   Prayer (theirs for him).
  | c |  xvi. 1-24.  Salutations.
```

Here notice how the smaller members correspond in all

20

perfection with each other. It can be seen only by carefully reading and comparing the very words themselves; and the reader can do this equally well for himself. It would necessitate our transcribing large portions of the Epistle were we to show this here.

If the Epistolary part is thus perfectly constructed, we are sure that we shall find the great doctrinal portion no less perfect.

Its great subject is the answer to the ancient question,

"HOW SHOULD MAN BE JUST WITH GOD?" (Job ix. 2).

And the answer is, that while God's wrath is revealed against all ungodliness and unrighteousness of men (i. 18), His righteousness also is revealed (i. 16, 17).

It is important to note that, in this great doctrinal division (a. i. 16—viii. 39), the expression, "righteousness of God" (*i.e.*, Divine righteousness, because it includes the death and resurrection of the believer in Christ), occurs *eight* times; while the word λογίζομαι (*logizomai*), variously translated *imputed, reckoned,* or *counted,* occurs *twelve* times, because it is in the perfection of sovereign government that God chooses to impute Divine righteousness to the sinner.

These numbers (*eight* and *twelve*) agree with the fact that this Divine righteousness is perfected and procured by the death and resurrection of Christ (*eight* being the number of resurrection): and that it is *imputed* by God to the ungodly in His sovereign power (*twelve* being the number of governmental perfection).

The righteousness of God has been procured and revealed and imputed to the sinner, and this is the believing sinner's justification before him.

It is the object of this great doctrinal division of the Epistle to explain and set forth this foundation truth.

It consists of two parts: the first ending with Rom. v. 11, and the second beginning with v. 12.[8]

---

8. J. N. Darby has well and carefully distinguished these two portions with their separate subjects.

21

Expansion of "a": i. 16—viii. 39.
Doctrine.

a | D | i. 16—v. 11. SINS. The products of the old nature-the fruits of the old tree.
   | E | v. 12.—viii. 39. SIN. The old nature itself—the old tree itself.

Simple as this appears to be, it is really the most important key to the whole teaching of the epistle. No commentary or exposition is worthy of the slightest attention, which does not mark this distinction and division which occurs between verse v. 11 and v. 12; and which is not governed by this fundamental division, which we have marked as D and E.

Up to v. 11 (D) the great subject is SINS, as distinct from SIN; *i.e.*, the outcome of the workings and manifestations of the old nature, as distinct from SIN, which is the old nature itself. This latter is treated of in v. 12—viii. 39 (E). The distinction is most marked, and must be carefully noted and studied.

Up to v. 11 (D) the fruits of the old tree are first dealt with; and we are shown the corrupt workings-out of the evil which is by nature in every man; and the principle on which God can justify sinners, Jew and Gentile. While from v. 12 (E) the old nature itself is dealt with, and we are told by precept and example what God has done with the old tree itself, and what *we* are to do with it, *viz.*, to reckon it as having died with Christ.

Up to v. 11 (D) we are viewed in our natural condition as *"in the flesh."* From v. 12 (E) we are viewed in our new position as *"not* in the flesh," but *in Christ.*

Up to v. 11 (D) it is *we* who are "in the flesh." From v. 12 (E) it is the flesh that is in *us.*

Up to v. 11 (D) we are viewed as dead in trespasses and sins; while from v. 12 (E) we are viewed as having died together with Christ, and risen again in Him in newness of life.

The different conditions in D and E are *two different planes.* The only change is in our standing. There is no change of nature; only change of position or standing before God. The evil nature remains, but its power is limited, and bounds are set to it. It no longer reigns. It is no longer the master, and never again can be. The flesh does not become spirit, but our relations to it are changed. We were in it. "We all had our conversation . . .in the lusts of our flesh, fulfilling the desires of the flesh and of the mind" (Eph. ii. 3). This is the plane, or condition treated of in D (i. 16—v. 11). But now, having died with Christ—on the cross—and having been (in the purpose of God) crucified with Him *there*, we have also been "quickened together with Christ," and now stand before God "in Christ," and walk in newness of life. This is the subject of E (v. 12—viii. 39).

These are the broad outlines of the great doctrinal portion of this Epistle. We must fill them in a more detailed manner as we proceed, but this is sufficient to enable us to see the great and broad foundation of church-teaching deeply and firmly and securely laid.

This is the first letter of the new alphabet, which is to spell out such wondrous truths and bring to us a new revelation never before made known in its rich details to the sons of men as it is in this epistle.

It is ignorance of this foundation truth, which is the parent of most of the errors and false teaching of the present day.

The two natures are two great facts. Their workings and manifestations are seen and experienced by all. Those on the one (the lower) plane exhibit the workings of the new nature; and the awful conflict between it and the old is made manifest.

Nothing can alter these facts. Nothing can eradicate the experiences produced by them. No system of theology can change or explain them. It is only when we have learned and understand the explanation which God has given us here in Rom. i. 16—viii. 39, and have thoroughly mastered His teaching concerning them, that we can have or know and enjoy "peace with God."

This is what we all crave. This is what we all seek. But only those find it who learn it in "what the Spirit saith to the churches."

The Epistle to the Romans.
(IV.) CHAPTER i. 16—v. II.

Having seen the division of the great doctrinal portion (i. 16-viii. 39) into two parts: "SINS" (i. 16-v. 11) and "SIN" (v. 12-viii. 39); let us now look at these two parts separately.

It will not be necessary for us to examine in such detail the other Epistles, or even the remaining portion of this Epistle. But, as this is the foundation of the whole—the basis on which all other truth depends, the subjective foundation on which the Mystery rests, we cannot be too careful in learning its lessons. And, moreover, as departure from this teaching, or failure to learn it, is the source of all error as to the standing and walk of the Christian, no subject can be fraught with such importance as this.

Coming, then, to the first with such of these two divisions which has been denoted by the letter D, we now give its structure: for it is impossible to get at the true *interpretation* without first seeing the *scope;* and it is almost impossible to get the true scope without first seeing the *structure.* We must, therefore, ask our readers for their close and patient attention.

The structure of D is in the form of *Epandos:* in which the *first* member (g) corresponds with the *fourth* (g): and the *second* (h), with the *third* (h), as follows:—

24

EXPANSION OF D. ROM i. 16-v. 11, "SINS."

The old nature: and the fruits of the old tree.

D | g | i. 16, 17. The *power* of God and the righteousness of God, declared in the Gospel of God, revealing a righteousness from God.

    h | i. 18. The *wrath* of god revealed against all ungodliness and unrighteousness.

    h | i. 19-iii. 20. The *wrath* of God described and set forth.

  g | iii. 21-v. 11. The *power* of God and the Righteousness of God described and set forth, imputing a righteousness from God on faith-principle.

In this division, marked D (i. 16-v. 11), we get the *fruits of the old nature* set forth and dealt with both in Gentile and Jew; and we are shown and instructed how, in spite of all, God can justify the ungodly and give a Divine righteousness to the unrighteous. And, further, how His wrath is revealed against all who have not His righteousness, but are trusting in their own.

In this first division, we have the foundation of justification securely laid. It is mainly *objective:* showing what Christ is, as *for us,* as dying for the ungodly; and providing a Divine righteousness as our alone *standing* before God.

While the second division, marked E (v. 12-viii. 39), is mainly *subjective:* showing what Christ is *in us,* and our *state* as to ourselves, we have died with Christ and risen again in Him; possessing in consequence a new nature, in the power of which those who are thus justified can walk "in newness of life." This is the foundation which must be laid before the Mystery can be revealed by God or understood by us. That is to say, the Gospel of the Grace of God is the subjective foundation of the Mystery.

It is scarcely necessary for us to expand with further minuteness all the various members in the above structure.

In "g," the great thesis as to the Righteousness of God is stated in two verses (i. 16, 17): and in "h" "the wrath of God" is as clearly declared in one verse (i. 18). Then, in "*h*" and "*g*," these are explained and described in detail; but in inverse order, and at greater length. Thus:

25

EXPANSION OF "*h*" (i. 19-iii. 20).

The wrath of God against the ungodliness and unrighteousness of man described and set forth.

h | i | i. 19-ii. 1. Man's "ungodliness" stated.
      j | ii. 4-11. God's wrath revealed.
   i | ii. 12-iii. 20. Man's "unrighteousness" proved and set forth.

The member "i" (i. 19-ii. 1) is a most marvellous and complicated structure, corresponding to the depths and intricacies of man's ungodliness. We must not impede the great argument by giving it here, but relegate it to a note.[9]

It is the member "*g*" which now claims our attention. It is in inverse order to "*h,*" as implied by the *Epanodos* of D.

EXPANSION OF "*g*" (iii. 21-v. II).

The power of God, and the Righteousness of God revealed.

g | r | iii. 21-31. God's righteousness revealed in grace, as to its source, from Himself. *Objective.*
     s | iv. 1-25. The justifying of the sinner. Stated, proved, and exemplified.
   r | v. 1-11. God's salvation revealed in power, as to its effects in us. *Subjective.*

Here, then, we have, at last, the great revelation of the Gospel

---

9. EXPANSION OF "i" (i. 19-ii. 1)
Man's ungodliness stated.

i | k | i. 19, 20. God's *power* know. Ungodliness, therefore, without excuse.
     l | n | 21. The *glory* of God rejected.
         o | -21. Consequent mental corruption
           m | p | 22, 23. God's *glory* degraded.
               q | 24. Consequent degradation of body: and abandonment by God.
           m | p | 25. God's *truth* degraded.
               q | 26, 27. Consequent degradation of bodily passions: and abandonment by God.
     l | n | 28- The *knowledge* of God rejected.
         o | -28-31. Consequent mental corruption.
     k | 32, ii. 1. God's *judgment* known. Ungodliness therefore inexcusable.

26

of God. It is the member corresponding to "g," and the full detailed explanation of i. 16, 17.[10]

Now, we are in a position to receive this revelation from God by the Holy Spirit. Here is the full statement:—

TRANSLATION OF "r" (iii. 21-31).
God's righteousness revealed in grace as to its source, from Himself. Objective.

"But, now, apart from law" (*i.e.*, without the deeds of the law (iii. 20); relating to man's side of the question (iv. 2; xi. 6. Gal. ii. 16; iii. 10. II, R.V.), not to God's side) **God's righteousness stands manifested, being borne witness to by the Law** (Gen. xv. 6, etc., for Genesis forms part of "the Law"), **and the Prophets** (Hab. ii. 4)—even a righteousness of God (*i.e.*, a Divine righteousness), **which is through faith in Jesus Christ** (*lit.*, of Jesus Christ. Gen., of reference, *i.e.*, with reference to or concerning Him, chap. i. 3; Mark xi. 22; Acts. iii. 16; Gal. ii. 16, 20; Eph. iii. 12; Phil. iii. 9) **toward all**[11] **those all who believe: for there is no difference! for all sinned** (or, sinned once), **and do come short of the glory of God; being justified** (or finding their justification) **without a cause** (δωρεάν, *dōrean*, see John xv. 25: "they hated me without a cause" **by His grace through the redemption** (deliverance by ransom), **which is by Christ Jesus: whom God did fore-ordain** (*i.e.*, purposed and set forth) **to be a propitiation** (*i.e.*, a mercy-seat or

---

10.   THE EXPANSION OF "g" (i. 16, 17)
The power of God, and the Righteousness of God declared in the Gospel of God.

g | t | 16. Salvation by faith through God's power in *procuring* righteousness.
    | u | 17- A Divine righteousness revealed by God ἐκ πίστεως *ek pisteos)* on faith-principle, as regards Himself.
    | *u* | -17- A Divine righteousness revealed by God εἰς πίστιν *(eis pistin)*unto faith, exercised in us.
  | *t* |-17. Salvation by faith through Tod's power in *imputing* righteousness.

11. Some ancient authorities add the words "and upon all," but they are omitted by Lachmann, Tischendorf, Tregelles, and R.V.

propiatiory. *ἱλαστήριον, hilasteerion*, occurs only here and Heb. ix. 5. It means the place or vehicle of propitiation) **through faith in His blood, for the display** (*i.e.*, or exhibition) **of His righteousness** (*δικαιοσύνη, dikaiosunee*. The death of Christ demonstrates it by the fact that sin cannot be passed over, for "He will by no means clear the guilty," Ex. xxxiv. 7), **because of the putting aside** (*πάρεσις, paresis, a putting aside:* not (*ἄφεσις, aphesis, a putting away*. Hence, the temporary suspension of punishment which may be inflicted at some future time. Here, inflicted at the cross; and thus exhibiting God's righteousness in visiting it on Christ) **of the sins done aforetime** (*i.e.*, before this revelation of God's righteousness) **through the forbearance of God: for a display, I say, of His righteousness at this present season that He Himself might be just** (or, shown to be just, in not clearing Christ when He took our sins upon Himself) **and also** (*i.e.*, and therefore) **a justifier of him that believeth** (*ἐκ πίστεως, ek pisteōs, i.e., putting away* the sins of him who takes his stand on faith-principle, apart from "works of the Law," to which *ἐκ πίστεως* is always opposed) **in Jesus (the Saviour)."**

Here, at the outset, in this grand definition of God's righteousness, is set forth the great fact that it is the blood of Christ and not the life of Christ; the death of Christ and not the incarnation of Christ; with which we, as sinners, must begin; and which constitutes the manifested or revealed righteousness of God. The reckoning is not between Christ and us, but between Christ and God. This is why it is called "God's righteousness" and not Christ's. Hence, it is said that God raised Him from the dead: for "it is God that justifieth" (vii. 33).

Having thus laid this foundation, God can now erect upon it all. His purposes according to His own will.

But Christ's death has another aspect with reference to us. It was the penalty (or wages) of sin. Hence, it was the triumph of sin and death and the Law over Christ. It is here, therefore, that *we* come in: and it is here, in this connection, that Christ is set forth as the *ἱλαστήριον (hilasteerion)* or mercy-seat. Now, the mercy-seat was the propiatory-lid or covering of the Ark of the Covenant on and before which the blood was sprinkled seven times by the high Priest

28

(Lev. xvi.). This is the place on which God stands in the act of justifying the ungodly.

And this is the word which the Holy Spirit chooses in order to explain the matter to us and to illustrate it. He begins here, with sins, and propitiation through the death and blood-shedding of Christ: and then, in chap. iv., He shows how works have no place in this justifying, for Abraham was a Gentile sinner (Josh. xxiv. 2), and "ungodly" when he was justified; and David describes the blessedness of the man whose sins are "covered" (i.e., atoned for). This covering embraces the two-fold fact that God's righteous-requirement had been satisfied, and His righteousness imputed to the sinner. Christ was "delivered [to death] for our offences (i.e., on account of them), and was raised from the dead for our justifying": i.e., for God's justifying of us, that God might be just even whilst He justifies. The word here is δικαίωσις (dikaiōsis) quite different from the other words employed. The Greek termination "-sis" answers to our English "-ing," and this word is used only of God's activity in justifying us. It occurs only here and v. 18, where "justification of life" means a life-long justifying, or a justifying which gives life."[12]

This section concludes with "r" (v. 1-11), setting forth the *subjective* effects of God's salvation in us, in all its blessed and wondrous results. We will give the first few verses, because these set forth the truth afterwards more fully developed and expanded in chap. vii.

EXPANSION OF "r" (v. 1-11).
God's salvation revealed in power, as to its effects in us.
Subjective.

"Having been justified, (or, on being justified then) **therefore by faith** (i.e., on the principle of faith as opposed to the works of the

---

12. See our next chapter for complete lists of these two words with their definitions.

law) we have[13] (not get, or obtain but possess), **peace with God through our Lord Jesus Christ, by whom we have obtained and possess** (aor. and perf., in one) **access** (or, introduction) **also** (this is a link with Eph. ii. 18 and iii. 12) **by faith, into this grace in which we stand** (fast and firm), **and we rejoice** (or boast). The Jewish καύχησις (kauchēsis) is boasting which is "excluded," iii. 27, because based on human merit; while the Christian kaucheesis is not excluded, because it rests on the grace of God and the Word of God) **in hope of the glory of God** (i.e., of God's presence which we hope to enter). **And not only so, but we rejoice also in our tribulations, knowing that tribulation worketh patience;** (endurance in holding out under trials), **and patience, approval; and approval, hope; and our hope does not make us ashamed** (i.e., does not disappoint or prove illusory) **because the love of God** (which He has to us) **has been shed abroad in our hearts by the Holy Spirit who was given to us,"** etc.

Thus, the first half (i. 16-v. 11) of this great doctrinal division (i. 16-viii. 39) ends.

The second half (v. 12-viii. 39) we shall reserve for our next chapter.

---

13. This Textual Critics and R.V. read ἔχωμεν (echōmen), *let us have, instead of* ἔχομεν (echomen), *we have.* But the documentary evidence is not sufficiently weighty to mar the whole of the context, which is all *doctrinal assertion* and not *practical exhortation.* A single stroke "w" for "o" is the only difference, and it was probably first made by some scribe who did not understand the scope of the passage. Even if ἔχωμεν, echomen the Subjective, were the original reading, it would be put, by *Enallage,* for the Indicative; as is often the case.

The Epistle to the Romans.

(3) ROM. v. 12-21.

We come now to consider the last half of the great Doctrinal division of the Epistle to the Romans (v. 12—vii. 39) which is indicated in the structure (Page 22) by the letter E; and we shall have first to discover its own peculiar structure; so that we may see its scope, *i.e.*, its great central aim and design, and the points to which this directs our attention. Then we shall be in a position to understand its statements and its words.

As this is the most important portion of the whole, we shall have to examine it with great minuteness, and seek to make it as plain as possible.

EXPANSION OF E (v. 12—viii. 39).
SIN.
The old nature—the old Tree itself.

E | v | v. 12-21. Condemnation to death through a single sin (τὸ παράπτωμα) of one man; but justifying unto life through a single righteous act (τὸ δικαίωμα) of one man.

　　w | vi. 1-vii. 6. We are not in sin, because we died with Christ.

　　w | vii. 7-25. Sin is in us, though we are risen with Christ.

　　v | viii. 1-39. "No condemnation" to those who are alive unto God in Christ Jesus, and in whom is the πνεῦμα χριστοῦ (*pneuma Christou*) or the new nature, because of condemnation of sin in the flesh.

From this we get a view of the whole division, and the four parts of which it is composed.

The great point for us to notice in it is, that we no longer read of SINS; but only of SIN. That is to say, it is not now the products of the flesh (*i.e.*, the old nature)—but the old nature itself: it is no longer the fruits of the tree, but the old tree itself. These two are called by various names.

The old nature is called "sin," "the flesh," "the body of sin," "the body of this death" (*i.e.*, this mortal, dying body), "the carnal mind," etc.

The new nature, which is imparted, is called "spirit," "the spiritual mind," "the inward man," "Christ in you," "$\pi\nu\epsilon\hat{\upsilon}\mu\alpha\ \theta\epsilon o\hat{\upsilon}$ (*pneuma theou*) Divine spirit," "$\pi\nu\epsilon\hat{\upsilon}\mu\alpha\ \chi\rho\iota\sigma\tau o\hat{\upsilon}$ (*pneuma Christou*) Christ-spirit (viii. 9). This does not mean the Holy Spirit, for there is no article. It is literally "spirit of Christ," or as we have expressed it, "Christ-spirit." The next verse (viii. 10) puts the meaning in another form, going on to the conclusion which flows from the statement—"and if Christ be in you, the body [$\mu\acute{\epsilon}\nu$, *indeed*] is dead because of sin; but the spirit (the new nature) is life because of righteousness." This Christ-spirit must be in us as the Holy Spirit's creation before He can bear witness with it. It is this "Christ-spirit" which is the great subject of viii. 1-15: and the "spirit" in these verses should be spelt with a small "s;" and not with a capital "S" till the Holy Spirit is spoken of in verse 16 (as we shall see when we reach chap. viii.).

But we are anticipating: only, however, because of the importance of distinguishing, all through this portion, between "flesh," or the old nature, on the one hand, which is spoken of as "sin"; and "spirit," which is spoken of as the new nature, *i.e.*, Divine nature.

The subject of this whole section therefore, after stating the facts as to the entrance of sin and death by one man, Adam, goes on to deal with the wondrous, effects of the Lord's death and resurrection upon "in," "and the effects of the communication of the new nature (*i.e.*, "the spirit of life which is in Christ Jesus") to the believer, giving him power to walk in the newness of this life. So that, as Christ "died unto sin," so does he in "spirit" live "unto God."

This last section is, as we have before said, *subjective*, and refers to *Christ in us* (*i.e.*, *identification* with us); whereas in the

32

former section (i. 16—v. 11), it is *Christ for us* (*i.e., substitution instead of us*).

Now let us look at the four members separately. We have underlined them above by the letters "v," "w," "*w*" and "*v*":—

EXPANSION OF "v" (CHAP. v. 12-21).
The first man and the second.

v | a | c | 12. By one man's "sin" (ἡ ἁμαρτία *hee hamartia*), all sinned, and death passed upon all.
　　　　　　d | 13. Sin not imputed where there is no law.
　　　　　　e | 14. The reign of death.
　　　　　b | 15. Not as by one sin, so the gracious gift.
　　　　　b | 16, 17. Not as by one man, so the gracious gift.

　a | c | 18, 19. By one man's righteous act (δικαίωμα, *dikaioma*) many made righteous (and the counterpart).
　　　　　d | 20. Sin imputed when law came (and the counterpart).
　　　　　e | 21. The reign of sin and death (and the counterpart).

Now this beautiful structure, instead of needing further explanation, really explains to us the great mysteries concerning the entrance and consequences of "sin" and "death" by Adam on the one hand, and of life and righteousness by Christ on the other.

We must notice that in all these structures the corresponding letters (roman and *italic*) belong to and mark corresponding subjects: so that, for example "c" and "*c*" not only correspond as to the subject, but are consecutive as to argument, all between them being practically in a parenthesis. And so with the other letters and verses.

Consequently, chap. v. 12 reads on to verses 18, 19, with which its corresponds; overleaping verses 13-17. Indeed these verses (13-17) are actually put in a parenthesis in the A.V.:—

12. **Wherefore, just as** (verse 12 commences the structure, and is, therefore, the introduction of the first member of the comparison;

33

the second being stated in the member corresponding with it in verse 18; it is not the conclusion of what has been already said) **by one man SIN** (*i.e.*, in itself, and in the sinful nature which it originated in us) **came into the world, and by means of sin** (as the appointed penalty, Gen. ii. 17; iii. 19), **death; and thus** (by this connection of sin and death) **death extended** (passed through) **unto all men because all sinned** (in Adam, and were born in sin. Compare Gen. i. 27 with v. 3) . . .[here comes in the parenthesis, verses 13-17, and then the second member of the comparison is continued in verse 18].

. . .

18. **Consequently, then as by means of one act of transgression** (this must be the meaning, according to the A.V. margin and the R.V. text, *i.e.*, one transgression not one man, because it would be in direct opposition to verse 17, where we have the word ἑνός (*henos*), three times, and each time with the article; to show that it there means one *man*, in contrast with this verse 18, where the article is purposely omitted, so as to exclude the man, and guide us to the true meaning). Judgement came **upon all men upon condemnation** (or sentence of condemnation, *i.e.*, death); **so by one righteousness act also** (*i.e.*, the obedience of Christ in death, referred to in verse 19) grace came **upon all men to a justifying** issue fraught with **life.** (As in verse 12 we have two evils, "sin" and "death," so we have, in verse 18, the two corresponding but opposite blessing, *viz.:* "justifying" and "life" as the act and gift of God, while in verse 19, we have the same two blessings in their operations as regards ourselves). **For as by the disobedience of the one man** (Adam) **the many were constituted sinners; so, too, by the obedience** (*i.e.*, the obedient righteous act explained in verse 18) **of the one** (Christ) **the many will be constituted righteous.**

Similarly, verses 13 and 20 must be read together consecutively. Also verse 14 and 21.

But we have omitted these, because verse 12 with verses 18 and 19, as rendered above, are the important portion. The Greek is elliptical as to its grammar, perfect as to its structure, and precise as to its employment of words.

It was the one act of the one man that brought in sin, and involved the penalty, *death*. It was the one act of the one man that

34

paid that penalty. The words δικαίωμα (dikaiōma) and δικαίωσις (dikaiosis) must be carefully distinguished in verse 18. Failure in distinguishing them leads to failure in apprehension of their teaching. These are not the words of Paul, but of the Holy Spirit. They are therefore chosen with absolute perfection, and employed with the utmost precision. The whole argument turns on their technical use.

The word δικαιοσύνη (dikaiosunee) righteousness, denotes the quality or attribute of righteousness. As God's righteousness it is the word which marks the condition of those who are accepted by God, in Christ.

δικαίωσις (dikaiōsis) justifying, denotes the action of the judge in declaring or pronouncing or recognizing a person δίκαιος (dikaios) right or just, as he should be. The termination -σις (-sis) marks the action as in progress, just as our English termination "-ing" does. Justifying is therefore, the meaning of the word in the only two places where it occurs, once in each of the two sections of this division, viz: in chap. iv. 25, Christ "was raised for our justifying," denoting the activity of God in justifying: and in this chap. v. 18, through the δικαίωμα (dikaiōma) or righteous act of Christ, a δικαίωσις (dikaiosis) or justifying action of the judge pronounces the sinner just, and confers life thus reversing the penalty of death (compare v. 12).

In verse 18 δικαίωμα (dikaiōma) is set in contrast with δικαίωσις (dikaiosis). Now the termination -μα (ma) denotes the thing done, the result or product of whatever the noun (or root means.[14] So that while the one (dikaiosis) denotes a justifying, the other (dikaioma denotes the just or right thing that is done.

No uniform rendering will therefore be sufficient for the translation of δικαίωμα, (dikaiōma), because it depends in each case on what the righteous act or thing is, that is done. The context alone can decide what righteous act it is. We give the five

---

14. For example—from the verb πράσσω (prassō) to do, we have πρᾶξις (praxis) the doing, and πρᾶγμα (pragma) the thing done.

From ποιέω (poieō) to make, we have ποίησις (poieesis) the making, and ποίημα (poieema) the thing made, etc., etc.

35

occurrences of the word in this epistle:—

i. 32. "Who knowing the judgement, *(i.e., the righteous sentence) of God*" concerning those who commit certain sins.

ii. 26. "If the uncircumcision keep the righteousness *(i.e., the righteous requirements) of the law.*"

v. 16. "The free gift is after many offences unto justification" *i.e., a righteous acquittal.*

viii. 4. "That the righteousness *(i.e., the righteous requirements) of the law might be fulfilled in us.*"

Now the meaning of the word is perfectly clear form the way in which the Holy Spirit uses it in all these passages. It cannot be different in the verse we are considering, ver. 18: "Even so, by *the righteous act* of one man also, grace came unto all men to a justifying issue fraught with life" and thus undoing the one disobedient act that introduced death (ver. 12).

We know what the one act of Adam was: but the question now is, What was the one righteous act of Christ? In the next verse it is called His "obedience" in contrast to the one act of Adam's disobedience. What was Christ's great act of obedience? We have the Divine answer—[15]

"He became obedient unto death, even the death of the cross" (Phil. ii. 8). That was the extent to which His obedience went, paying the penalty of sin. That was the great propiatory act which "God hath set forth to be a propitiation through faith in his blood" (iii. 25), which the corresponding member and subject which is

---

15. It occurs five times elsewhere (or ten times in all): viz,

Luke i. 6. "Walking in all the commandments and ordinances (*i.e., the righteous requirements* ordained) of the Lord, blameless.

Heb. ix. 1. "Then verily the first covenent had also ordinances (*i.e., righteous requirements*) of Divine service.

Heb. ix. 10. "Which stood only in meats and drinks, and divers washings and carnal ordinances (*i.e., righteous requirements,* margin, *rites or ceremonies*).

Rev. xv. 4. "For thy judgements (*i.e.,* thy righteous judgements) are made manifest.

Rev. xix. 8. "The fine linen is the righteousness (*i.e., are the righteous awards*) of the saints," *i.e.,* not their own righteousness, but the award given to the saints.

36

being here explained.

The attempt to get rid of this great central truth, or to minimize it, is one of the saddest blots on man's "theology". Here we have the death and bloodshedding of Christ set forth as the one ground on which God can justify us and constitute us righteous in His own righteousness. Righteousness does not come by law-keeping as Gal. iii. 21 so emphatically declares.

"For if there had been a law given, which could have given life, verily righteousness should have been the law." Therefore it could not have come to us by Christ's law keeping apart from His death and blood-shedding. Christ's obedience formed His own righteousness, in order to give virtue to His sacrifice; for the sacrifice must be "without spot or blemish." It was not the spotlessness of the sacrifice which made the atonement, but its blood. "The wages of sin (not sins) is death:" and life can come now only through death; and, Christ having died, the gift of God—eternal life comes to us through that death; and our righteousness comes through Christ's death, and not "by the law;" not by His law-keeping but by His suffering the penalty of the law and receiving in His own person "the wages of sin," that we might have life through his death, and not through His life.

If Christ's obedience during His life was our obedience, then we stand as He stood. And if so why did He die? How could there be any penalty? Penalty for what? If He fulfilled all righteousness and His people stand before God as Christ stood, how could there possibly be any penalty? Christ did not die for himself as we are plainly told. He died for others—for us: but if we "fulfilled all righteousness" in Him, why should He have died for us.

No! His obedience in life gave virtue and efficacy to His sacrifice, and His death gives us righteousness. *We* begin with Him in iii. 24, 25, at, and as, the mercy seat; and then we see how, after that (in chap. v. 18, 19), the glory of His person gave perfection to His work, and all is given to us in Him.

If Scripture teaches us anything it teaches us this, that the only title to acceptance with God, is in and by the sacrifice of Christ once and for ever offered on the Cross.

We are accepted in all His acceptableness, but only by

imputation. The justifying of Rom. v. 18, comes through the propitiation "in his blood" as stated in iii. 25 and v. 9. All the value of his obedience centres in His death. This is the meritorious ground on which alone we can stand in righteousness before God.

The Epistle to the Romans.

In our last chapter we dwelt on the first great member (v. 12—21) of the second half (v. 12—viii. 39) of the doctrinal portion of the Epistle.

There are four such members, and we now come to look at the second member (vi. 1—vii. 6) marked "w" in the structure of this division on page 31.

This second member also yields its treasures when we examine its own peculiar structure, which gives us the key to the particular point which it is designed to impress upon us.

EXPANSION OF "w" (vi. 1—viii. 6).
The subject of which is
We are not in "sin," because we died with Christ.

w | f | vi. 1-11. Death to "sin," and Life in Christ. *Association with Christ in death and life.*

    g | 12-24. Sin no more dominion, because no longer under law, being alive from the dead.

       h | 15-16. The old master and servant.

       h | 17-19. The new master and servant.

    g | 20-23. Free from "sin" and alive from the dead (Illustration of "g," by master and servant).

  f | vii. 1-6. *Association* with Christ in death and *life*. (Illustration of "f," by husband and wife).

We have to bear in mind that the great subject of this whole division is SIN and not *sins*. The old nature (which is called "sin"), and not its results. The old tree, and not its fruits.

Having learnt the great fact, *objectively*, as to the entrance of "sin," and its penalty, death (v. 12-21), we come in this member (vi.

1—vii. 6) to be taught directly as to "sin" itself subjectively, in its special relation to ourselves and our experience.

In no department of Theology is seen more clearly how opposite is the teaching of Romans, here, to that which is of man and of *human* reasoning. Romans' teaching is that all are absolutely ruined by sin, and wholly unable to restore themselves to Divine favour. The popular teaching is that man is not wholly ruined, and that therefore he is able to do something to regain the Divine favour, and promote his own happiness by progress in virtue and knowledge.

Having learnt this opposition in Rom. i. 16—v. 11, as to justification *objectively*, we are now to be Divinely taught as to its bearing on the believer *subjectively*.

The subject is opened by stating an objection which, from that day to this, is the first manifestation of the natural man's enmity to salvation by free grace. It is most plausible: If the sinner is justified without works; and if, where sin abounded, grace has much more abounded, may we not continue in sin that grace may still more abound and be still more abundantly displayed?

Let any of our readers state the doctrines of grace to a natural man, and he will be found at once to use this objection in retort. It will come naturally and spontaneously from the natural heart.

But before we consider the Divine answer to it, it will be necessary for us to notice how the first member "f" (vi. 1—11) of the structure given above is itself constructed.

THE EXPANSION OF "f" (vi. 1—11).
Death to "sin" and Life in Christ. Association with Christ in Death and Life.

f | i | vi. 1-3. Death to "sin" cannot entail life in sins.
  | j | 4-7. By *association* with Christ in His death and *life* there cannot be continuance in sin.
  | j | 8-10. By *association* with Christ in death and *life* there must be life with God.
  | i | 11. Death to "sin" entailing life with God.

Now we are prepared to understand the words employed, having before us in this structure the scope and design as the key to their meaning. The words, looked at from this point of view, interpret the truth to us; instead of our having to interpret the words according to our ideas of truth.

TRANSLATION OF "i" (vi. 1—3).
Death to "sin" cannot entail life in sins.

What, then, shall we say? Are we to go on in (the commission of) **sin in order that (God's) grace may abound? Far be the thought!**[16] **How shall** (such as) **we who died** (in person of our substitute, Christ) **to sin** (still) **live in it?** or (if you do not understand this) **are ye as ignorant that as many of us as were baptized unto Christ Jesus unto His death were baptized.**

The question is merely asked as to whether as many of those who had been baptized really knew what it meant? When Christ was on earth He said: "I have a cup to drink that ye know not of"; "I have a baptism to be baptized with" (Matt. xx. 20-22; Mark x. 38, 39). That cup was his death (Matt. xxvi. 39). That baptism, then, must have been His burial (for it was something which the sons of Zebedee could undergo). Christ went under, not the water, but the earth. And as many as had been baptized unto Christ are reckoned as having been buried with Christ. It was a figurative burial, whereby the person professed to become the disciple of Christ, owning Him as Lord; no longer to live in the service of sin; but, as associated with the One who had died and was buried, he professed to have died with Him and to be alive to God in Him, to serve God who had done so great things for him, in Christ who died and was risen.

We have here the first preliminary statement of the great fact which is to be developed later on in the teaching given to us in Ephesians and Colossians.

This the only reference to baptism in Romans. Paul had administered both circumcision and baptism during the first portion of his ministry "to the Jew first" among the synagogues. He refers to what

---

16. Fourteen out of the fifteen occurrences of this expression occur in these Church Epistles—10 in Romans, 3 in Gal., and 1 in 1 Cor.

41

he, as a Jew, had received and practised; and he draws an argument from it.

But we hear no more of it. For when he comes in Ephesians and Colossians to speak of "the Body of Christ," and the Headship of Christ, it is Christ who is the Baptizer with the One Spirit.

Speaking of Baptism in Romans, he does not teach the Mystery, but he connects it with "the gospel promised afore." But speaking of the Headship of Christ, it is the baptism with the Holy Spirit which he connects with it. In other words the old ordinance of baptism is connected with the Gospel "promised afore" (Rom. i. 2), while the further revelation (in Eph. and Col.) is connecting the One Spirit by the one Lord into the One body and is connected with the Mystery never before revealed. The Mystery is mentioned in this epistle in its closing words as forming the starting point of, and connecting line with, the further teaching to be given in Ephesians.

TRANSLATION OF j vi. 4-7.
*By association with Christ in His death and life there
cannot be continuance in sin.*

We were buried, then, with Him by our baptism unto (His) death to the end that like as Christ was raised up from among the dead by the glory (*i.e.*, the glorious power) **of the Father, so we also should (get to) walk in newness of life** (*i.e.*, life-newness, or, freshness, with emphasis on newness). **for if we are become planted together[17] in the likeness of His death we shall exist (in**

---

17. To plant and to build are terms used by God throughtout His word for the setting of a People or a Nation as a corporate unity on the earth (Exod. xv. 17, Jer. xviii. 9, Amos ix. 15). The same words are used by the Holy Spirit in 1 Cor. iii. 6—10 in reference to the preaching of the Gospel "to the Jew first." "I have planted"—"as a wise master-builder I have laid the foundation." By the baptism of Jews and Gentiles in confession of Jesus as Lord and Christ, those who before were separated as circumcised were "planted together," and became "members one of another." The church so constituted contained persons of two nationalities, recognised as "one body in Christ," though all that this meant could not yet be explained, for the Headship of Christ was not yet preached.

The force of this Scripture, Rom. vi. 5, lies in the contrast between the two verbs, "we are become" γεγόναμεν (past), "we shall be or exist" ἐσόμεθα (future). The saints had become "one body" on earth by baptism unto Christ's

42

the likeness) **of the resurrection** (of Him, *i.e.,* His resurrection) **also; knowing this, that our old man**[18] **was crucified together with** (Him) **to this end, that** (the domination of) **the body of sin,** (this slave of sin) **might be brought to nought** (or rendered inoperative) **that no longer should we be slaves to sin. For he that died** (or had once for all died, *i.e.,* with Christ, ver. 8) **is cleared** (justified) **from sin."**

Here, noted again it is "sin," not sins. It is the old man and the old tree that is being dealt with. The whole passage is so clear that it required no explanation at our hands. It was written in order to explain these wondrous truths to us. He who has once died (as the believer has in Christ) has already suffered the penalty, and received the wages of "sin." He is therefore cleared, and thenceforth discharged from all its legal claims. But it is in Christ that he died, *and is reckoned to have died with Him, as expressed in the* counterpart of His death.

What the consequence of this is, is explained in
"j" (vi. 8-10).
By association with Christ in death and life, there must be life with god.
"Now if we did die together with Christ we believe that we shall live also with Him (the future tense is used here to show that though this is spiritual now, it will soon be gloriously literal and real) **knowing** (as we do) **that Christ, having been raised from among the dead, dieth no more: death hath dominion over Him no more. For** (the death) **He died, He died once for all** (as the penalty due) **to sin, but in that He liveth, He liveth** (with respect) **to God."**

---

death. This was temporary. They were to exist in the likeness of His resurrection by the baptism with the Spirit whereby he was raised from among the dead, a Spiritual body no longer associated by an ordinance upon the flesh), but by the indwelling Spirit united to Christ and one to another. [They were afterward, taught that Christ had abolished in His flesh the law of commandments in ordinances (Eph. ii. 15).]

18. In these epistles only here, and Eph. iv. 22, and Coloss. iii. 9.

This is the consequence of Christ's death as regards himself; and now the actual result of it to us and as regards ourselves in our own experience is stated in the fourth member.

"i" (vi. 11).
Death to "sin" entailing life with God.

"Likewise reckon ye also yourselves (as[19]) dead persons (with reference) **to sin** (not sins!) **but alive** (<i>i.e.,</i> living persons) (with respect) **to God, in Christ Jesus."[20]**

This again interprets spiritual facts to us; and needs no human comments, which only darken the meaning and impede the flow of the doctrine.

Now we come to the second member of the larger section.

"g" (vi. 12-14).
"Sin" (the old man) no more to have dominion.

g | k | 12. Sin not to reign in mortal body (exhortation).

    | 1 | 13-. The members therefore not to be surrendered as instruments of unrighteousness (negative).

    | <i>l</i> | -13. The members to be surrendered to God as instruments of righteousness (positive).

    k | 14. Sin not to lord it, because no longer under law but grace (reason for exhortation in ver. 12).

The translation of "g" (vi. 12-14).

"Let not therefore sin (your old nature) **reign in your mortal body so as to obey its desires, neither present ye [21]** (or be presenting) **as instruments** (or weapons for it to use) **of**

---

19. The verb, <i>to be</i>, is omitted by all the best Greek Texts.

20. The words, <i>our Lord,</i> are evidently the addition of a later scribe, and are omitted in all the best Texts.

21. Present tense, <i>be presenting,</i> with a continuous present sense, meaning <i>it is at no time to be done.</i>

44

unrighteousness to sin. But present[22] yourselves unto God as alive from among the dead, and your members as instruments (or weapons) of righteousness unto God. For sin (your old nature) will not be your lord (with emphasis on your); for ye are not under law but under grace."

The third and fourth members which go together.
h, vi. 15, 16 and *h*, vi. 17-19.
The subject illustrated.

h | m | 15, 16. Acts of obedience indicate the master served.
     n | 17. Change of acts of obedience.
     n | 18. Change of master served.
   m | 19. The master served indicated what the acts of obedience should be.

The translation of h, and *h*; vi. 15-19.
What then? Shall we sin (or are we to sin, Sub. aor. According to L T Tr A) **because we are not under law, but under grace? Far be the thought! Know ye not that to whom ye present yourselves as servants for obedience, ye are servants to him whom ye obey: whether of sin** (*i.e.*, the old nature) **unto death, or of obedience unto righteousness. But thanks be to God that** (although[23]) **ye were servants of sin, yet ye obeyed from the heart that form of teaching in which ye were instructed** (lit. To which ye were delivered). **Having then got your freedom from sin** (*i.e.*, from the dominion of the old nature) **ye are made servants of righteousness. I speak after the manner of men on account of the weakness of your flesh: for as ye once presented your members in bondage to uncleanness and to lawlessness to (work)**

---

22. Aorist tense, which refers to the act itself as a once accomplished fact: lit. *Have presented yourselves once for all.*

23. The δε (*de*) *but,* in the latter part of the clause implies the ellipsis of μέν (*men*) *though,* in the former part.

lawlessness; so now present[24] your members in bondage to righteousness (work) **holiness.**

Having thus got our freedom (as verse 18 explains) from the lordship of sin (*i.e.,* from the dominion of the old nature we have become the bond-servants of righteousness).

Further illustration of this great fact is afforded by

The fifth member "*g*" (vi. 20-23).
(Illustration of "g" (vi. 12-14), Master and Servant).

```
g │ o │ q│  20-. Servants of "sin."
  │   │  r │  -20. Free men as to righteousness.
  │   │     p │ 21. The fruit shame, and the end death.
  │ o │    r │ 22-. Free men from sin.
  │   │ q │ -22-. Servants of God.
  │   │      p │ -22, 23.  The fruit, holiness, and the end
  │   │        │ eternal life.
```

The following is the translation of "*g*" (vi. 20-23).

"For when ye were servants of sin (*i.e.,* the old nature) **ye were free in the matter of righteousness. What fruit then had ye at that time in the things of which now ye are ashamed? For the end of those things is death** (vi. 23). **But now, having got your freedom from sin** (your old nature) **and once made servants to God, ye have your fruit unto holiness, and the end eternal life** (vi. 21). **For the wages of sin** (the old nature) *is* **death, but the free gift of God is eternal life in** (and through) **Jesus Christ our Lord."**

We pass on to the last member of this section, *viz:* The first six verses of chap. vii. which correspond with vi. 1-11.

Just as in the previous section on *justification,* two illustrations were given in (1) Abraham, (2) David (chapter iv): so here in this section, as to *the effects of justification,* there are also two

---

24. Again we have the aorist tense, marking the act as done once for all, *have them presented.*

illustrations: (1) master and servant (vi. 16-23), and now (2) man and wife (vii. 1-6).

EXPANSION OF "*f*" (vii. 1-6).
Illustration of "*f*" (vi. 1—11) *Man and Wife.*

f | s | vii. 1. Lordship of the law during life.
     t | u | 2. Death releases from its claim.
        v | 3. Result (Re-marriage lawful).
     t | *u* | 4-. We dead to the law in Christ.
        v | -4. Result (The way open for union with Christ in resurrection.
   s | 5-6. Clearance from the law of death.

The following is the Translation of *f* vii. 1-6.

"Are ye ignorant, brethren (for I speak to them that know) (or have learnt) law (*i.e.*, understand through having learnt how law works, and what are its effects) **how that the law is lord over a man as long a time as he may live? For the married woman is bound by law to her living husband** (*i.e.*, so long as he is alive) **but should the husband die she is free from the law of (or, as to) the husband. So then, if while the husband is alive she be (married) to another man, she will be called an adulteress: but should her husband die she is free from the law, so as not to be an adulteress though she be (married) to another man.** (And it goes without saying that, if she die herself, of course she is free.[25]) **Wherefore, my brethren, ye too were once for all dead to the law by the body of Christ, that ye should be** *joined* **to another, even to Him that was raised up from among the dead, in order that we may bring forth fruit to God. For when we were in the flesh the sinful passions** (with emphasis by *Enallage* on "sinful,") **which were called out through the Law wrought in our members to bring forth fruit unto death: but now we have been (once for all)**

---

25. By the figure of *Enthymena* one of the premisses is omitted, and the writer passes on to the *conclusion*. This explains the change: for it is we who died in Christ, and are therefore free from the law *in order that we may be* united to Christ in resurrection.

47

cleared from the Law, having died to that in which we were holden: so that we serve in newness of spirit, and not in boldness of letter."

It is difficult to express this in English. But it means that we now serve, not as we once used to do the letter of the Law; but, following the instincts of the new (spiritual) nature our obedience is quite a different thing altogether. Once we used to obey because of some vows and resolutions which we had made; but now we serve according to the new instincts of our spiritual nature, and on quite a new and different principle.

This completes and exhausts the expansion of w. (vi. 1—vii. 6), the second member of this last great doctrinal division. It is a revelation of new and wondrous truth which directly concerns the Church of God; and is the voice and instruction of the spirit to those who are members of that Church.

The Epistle to the Romans.

Rom. vii. 7-25.

We now come to the *third* member of the second division of the great doctrinal portion of this Epistle. (See page 31). Its structure is as follows:—

> "*w*." ROM. vii. 7-25.
> *Sin is in us though we are alive to God in Christ.*

w | x | 7-12. The Law: its conflict with the *Old* nature.
| | y | 13-16. Manifestation of the Law in the conscience (the consent).
| | y | 17-20. Manifestation of the law in the experience and the life (the doing).
| x | 21-25. The Law: its conflict with the *New* nature.

This section sets before us the true action and effects of the Law; its conflict with the old nature and the new ("x" and "x"), and its action on the conscience and on the life ("y" and "y").

The soul is now established in its standing before God, as having died with Christ, and as having a life in association with Christ. Its *relationship* to the Law has now been settled. The old nature is to be reckoned a having died, in Christ, to all its claims. But its workings are still experienced. Its action is still felt. What is the cause of this? We are now to have God's answer to this important question: and the answer is that "Sin," *i.e.*, the Old nature, is in us, notwithstanding we have life in Christ, Who died unto sin and lives unto God.

The previous member, vi. 1-vii. 6 (with which vii. 7-25 corresponds), showed that we are not in "sin": *i.e.*, not reckoned as

49

being any longer in the flesh, or in our old natural state; inasmuch as we are reckoned by God, and are to reckon ourselves, as having died with Christ. Now we are to learn the converse of this. **"Once we were in the flesh"** (vii. 5), **and then the sinful feelings (or instincts) which were brought out by the law wrought in our members to the bringing forth of fruit for death.** But now, (the fact is) **we were cleared** (by identification with Christ in His death) **from the law, on dying to that wherein we were held, fast, so that we should serve in newness of spirit, and not in oldness of letter"** (compare ii. 29 and 2 Cor. iii. 6: *i.e.*, on a new plane, of which the essence is "spirit," or the new spiritual nature, so that things are now done spontaneously in fulfilment of the new spiritual desire, and not on the old principle of duty, characterized by a bondage to the letter). The basis of the whole service is changed. We do not now serve because of vows, or pledges, or resolutions, which were bondage; but, in a liberty which is the outcome of the New nature ("spirit") which has been implanted in us.

This action of the Law with respect to the two natures is now to be shown.

In "x" (vii. 7-12) we see its conflict with the *Old nature* before regeneration.

In *"x"* (vii. 21-25) we see its conflict with the *New nature* after regeneration.

While, between these, we have its manifestation within us; in "y" (13—16) in the *conscience,* and in "y" (17-20) in the consequent experience in the *life and walk.*

Nothing can be more important than clearness of view as to this revelation from God-the Divine unravelling of the experiences of every soul which is the subject of Divine grace.

The whole of this member ('x') is in the first person, and its structure is as follows:—

"x." ROM. vii. 7-12.

The Law: its conflict with the old nature.

x | a| 7. The Law not sin.
    b | 8. Sin using the commandment as a point of attack.
      c | d | 9-. Alive without sin.
           e | -9-. Revival of sin.
           f | -9. Result: death.
      c | d | 10-. Commandment ordained to life.
           e | -10-. Discovery on account of sin.
           f | -10. Result: death.
    b | 11. Sin using the commandment as a point of attack.
  a | 12. The Law holy.

Verse 5 had just declared that "when we were in the flesh the instincts of our sins were stirred through the law." This section therefore takes up this point and commences with the same question as the corresponding section (or member, vi. 1). **"What then shall we say? Is the Law sin? Far be the thought; nay, I had not known** (or recognized) **sin** (*i.e.*, known it to be sin), **except by Law, for I had not recognized appetite** (*i.e.*, the desire of the Old nature) **to be sin unless the law had said, 'Thou shalt not covet.'**

8. **But I say that sin, having got a point of attack through the commandment, worked-out in me every kind of appetite. For apart from Law sin is dead.**

9. **I, however** (in my Old nature) **was alive, apart from law, once; but as soon as the commandment came sin revived, and I died.**

10. **And the commandment, that was intended to give me life, was itself found to be my death.**

11. **For sin, having got a point of attack by the commandment, beguiled me, and by it slew me. So that the law** (as a whole) **is holy, and each mandate holy, and just, and good."**

Having thus seen the conflict of the law with the Old nature, we are now to see, in

51

The manifestation of the law in the conscience.

y | g | 13. Manifestation to the conscience of the evil of sin.
    h | i | 14-. *The Law* spiritual.
        j | -14. *The man* sinful— fleshly.
    h | i | 15-. The will like-minded with *the Law.*
        j | -15. The will like-minded with *the man.*
  g | 16. Consent of the will to the good in the Law.

The translation is as follows:–

13. **Is goodness then, to me, become death? Far be the thought. Nay; it was sin** (*i.e.,* the Old nature) **in order that it might be seen to be sin** (and to bring its own self to light), **working out death in me through that which is good, in order that sin might become overwhelmingly sinful through the commandment.**

14. **For we know that the law is spiritual, but I myself am fleshly** (*i.e.,* made of flesh), **having been sold under** (the power of) **sin** (the Old nature).

15. **For what I carry out** (same words as ver. 13, *working out*) **I do not approve**[26]**: for not what I will practise I but, what I hate, that I do.**

16. **But if what I do not will, this I do, I consent to the law that it is good** (or right).

This completes the manifestation of the law in the conscience. And now we have in

---

26. The Greek means *I do not know,* but it includes here to know in the sense of approving, like the old English *allow (i.e., allaud, to praise, or approve,* as in Psa. xi. 6, P.B. Version, "the Lord alloweth the righteous."

"y." ROM. vii. 17-20,

The manifestation of the law in the life and experience.

y | k | 17. No more I myself that do evil, but Sin that dwelleth in
         | me.
         l | 18-. No good in me as to my flesh.
            m | -18-. Will favours good, but it has no ability.
            m | -18.   Will favours good, but it is not performed.
         l | 19. Evil is what I perform.
      k | 20. No more I myself do evil, but Sin that dwelleth in me.

The following is the translation:–

17. **Now, however** (*i.e.,* this being the state of the case), **it is no longer I myself who am carrying** (or working) **it out, but the indwelling sin within me** (*i.e.,* my Old nature).

18. **For I know that in me, that is, in my flesh** (my Old nature), **good does not dwell: for to will is present with me, but how to carry out the good I do not find.**

19. **For it is not what I do, that I will; but, the evil which I do not will, this I practise.**

20. **But if what I do not myself will, this I do, it is no longer I myself who carry** (or work) **it out, but the indwelling sin in me** (*i.e.,* my Old nature "sin" which dwelleth in me).

Having had in "x" (vers. 7-12) the Law's conflict with the Old nature, we now come to

"x." ROM. vii. 21-25.

The conflict of the Law with the new nature.

x | n | 21. Two opposing principles present in the one man.
         o | p | 22. Delight in God's law.
              q   23. Present conflict.
         o | *p* | 24.- Distress at sin's law.
              q | -24, 25-. Future deliverance.
      n | -25. Two opposing services continued in the one man.

The following is the translation:—

21. **It follows then that I find this law with me who will to do the good,** [I find, I say] **that the evil is present with me.**

53

22. **For I delight in the law of God according to the inward man** (*i.e.,* the new nature).

23. **But I see a rival law in my members, carrying on war against the law of my mind** (*i.e.* my new nature), **and aiming at leading me captive to the law of sin** (*i.e.,* to my Old nature) **that is in my members.**

24. **O wretched man that I am, who shall rescue me out of this body of death?** (*i.e.,* out of this mortal body).

25. **God—I thank Him,** [*He shall deliver me*] **through Jesus Christ our Lord. It follows then that I myself serve with the mind indeed** (*i.e.,* with my New nature), **God's law, but with the flesh** (*i.e.,* with my Old nature), **sin's law.**

Thus does the Holy Spirit lay bare to our view His own explanation of the origin and nature of the experience possessed by every soul which is the subject of the grace of God, and which has the gift of the New nature as the result and sign of God's justifying.

In this section, it is not the experience of one man in two successive stages of his experience, but it is the co-existence of the two experiences in the one man at the same time.

Those who fail to learn this lesson as to the conflict of the Law, first with the old nature (vii. 7-12), and ever afterwards (21-25) with the New nature, will not only be in constant perplexity themselves, but will fall into that error of doctrine which is corrected in the Epistle to the Galatians, chap. iii. 3.

Having begun with truth as to the New nature (called "spirit") they will, if they depart from it, seek to improve the Old nature. This is the error which Gal. iii. 3 corrects, **"Are ye so senseless? having begun in spirit** (in the New nature) **are ye now being perfected in flesh** (*i.e.,* in the Old nature)?

This is what thousands are doing everywhere around us. They are seeking to perfect, or, at least, to improve, the old nature. Not seeking the truth or reality of the two natures. they are seeking to improve the only one which they are acquainted with. This is ever the work of all who are ignorant of what the Spirit is saying to the churches. Be they Buddhists, Romanists, Perfectionists, they are all alike endeavouring to convert the "flesh" into "spirit," to subdue the "flesh," and by all kinds of arts, and articles, and rules, and regulations, pledges and badges, to improve the Old nature. All, alike, formulate "rules for holy living," ignorant of the fact which lies before us in this Scripture that the Old nature knows no rules, and that the New nature needs no rules. Instead of reckoning the Old nature to have died with Christ, they are ever seeking *to put it to death!* Instead of reckoning that it was crucified with Christ upon the cross, they are exhorting us to crucify it for ourselves. When God crucified it with Christ He did it once for all. But those who know nothing of this tell us to crucify it. They do not tell us, how we are to do it; but, knowing how futile is the effort, they tell us we must do it every day. But, no! once would be enough if it could be done at all. And, thank God, it has been done. HE has done it Himself on Calvary; and now, we, in spite of all our conflict, in spite of the flesh (the Old nature) lusting against the spirit (the New nature) and the spirit against the flesh; in spite of the fact that these are contrary the one to the other, so that we cannot do the evil which the flesh would have us do, and we cannot do the good that the spirit would have us do; in spite of this conflict, we find "peace with God," and rest in the truth—that the child of God has his Old nature, which can produce no good thing—and he has a New nature, which "doth not commit sin" (1 John iii. 9), "sinneth not" (1 John v. 18). And, further, that God reckons the Old nature as having died with Christ and as having therefore no more dominion over us, though the conflict in actual experience is ever present with us.

Those who learn this lesson have learned that the Old nature is so bad that nothing can ever improve it, and that the new nature *is so perfect* that it needs no improvement.

It is "spirit," and its life cannot be "deepened."

It is "newness of life," and cannot be made "higher."

The only way to mortify, now, "our members which are upon the earth," *i.e.,* the organs though which the Old nature works, is to "set our affections" (or "mind") on the things which are above; on these blessed realities which God here brings before us as being involved in "His calling." The more we know of His wondrous calling the more shall we walk worthy of it. But to occupy ourselves with (or to mind) our "walk" is to "mind" the "earthly things"; and it will never improve that walk, and will but defeat the very object we seek to obtain.

The Epistle to the Romans.

Romans viii.

We now come to the important eighth chapter, which in our structure on page 31 was marked by the letter *"v,"* and seen to correspond with "v," (chap. v. 12—21); the subject of "v" being *"condemnation,"* and that of *"v"* (viii. 1—39) being *"No condemnation."*

"v" (v. 12—21) shows us how *"condemnation"* was brought in by one man, Adam, and to all who are in the first Adam.

"v" (viii. 1—39) shows us how there is now *"no condemnation"* to those who are in Christ Jesus, the last Adam.

The expanded structure of *"v,"* (Rom. viii. 1-39), is as follows:

v | a | viii. 1-4. "No condemnation" for those who are in Christ: and the reason.
| b | 5-15. The "spirit" (or New nature) in us: now leading *us.*
| *b* | 16-27. The Holy Spirit's witness with our "spirit" (or New nature), leading *it.*
| *a* | 28-39. No separation from Christ for those who are in Christ: and the reason.

The first great truth which comes out in this structure is this: that in "b," (viii. 5-15), the subject is the New nature in us, which is called "spirit"; in contrast to the "flesh," or the Old nature. But in *"b,"* (viii. 16-27), the subject is the Holy Spirit Himself as a Person.

As the Holy Spirit is not the subject in verses 1-15, the word spirit should begin with a small "s," and not a capital "S," in that section.

57

The reader must remember that there is absolutely no authority whatever as to whether the word "spirit" should begin with a capital letter or not. There is nothing in the Greek to show it, and translators differ among themselves. The humblest Spirit-taught reader is able to judge as well as the greatest of Greek scholars. The point must be decided wholly by the *scope* of the passage; and the scope can be found only from the structure.

The structure, therefore, at once revolutionizes the common interpretation of this chapter; and leads us into the true meaning of what the Holy Spirit is saying to the churches.

It will therefore be necessary for us to set this chapter out come what fully, in order to establish our case.

The four great members of which this chapter is composed are so large as to suggest at once that they must have each its own separate and important structure, giving in turn its own key to the space of the various sections.

Thus the structure of the seven epistles as a whole is the key to the interpretation of each epistle separately.

The structure of each epistle becomes the key to the interpretation of its various members: while the structure of the various members gives the scope of the several passages, and leads to the true interpretation and translation of its phrases, and the meaning of its words. We first take

"a" (viii. 1-4).

"No condemnation" and the reason.

a | c | 1. No condemnation to those in Christ.

  d | 2. The law of the "spirit" (or the New nature) sets us free from the claims of the Law.

  c | 3. Condemnation of sin in the flesh (the Old nature) by God sending His Son in the likeness of sinful flesh.

  d | 4. The law of the "spirit" (or the New nature) fulfils the righteous requirements of the Law.

In these four brief statements all the arguments of the foregoing chapters are summed up; and we are introduced to the glorious consequences which flow from their teaching.

The word "therefore" refers back (according to the structure on page 31), to the end of "v" (chap. v. 12-21), and takes up the

58

argument from that point. The subject of "v" (v. 12-21), as we have seen, is *"condemnation"* for all who are in the first man, Adam. The subject of *"v"* (viii. 1-39), which corresponds with it, is *"no condemnation to those who are in Christ."* It is remarkable that the word *κατάκριμα (katakrima) condemnation,* occurs only in these two corresponding members in the whole New Testament, viz: v. 16,18 and viii. 1. It thus forms a link between the two members.

The word "therefore" refers to this fact: that as Christ by His obedience unto death caused grace to reign, because of righteousness, unto eternal life by Jesus Christ. . . . "therefore, there is no condemnation to them which are in Christ Jesus." The structure of the whole epistle puts chap. vi. 1 to vii. 25, practically, into a parenthesis.

Chap. viii. begins in the Greek with the negative, which, by the figure *Hyperbaton,* is thus emphasized by being put out of its ordinary place.

THE TRANSLATION OF "a" (viii. 1-4).

No condemnation, it follows, is there (or can there be) now to them that are in Christ Jesus.[27]

For the law of the spirit of life in Christ Jesus, (*i.e.,* the New nature—eternal life in Christ), **set me free from the law of sin (the Old nature) and of death.**

For, what the law could not do in that it was weak through the flesh, God, by sending His own Son in the likeness[28] of sinful flesh, and for sin, did: namely He condemned sin in the flesh.[29]

---

27. The remainder of this verse goes out according to all ancient authorities and Textual critics. It was doubtless copied by some scribe from verse 4, to which it properly belongs. The truth of verse 1 is therefore not to be made less absolute or limited by this addition.

28. Not *sinful flesh;* for "in Him was no sin," nor the likeness of flesh, for His was real flesh; but the likeness of sin's flesh.

29. *i.e.,* He exhibited in the perfect humanity and perfect walk of His Incarnate Son, a *living* condemnation of sinful flesh: and in His *atoning death* He exhibited the full and final condemnation of it.

That the righteous requirement of the law might be fulfilled in us who do not walk according to flesh (the Old nature) but according to spirit (*i.e.*, according to the aspirations of the New nature).

THE EXPANSION OF "b" (viii. 5-15).

The spirt-life (or New nature) in us, now leading us.

b | e | 5-7. The carnal mind is death; the spiritual mind, life.

f | 8. Those in the flesh (or Old nature) cannot please God.

g | 9-. We not in the flesh if Divine spirit-life dwells in us.

h | -9. If the Christ-spirit (the New nature) is not in us, we are not His.

h | 10. If Christ be in us; then, though the body is mortal, this spirit-life (or New nature) is immortal.

g | 11. Our flesh to be raised from the dead if Divine-spirit life dwells in us.

f | 12. We are not debtors therefore to the flesh (and therefore can please God).

e | 13-15. The carnal life is death; but spiritual death-writing (*i.e.*, reckoning the old nature as dead, and thus mortifying it—vi. 11) is life indeed. For as many as are led by Divine spirit these are sons of God.

Now we give the

TRANSLATION OF "b" (viii. 5-15).

For they that are (or, who live) **according to flesh** (*i.e.*, the Old nature) **do mind** (or set their affections on, as in Col. iii. 2), **the things of the flesh; but they** that are (or, who live) **according to spirit** (*i.e.*, the New nature), do mind **the things of the spirit** (or New nature). **For the mind** (or desire or aim) **of the flesh** (or Old nature) **is** (*i.e.*, works out or ends in) **death, but the mind** (desire or aim) **of the spirit** (the New nature) **is** (*i.e.*, works out or ends in) **life and peace.**

Because the mind (the carnal principle) of the flesh is enmity (hostility) toward God; [What proves this?] for it is not under subjection to (does not submit itself to) the law of God, neither indeed can it.

But they who are in flesh (or the Old nature) cannot please God.

But ye are not in flesh (in the Old nature) but in spirit (in the New nature) if indeed Divine spirit (or the New nature) dwell in you.

But if anyone has not Christ-spirit (*pneuma-Christou,*[30] *i.e.,* the New nature which is in us by Divine power) he is not His.

Whereas if Christ is in you, the body indeed is dead, (*i.e.,* mortal) an account of sin (*i.e.,* the Old nature), but the spirit is life (*i.e.,* immortal), on account of righteousness.

But if the spirit (*i.e.,* the New nature, the gift) of Him that raised up Jesus from among the dead, dwells in you, He that raised up Christ Jesus from among the dead will make alive your mortal bodies too on account of His spirit (*i.e.,* the New nature which is from Him), that dwells in you.

It follows then, brethren, that we are debtors, not to the flesh (the Old nature) to live according to flesh.

For if ye are living according to flesh (the Old nature) ye are sure to die:[31] but if by spirit (*i.e.,* by the New nature) ye are killing the deeds of the body, (by reckoning according to vi. 11), ye will live.

For as many as are led by Divine-spirit (*i.e.,* the New nature), these (and no others) are sons of God.

For ye did not receive a spirit of bond-service (Gal. iv. 24) again unto (*i.e.,* so as to produce) fear, but ye received a spirit of sonship (see same word in Gal. iv. 5, and Eph. i. 5), whereby we cry Abba, *i.e.,* Father.

We now come to "*b*" (viii. 16-27), and here, for the first time in

---

30. See above, page 32.

31. Lit. *about to die; i.e.,* indicating a sure effect from a given cause; R.V., "*Ye must die.*"

61

this chapter, we have the Person of the Holy Spirit mentioned. Its structure is very simple:—

EXPANSION OF "*b*" (viii. 16-27).

The Holy Spirit's work in us: leading the new nature.

b | i | 16-18. The Holy Spirit Himself in us. His witness with our New nature, as to our *standing* as sons of God.
  | | j | 19-21. The manifestation of this sonship in coming glory. Creation's groaning for it.
  | | *j* | 22-25. The manifestation of this sonship in resurrection-glory. Our sympathetic groaning with creation.
  | i | 26, 27. The Holy Spirit Himself in us. His helping power in us as to our *state,* and His intercession for us.

TRANSLATION OF "*b*" (viii. 16-27).

The Spirit Himself joins our spirit (or New nature) **in witnessing that we are God's children too. But if children, heirs also, heirs indeed of God, and joint-heirs with Christ; if we suffer together with Him, that we may be glorified together also with Him. For I reckon that the sufferings of this present time** (or appointed season) **are not worthy of comparison** (or to be compared) **with the glory to be revealed unto us** (or, with regard to us).

For the earnest expectation (*i.e.,* the anxious looking out with outstretched head) **of the creation waiteth for the revealing** (ver. 18) **of the sons of God. (For the creation was made subject to vanity not of its own will, but by reason of Him Who subjected it)**—waiteth, I say, **in hope, because the creation itself also shall be set free from the bondage of corruption into the glorious freedom of the children of God.**

22-25. **For we are conscious that the whole creation groans together, and travails together until now, and not only the whole creation, but ourselves also who have the first-fruit of the Spirit; even we ourselves groan within ourselves, awaiting** our sonship manifestation, that is to say, **the redemption of our body** (in a glorious resurrection and transformation). **For we were saved in**

62

hope (not "by hope," but by faith. In hope, as the sphere: or, now like the creation, we wait in hope for the completion of that for which we were saved, as in 1 Pet. i. 5). **But a hope that is seen is not hope, for what anyone sees why does he hope also for? But if we hope for what we do not see, we wait for it in patience.**

And in like manner the Spirit too joins in helping (or takes up our cause, *i.e.,* joins His help to) **our weakness. For what to pray for as we ought we are not conscious** (do not know by intuition), **but the Spirit Himself maketh intercession with unspoken groanings. But He** (the Holy Spirit) **Who searches the hearts knows what is the mind of the spirit** (the New nature) **because according to God's** will (*i.e.,* in a Divine manner) **He intercedes on behalf of saints.**

We come now to the last section of this great doctrinal division of the epistle to the Romans, *viz.,*

"a" (chap. viii. 28-39).
No separation from Christ.
(Which stands out in correspondence with viii. 1-4, *No condemnation in Christ).*

This last member, *"a"* (28-39), of this chapter is the culmination of the whole: — the height of the standing which is given in grace to the lost sinner who has been justified and saved in Christ.

It is divided into two parts, *God's purpose,* and *God's love.* This is the source and origin of all.

It is "God's Gospel" (i. 1) which is here being declared and revealed. It has its origin in God. Nothing lower than this. But this is reserved for the close, that it may shed back its light on all that has gone before. The Epistle began by declaring that those who are addressed are, "by Divine calling, saints." Now, at the end, we have this calling stated more fully as being the outcome of God's *purpose* and of God's *love.*

The following are the two divisions of

"a." Rom. viii. 28-39.

a | X | 28-32. God's *purpose* as affecting our *standing.*
  | Y | 33-39. God's *love* as affecting our *state.*

These may be expanded as follows:—

X. Rom. viii. 28-32

God's purpose, as affecting our standing.

X| k | 28 God's purpose in working "all things' together for good to His People.
     | l | 29, 30. God's purpose for us in conforming us *to* His Son.
     | *l* | 31, 32 . God's purpose for us in giving His Son to us.
  | k | 32. God's purpose to give "all things" to His People with Christ.

Here we have the *purpose* of God set forth as embracing all things that concern Christ and His People. In "k" and "*k*" the "all things"; and in "l" and "*l*," "His Son."

THE TRANSLATION OF "X" (CHAP. viii. 28-32)

But (though we do not know, *i.e.,* though we have no instinctive or intuitive knowledge what to pray for 'as is right,' *v.* 26) **we do know** (*i.e.,* are conscious) **that all things work together for good to those who love God,** namely, **to those who according to** His **purpose are called. Because, who He fore-knew, He fore-ordained also to be conformed to the image of His Son; so that He should be the first-born among many brethren. But whom He fore-ordained, them He called also; and whom He called, them He justified also; and whom He justified, them He glorified also.**

What then shall we reply to these things? If God be for us, who can be against us? He that spared not His own Son, but delivered Him up to death for us all.

How shall He not with Him also, freely give us all thing?

64

Y. Rom. viii. 33-39
God's love, as affecting our state.

Y | m | 33. God's love, in Himself, in justifying us, our security against all who would *accuse.*

    n | 34. Christ's love to us (in death and resurrection, ascension and intercession) our security against all who would *condemn.*

    n | 35-37. Our love to Christ our security in all trouble arising from the *operations of things:* "or."

   m | 38, 39. God's love, in Christ, our security against all trouble arising from *the nature of things:* "nor."

Here in "m" and *"m"* we have *God's* love; while in "n" and *"n"* we have *Christ's* love.

In "m" and "n" we have *persons;* while in *"n"* and *"m"* we have *things.*

But all is in relation to Divine love, as being our alone security. Nothing in or of ourselves can secure us. All our security arises not from what we do, but from what He is.

The following is the translation:—

Who shall impeach God's elect? Shall God that justifies? (Isa. 1. 7-9).

Who is he that condemns? Is it Christ Jesus who died? Yea, rather that was raised up, who is at the right hand of God; Who intercedes also for us?

Who shall separate US (emphatic) from the love of Christ (i.e., our love to Christ)? Shall tribulation, or distress, or persecution, or famine, or nakedness, or peril, or sword? As it is written "For thy sake are we killed all the day long:" "We were accounted as sheep for the slaughter" (Ps. xliv. 22). Nay, in all these things we more than overcome through Him that love us (Job, xxiii, 10, 1 Cor. xv. 54) For I am persuaded that neither death, nor life, nor angels, nor principalities, nor powers, nor things present, nor things to come, nor height, nor depth, nor any other created thing will be able to separate us from the love of God, that is in Christ Jesus our Lord.

65

Thus ends the great doctrinal portion of the epistle, which reveals and declares the Gospel of God: taking the sinner up from the depth of his ruin and degradation in which the first chapter finds him, and leaving him in the secure possession of unalloyed blessing. His perfect *standing* in Christ is set forth; his imperfect *state*, in himself, is described: while the secret springs of his experience are laid bare and explained by God who alone knows what the human heart is. Here it is searched and known; and here we have the key to mysterious paradoxes put into our hands.

If we learn the lesson as to what the Spirit is here saying to the churches, we shall escape the practical "reproof" conveyed in the Epistles to the Corinthians, and the doctrinal "correction" administered in the Epistle to the Galatians.

The Epistle to the Romans

THE REST OF THE EPISTLE

Before passing on to the other Epistles we must complete the structure of the rest of the Epistle to the Romans, and learn some of the lessons taught thereby.

It will not be necessary for us to enlarge on the *practical* portion, which commences with chapter xii.; as that is dealt with by preachers, speakers, and writers, every day, and on every hand, who, for the most part, treat the Epistle as though it commenced there, and contained none of those great foundation truths which we have been seeking to set forth.

But we must present the structure of the great Dispensational portion contained in chapters ix., x, and xi:

Its place, with reference to the whole Epistle, will be seen by referring to the structure on page 18, and there marked "b."

ROMANS ix.-xi. *Dispensational*

A| ix. 1-5. Paul's sorrow regarding Israel's failure.
   B | a | 6-13. God's purpose had respect only to a portion.
         b | 14-29. God's purpose regarded only a remnant
            C | c^1 | ix. 30-33. Israel's failure in spite of the Prophets.
                c^2 | x. 1-13. Israel's failure in spite of the Law.
                c^3 | x. 14-21. Israel's failure in spite of the Gospel.
   B   *b* | xi. 1-10. God's purpose regarding the remnant accomplished.
      a | 11-32. God purpose will ultimately embrace the whole.
A| 33-36. Paul's joy regarding God's purpose.

It is absolutely necessary that we should carefully and rightly divide off the Doctrinal portion from this which is Dispensational. Both are true and perfect in their place; the former, as to the standing of the Church in Christ; the later, as to God's dealings with Jew and Gentile.

In xi. 13, it says emphatically, "I speak to you Gentiles." If, therefore, we mix up what is said of and to the Gentiles, as such, with what is said of the Church, there can be nothing but confusion.

The Gentiles, as such, are warned (xi. 22) as to their use of the place of privilege which God has given them (while Israel is for a time cast off),[32] and exhorted to continue in the goodness accorded to them, "otherwise thou also shalt be cut off." Now, to use this truth to destroy the truth of chap. viii, in which the believer is taught that nothing can separate, or cut him off, from the love of God in Christ, is to fall into the snare of the devil, and to make void the Word of God. *To use one truth to destroy another truth* is the most subtle of all Satan's devices; and unless we rightly divide God's Word of Truth, we are in imminent danger of falling into this snare.

The warning given to Gentiles, as such, is true, and is truth.

The assurance of the Christian's security in Christ is true, and is truth.

Let us then heed these separate truths, as they are divided off, according to the structure.

It may be well to give the expansion of the various members of this dispensational portion, which is so exquisitely constructed.

---

32. The national privileges of Israel are stated in Rom. iii. 1, 2; ix. 4, 5.

The first member "A" (ix. 1-5)

Paul's sorrow regarding Israel's failure.

A | d | 1-3. Paul's kinship to Israel according to flesh (κατὰ σάρκα). His former wish to be accursed., and his present sorrow.

    e | 4. What belongs to Israel.

    e | 5-. Who belong to Israel.

   d | -5. Christ's kingship to Israel according to flesh (κατὰ σάρκα). His eternal existence as God over all, blessed for ever.

Here in "d" and "*d*" we have a wonderful contrast between Paul's kinship to Israel and Christ's. Paul had uninterrupted pain in his heart for his brethren as to the present and as to the past. Note the parenthesis—(for I used to wish, I myself, to be anathema, from Christ). This is a pure parenthesis. This particular form of it is called *Epitrechon*.[33] *i.e.*, a running remark thrown in, without interfering with the thought or sense of the passage itself. While speaking of his present continual sorrow, he throws in a remark as to his past sorrow. The word ηὐχόμην *(eeüchomeen)*, is in the imperfect tense. It may well be translated by the English, "I used to wish," as descriptive of his past condition. The order of the words (according to Lachmann, Tischendorf, Tregelles and Alford) being "I used to wish to be anathema (*an accursed thing*), I myself [*for ever separated*] from Christ."

The contrast is between Paul, a man, with all his infirmities, accursed; and Christ, God over all, blessed for ever.

---

33. See *Figures of Speech*, page 472.

Expansion of "a" (ix. 6-13).
God's purpose had respect only to a portion.

a | f | 6. The Word of God not failed.

  g | h | 7, 8. Election and calling of the seed out of different women.

       i | 9. What was promised.

  g | h | 10, 11. Election and calling out of the seed of the same woman.

       i | 12. What was prophesied.

  f | 13. The word of God confirmed.

Expansion of "b" (ix. 14-29)
God's purpose regarded only a remnant.

b | j | 1 | 14-16. Divine election justified by Scripture. Election of a portion from the Jews.

         m | 17, 18. Divine election justified by Scripture. Gentiles hardened for the sake of the Jews.

             k | 19-21. Divine election not to be challenged by the conscience. "Thou wilt say."

             k | 22-24. Divine election benevolent so far as apprehensible by the conscience [*What hast thou to say?*]

  j | m | 25, 26. Divine election justified by Scripture. Jews hardened for the sake of the Gentiles.

     l | 27-29. Divine election justified by Scripture. Election of a remnant from the Jews.

Expansion of "c¹" (ix. 30.33).
Israel's failure, in spite of the Prophets.
(Isa. viii. 14; xxviii. 16).

c¹ | n | 30. No *running* or *willing* in the believer (from verse 16).

     o | 31, 32-. No believing in the *runner* or *willer*.

     o | -32, 33-. Stumbling in the runner or willer.

   n | -33. No stumbling in the believer.

70

Expansion of "c²" (x. 1-13)
Israel's failure, inspite of the Law.

c² | p | x. 1-3. Israel's blindness as to salvation through faith unto justification.
| | q | 4. Christ, the end of (all claims of) the Law for righteousness to every one who believeth.
| p | | 5-10. The teaching of the Law, as to salvation through faith unto justification.
| | q | 11-13. The teaching of the Prophets as to Christ, being the end of all law for righteousness, to everyone who believeth.

Expansion of "c³" (x. 14-21)
Israel's failure in spite of the Gospel.

c³ | r | x. 14, 15. God's setting aside of the nation of Israel vindicated, because the Gospel was preached to them.
| | s | 16. Israel not excused, because they did not yield faith-obedience.
| r | | 17, 18. God's setting aside of the nation of Israel vindicated, because the Gospel was heard by them.
| | s | 19-21. Israel not excused, because their Scriptures had warned them that that setting aside would be the consequence of their lack of faith-obedience.

Expansion "b" (xi. 1-10).
God's purpose regarding the remnant accomplished.

b | t | xi. 1-3. What the majority of the nation of Israel did. They rejected God.
| | u | 4-6. A Remnant reserved, according to God's election of grace.
| | u | 7-. The Remnant obtained that which the nation of Israel did not obtain.
| t | | -7-10. What befell the majority. God hardened them.

In this member "b" (xi. 1-10), and "b" (ix. 14-29), with which it corresponds, we have an important revelation respecting the "Remnant." A revelation which explains the Lord's words in Matt.

71

xi. 43. "The kingdom of God shall be taken from you, and given to a nation bringing forth the fruits thereof." The new nation of Israel will be made out of this "Remnant." This Remnant was originally part of His purpose, and that purpose will be accomplished, and result in blessing to Israel and the World.

This is shown in the next member "*a*" (xi. 11-32).

EXPANSION of "*a*" (xi. 11-32).

God's purpose will ultimately embrace the whole.

a | X | a | xi.   11.   Salvation to the Gentiles the means of provoking Israel to jealousy.

b | 12.   If benefit accrues to the world through Israel's fall, greater benefit will accrue from their fulness.

a | 13, 14.   Apostleship of the Gentiles the means of provoking Israel's rejection, to jealousy.

b | 15, 16.   If benefit to the world accrues through Israel's rejection, greater benefit will accrue through their reception.

Y | c | 17, 18.   The wild olive-sprout, grafted in, urged not to boast against the branches.

d | 19, 20.   The wild olive urged to fear.

d | 21, 22.   The Reason why.   The wild olive-graft urged to fear: for God, who spared not the natural branches, may also cut him off.

c | 23, 24.   The Reason why.   The wild olive-graft urged not to boast against the natural branches: for God may engraft them in again.

Z | e | g | i | 25-.   Hardening in part happening to Israel, the means.

k | -25.   The completion of Gentiles in consequence.

h | 26, 27.   The salvation of Israel in consequence.

f | 28-.   Gospel standpoint: Israel enemies.

f | 28, 29.   Election standpoint: Israel beloved.

e | *g* | k | 30.   Mercy to Gentiles, the consequence.

i | 31.   Disobedience of Israel, the means.

h | 32.   Mercy   upon   all   through disobedience of all.

73

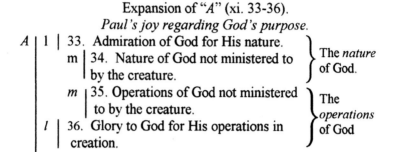

Expansion of "*A*" (xi. 33-36).
Paul's joy regarding God's purpose.

A | 1 | 33. Admiration of God for His nature.
    m | 34. Nature of God not ministered to by the creature. } The *nature* of God.
    m | 35. Operations of God not ministered to by the creature. } The *operations* of God
    l | 36. Glory to God for His operations in creation. }

Thus we reach the end of the dispensational portion of the Epistle to the Romans. The mysterious truths involved in Israel's fall, as the reason why the salvation of God is sent to the Gentiles, are explained as far as may be to finite minds and intellects. The Acts of the Apostles closes with the declaration as to the sending of this salvation to the Gentiles. Romans i.-viii. explains what this salvation is and what it contains. While chapters ix.-xi. take up the dispensational problems involved in this transfer.

It now only remains for us to complete this Epistle by giving the structure of the Practical division, xii. 1—xv. 7. (The latter Epistolary portion, xv. 13—xvi. 24, has already been given (page 20), and the remaining Dispensational portion (xv. 8-12) does not require further expansion.)

The structure of this practical division:
"*a*" Rom. xii. 1—xv. 7 (see page 18)

a | d | xii. 1, 2. Personal and Individual.
    e | 3-8. Ecclesiastical.
      f | 9-21. Social.
        g | xiii. 1-7. Civil.
      f | 8-14. Social.
    e | xiv. 1-23. Ecclesiastical.
  d | xv. 1-7. Personal and Individual.

The same warning as to "rightly dividing the Word of Truth" applies to this practical portion of the Epistle. It commences with the words: "I beseech you therefore," etc.

Now the structure shows us that it does not refer back to the end of chapter xi., but to the end of that member ("a," i. 16—viii. 39) with which it corresponds. So that xii. 1 reads on from viii. 39. And the connection is—Seeing that nothing can separate us from the love of God in Christ, therefore it is we are besought as to our practical walk. We are not to read this, which affects our *state*, into that which concerns our *standing*. Our *standing* is sure, and quite independent of all else. But, being what it is, our walk should be worthy of it. Hence, then, these exhortations and practical instructions.

Let, us, then, rightly divide the Word of Truth, and not use truth as to our *state* to upset that which is equally truth as to our *standing*.

The importance of thus rightly dividing is seen in the final member (xvi. 25-27) of the Epistle, as in every other. Here we have *the Mystery* in contrast to "God's Gospel" (in i. 1-6). There are those who wilfully close their eyes and perversely refuse to see the difference between these two. But the Word is clear for all who have the eyes of their understanding opened. Eph. i. 18 declares the necessity of this for the understanding of the Mystery which is the great subject of Ephesians, as we shall see. If any say they cannot see it, it is an honest confession that their eyes have not yet been thus opened. They are not compelled to make that confession; but, if they do, we can only express our sorrow for them, and thank God for the blessed answer of the prayer in Eph. i. 16-23 in our own experience. If any have not yet this experience, we exhort them to continue to pray this prayer.

It surely must be clear to the simplest honest mind that "God's Gospel," which is expressly stated to have been *promised afore by His prophets in the Holy Scriptures,* " cannot possibly be the same as "the Mystery which was *kept secret since the world began, but is now made manifest by prophetic writings.* "[34]

---

34. The Greek is γραφῶν προφητικῶν *(graphon propheetikōn).* There are no articles: and it is not the Old Testament prophets who are referred to here, but the Prophets as well as the Apostles who were given after the Ascension of Christi into Heaven (Eph. iv. 8-13). The expression is to be carefully

75

If they be the same, then language is useless for the purpose of revelation. If this be "doctrine and instruction"—what is the special instruction conveyed by stating that "promised afore" means "kept secret from times eternal" (R.V.) until now?

What answer could be given to the Infidel, who, believing what is taught by some Christians, as to this mistaken identity, exposes such a discrepancy as is thus created?

No: we abide by the teaching here given, that "the Mystery" was a revelation made to Paul (2 Cor. xii. 1, 7; Gal. i. 12, etc.), after his Divine calling to be an Apostle.

Some brethren mistakenly suppose that we are teaching "another gospel" when we maintain this; and cry out that "there is only one gospel" which we are thus undermining. We have only to define our terms, and the baselessness of this fear is at once seen. What does the word Gospel mean? Every one will answer, truly, *"good news."* Then surely it depends on what the good news is about:

There is the "good news" of "the *grace* of God" to lost and unworthy sinners as revealed in this Epistle. *That* is "good news."

There is "good news" concerning *the Kingdom*: for though rejected by Israel, and still in abeyance, it is yet to be set up in power and great glory: *that* is good news.

There is "good news" concerning *the glory*: for Christ's mission did not end with His sufferings, but there is "the glory which should follow." That is "good news."

So, in like manner, there is "good news" concerning *the Body of Christ*, of which His People now are the members on earth, and He is the great and glorious Head in heaven. This is "good news," and it is part of the Gospel. Being specially committed to Paul, he sometimes speaks of it as "my" Gospel, as distinguished from that

---

distinguished from that used in connection with "the gospel" (i. 2), which is διὰ τῶν προφητῶν αὐτοῦ ἐν γραφαῖς ἁγίαις, dia tōn propheetōn autou en graphias hagiais), by His prophets, in holy writings: viz., those well known as such in the Old testament. Whereas the word "prophets" in xvi. 26 is not a noun at all. It is an adjective, and should be translated *by prophetic writings, viz.,* the New Testament prophets so frequently spoken of in the New Testament Scriptures. (See *The Mystery*, pages 17, 18 and note).

committed to the twelve. He speaks of it as "my Gospel" here (xvi. 25). And, whether this refers to the Mystery, and the καί *(kai)* should be rendered *even* (as it sometimes is):— "Even the preaching of Jesus Christ, according to the revelation of the mystery;" or, whether it refers to "God's Gospel" of grace (i. 1), and the καί *(kai)* should be rendered *and* (as it usually is):— "And the preaching," etc., the conclusion is the same: that "the Mystery," always hitherto hidden, cannot be the same as that which was "promised afore."

What the Mystery (or Secret) is, it is not the purpose of the Epistle to the Romans to teach. The subjective, doctrinal foundation for it is laid; and it is merely mentioned at the close in order to complete the beautiful structure of the Epistle, and to prepare the way for it to be taken up in the Ephesians; where it is fully dealt with as the next great lesson to be taught in Romans must first be experimentally received and learned, before we can pass on to the more advanced lessons of Ephesians. Having learned what it is to have died with Christ, and to have been raised with Christ; we are, in Ephesians, further taught what it is to be now already seated in the Heavenlies in Christ.

Hence it is that the "Doctrine and Instruction" (of 2 Tim. iii. 16) now passes on to the Epistle to the Ephesians. Romans viii. is the foundation on which it is built; and Romans xvi. 25 is the point from which its revelation starts.

But, before we take up that epistle, we have to consider the pair which come between, and exhibit departure from, and failure with respect to, the teaching of the Epistle to the Romans, viz., Corinthians and Galatians.

The First Epistle to the Corinthians.

Its structure and Scope.

We have seen, by the structure (page 10) which shows the order and arrangement of these seven epistles of the Holy Spirit to "the churches," that Corinthians and Galatians follow the Romans, and that they both manifest departure from, and failure as to the "doctrine" and "instruction" contained in the Epistle to the Romans. The Epistles to the Corinthians are characterised by "reproof," and that to the Galatians by "correction." The former as to *practice,* the latter as to *doctrine.*

These three Epistles form, therefore, a group by themselves, definitely marked off from the other four. These three contain more quotations from the Old testament than any other three. This is the one feature which gives them the same character, and unites and links them together, while it separates them from all others.

To take the Corinthians first (both Epistles); we shall have to discover their great distinguishing feature or scope.

This can be done only by noting their structure, and comparing the different members and their subject matter:—

1 CORINTHIANS, AS A WHOLE.

A| i. 1-9. Epistolary. Salutation. Introduction.

B | a | i. 10-iv. 16. Ministerial reproof and explanations.

      b | c | iv. 17. Mission of Timothy to bring before them the remembrance of Paul's *"ways"* and *teaching.*

             d | iv. 18-21. Visit of Paul promised.

          C | v., vi. Things reported to Paul.

          C | vii., viii. Things enquired of Paul.

B | a | ix.-xv. Ministerial reproof and explanations.

      b | d | xvi. 1-9. Visit of Paul promised.

         c | xvi. 10-18. Mission of Timothy.

A | xvi. 19-24. Epistolary. Salutation. Conclusion.

From this simple, yet beautiful structure, we note at once the absence of "doctrine" and "instruction," as such; and the large part of the Epistle that is occupied with "reproof," and the setting right of what is wrong. Nearly the whole of it is thus occupied. Chapter after chapter is taken up with reproof and ministerial explanations.

Even the parts which look like doctrine or instruction are introduced by way of *reproof.* In chap. xiii., charity is enlarged upon, but it is "a more excellent way" than that which he had been dwelling upon in chap. xii. They might covet "spiritual gifts," but it was better to covet Divine love with all its grace and powers.

In chap. xv., the resurrection is taught, but it is introduced by way of *reproof* because some among them had said: "There is no resurrection of the dead" (ver. 12), and has asked: "How are the dead raised up" (ver. 35).

Everywhere, this is the tone which pervades the whole Epistle. In Romans, the teaching is positive; here, it is negative. In Romans, the teaching is put forth as something to be learned and understood: here, it is presented as something which had been taught, but departed from.

There are points of contact, many and marked. But it will be noted that what is stated dogmatically in Romans is treated apologetically in Corinthians; and obliquely rather than directly. For example:

In Rom. iv. 15; v. 13; vii. 5,7, 13, we have the direct teaching that without law there can be no transgression; but in 1 Cor. xv. 56, it is introduced as part of the argument to show what resurrection does for us in destroying death and sin and law.

In Rom iii. 27, we have the direct statement of a fact that all boasting is excluded. In 1 Cor. 29, it is brought in indirectly, as a reason for what has been said "that no flesh shall glory in His presence.

In Rom. viii. 38, etc., nothing is able to separate us from the love of God in Christ, "neither things present nor things to come," etc., etc., but in 1 Cor. iii. 22, the same fact is introduced as a reason why they should not "glory in men, for all things are yours, whether . . . things present or things to come," etc.

In Rom. viii 30, we have the direct statement that whom God "did predestinate them He called also; and whom He called them He justified also; and whom He justified them He glorified also." But in 1 Cor. vi. 11, the same thought is introduced indirectly. The Corinthians "did wrong and defrauded" their brethren, as the unrighteous and ungodly did; and after describing their characters the Holy Spirit says: "And such were some of you; but ye were washed, but ye were sanctified, but ye were justified in the name of the Lord Jesus and by the Spirit of our God" (R.V.).

In Rom. vii. 24, 25, we are taught directly that there is a deliverance from this dying, mortal body, and that God will in due time accomplish that deliverance; but in 1 Cor. xv. 57, it is introduced indirectly as one of the glorious results of resurrection: "But thanks be to God which giveth us the victory through our Lord Jesus Christ."

In Rom. xiv., we have definite positive, practical instruction as to our walk before those who are "weak in the faith"; and amongst other things, the principle is laid down as to matters that offend the weak conscience of a brother in Christ, inasmuch as "none of us liveth to himself." Meat or wine could hardly be obtained, except that which had been offered to idols. As to the eating of this, the question is settled in Rom. xiv. It is not wrong in itself, but if a brother's weak conscience considers it to partake of idolatry, and regards it as "a thing offered to an idol" and, therefore, as an insult to God; then we are not to touch it in his presence and cause him to stumble. But in 1 Cor. viii., the same matter is treated of from a different standpoint. It was one of those questions which the Corinthian saints had enquired of Paul (vii. 1) as a practical question; and it at once becomes a personal question, and is dealt with by way of reproof. "Take heed" (ver. 9). "When ye sin so against the brethren and wound their week conscience, ye sin against Christ." It is not treated of merely as something they were not to do (as in Romans), but as something they had done.

In Rom. vi. and vii., the conflict between the New nature and the Old is explained and set forth in all detail. In 1 Cor. ix. 26, 27, an example of it is given, showing how he maintained this conflict in himself, because he did not wish his ministerial labour to be thrown away, but to be such as God would approve.

In Rom. v. 12-21, we have the "first man" and the "second man"; the first Adam and the last Adam and all the wondrous contrast between them, showing how death entered by one and life comes by the other. In 1 Cor. xv. 21, 22, 45, these two federal heads are referred to not as a plain direct statement of doctrine, but indirectly as part of an argument: "For since by man came death, by man came also the resurrection of the dead. For as all in the Adam die, even so shall all in the Christ be made alive."

We have seen how, in Rom. xvi. 25, 26, "the Mystery" is referred to and stated as a fact. The time was come for it to be made known, that the saints might be established as the Church of God, apart from the *earthly* hope of Israel as a nation, *now,* that as a nation Israel was cast-off. The saints were to know a higher and a *heavenly* calling. But in 1 Cor. ii. the reasons are given why, when the apostle was at Corinth, he could nor preach "the Mystery" to the saints there.

Their state was a contrast to what it should have been: they failed to exemplify in practice the elementary truth that they had received; even now they need *reproof* before he can communicate that of which he is about to write to them. Instead of recognizing that they were "one body in Christ" and "members one of another" (Rom. xii. 5), they were forming separate "Bodies" of their own, and classing themselves under different teachers, and everyone said "I

am of Paul; and I of Apollos; and I of Cephas" (1 Cor. i. 12).
Instead of reckoning themselves as having died with Christ to sin,
since he had died for their sins (Ch. xv. 4), they were living in sin.
Instead of separation from the world by the cross of Christ, they
were placing themselves under its authority (Ch. vi. 1). He may
well ask: "Is Christ divided?" (ver. 13). No wonder he could not
preach "the mystery" to them. They were not in a fit condition to
receive this wondrous truth. This member (i. 10-iv. 16), which is
taken up with ministerial explanations, commences with a reference
to this their condition. The commencement of any book of the Bible
or of these Epistles is always important as furnishing a key to the
whole. This Epistle commences (after the Epistolary salutation) at
verse 10: "Now I beseech you, brethren, by the name of our Lord
Jesus Christ, that ye all speak the same thing, and that there be no
divisions among you; but that ye be perfectly joined together[35] in the
same mind and in the same judgment, for it was declared unto me of
you, my brethren, that there are strifes among you."

This is why he could not preach "the Mystery" to them. For He
goes on to say in chap. ii. 1, 2: "And I, brethren, when I came to
you, came not with excellency of speech or of wisdom, declaring
unto you the Mystery of God.[36] For I determined not to know[37]
anything among you, save Jesus Christ and Him crucified." That is
to say, owing to their divisions, and their being taken up with their

---

35. κατηρτισμένοι (kateertismenoi). The word refers to the mending of
what is broken (Matt. iv. 21), the restoring of what is marred. As 1 Cor. begins,
so 2 Cor. ends. For in 2 Cor. xiii. 11, this is the final word: "Be perfect," i.e., be
restored, be perfectly joined together (1 Cor. i. 10).

36. This is the correct and true reading here, and the Revised Version so
gives it. The mistake is very slight, μαρτύριον (marturion) was written by
some scribe for the more ancient reading μυστήριον (musterion), a mere
interchange of two letters. The scribe, like the Corinthians, was doubtless
ignorant of the doctrine, and so, thinking it to be a mistake, put the word
marturion, testimony, which he could understand. The Revised Version had no
motive in putting "mystery" beyond giving the most ancient and correct reading.

37. Lit. "I did not judge [it well] to know."

82

own "Bodies," they were not in a fit condition, spiritually, to receive the revelation of the Mystery, which is the one body of Christ, of which He is the glorious Head in heaven, and His people the members of it on earth. This is a spiritual Body. This is a spiritual union and a spiritual truth. It can be declared[38] only to spiritual persons.

Hence, he goes on to say (ii. 13-15): "And I brethren, could not speak unto you as unto spiritual persons but as unto carnal, even as unto babes in Christ. I have fed you with milk, and not with meat, for hitherto ye were not able to bear it, neither yet now are ye able, for ye are yet carnal; for whereas there is among you envying and strife and divisions, are ye not carnal, and walk according to man? For when one says I am of Paul; and another, I am of Apollos, are ye not men?[39] (iii. 1-4).

It is clear that this is the scope of 1 Cor. ii. and iii. So that the statement of chap. ii. 2: "I determined not to know anything among you save Jesus Christ and Him crucified," is wholly misunderstood when taken apart from its context, as though nothing came before it, and nothing came after it; treating it as though it were the very end and height of Apostolic example instead of the very beginning.

It is a sad exhibition of the low estate of Biblical study when this text is thus misused and set up as a model to be followed, instead of set forth as a condition to be deplore.

These saints in Corinth were so carnal that they could not

---

38. This must be the meaning of 1 Cor. ii. 13. The verb συνκρίνω (*sunkrinō*, occurs only here, and in the next epistle (2 Cor. x. 12). It means *to mix* or *put together*. This may be for the purpose of comparing, or of expounding or interpreting. In Daniel the nouns σύγκριμα (*sunkrima*) and σύγκρισις (*sunkrisis*), are frequently used of *interpretation* and *interpreting*. It is used for the Hebrew שׁרפ (*parash*), to *make clear* (Neh. viii. 8), *declare* (Num. xv. 34), *mark out distinctly* (Num. xv. 34). Hence it means, here, *declaring*, the two adjectives which follow are, one in the accusative plural (*feminine*), and the other dative plural (*masc.* or *neuter*); and the three words mean: "declaring spiritual [*things*] to spiritual [*persons*]." See the R.V. in margin.

39. Lachmann, Tischendorff, Tregelles, Alford and R.V. read: ἄνθρωποί (*anthropoi*), men, instead of σαρκικοί (*sarkikoi*), *fleshly or carnal*.

understand or receive truths which can be "only spiritually discerned." They were so divided up into parties that the Apostle could not teach them concerning the higher and deeper truths connected with their union with Christ. Without the preaching of "Jesus Christ crucified," there could be no preaching at all. But beyond this, there was the preaching of Christ risen from the dead, and all that that means for those who died with Christ, are risen again in Him: and there is the preaching of Christ's coming again from heaven with all the wondrous power of this truth for those who are waiting for God's Son from Heaven. The Apostle, therefore, judged it well not to know anything among them, "except Jesus Christ and Him crucified;" and this, for the special reason stated, that he "could not speak unto them as spiritual persons, but as unto carnal, even as unto babes in Christ." This resolve and determination on his part tells its own tale as to the condition of these Corinthian saints. They were not walking according to the light of Rom. v.12—viii. 39; not appreciating their marvellous standing as risen with Christ; not walking "in newness of life."

"The Mystery" involves the full truth of this new and heavenly standing. It involves truth far beyond substitution in death; it involves *union with Christ* in all the value of his death, burial, and resurrection. It embraces the truths connected with His ascension and coming again. It involves not only our present stand in Christ, but the hope of our union with Christ in glory, when He shall come to be glorified in His saints.

Imagine the loss of these powerful influences on the life and walk of a Christian! We cannot be surprised at the practical *reproof* needed by these Corinthian saints. For what can be expected in the way of power or holiness in those who are ignorant of this standing, and of this blessed hope! No wonder we see such wide-spread distress at the unsatisfactory walk of many Christians; and no wonder that, from ignorance as to the cause of it, we see so many vain attempts in the present day to bring about this improvement in the Christian walk by other means and methods, instead of going back to the root of the mischief.

The object, therefore, of this first Epistle to the Corinthians is thus to lead them back, and to lead them on by the reproof administered to see what *Jesus Christ and Him risen again* means; and to teach them in his Epistle (chap. xii.) Something of "the Mystery" which he could not announce to them when he first visited them, and planted the church of Christ among them.

The Second Epistle to the Corinthians.
Its Structure and Scope.

The Second Epistle to the Corinthians has precisely the same scope as the First Epistle.

An examination of its structure shows us that the great bulk of it (more than one-half) is taken up (as the First Epistle is) with Ministerial explanations and Epistolary matter; and this by way of reproof for failure as to the teaching given in the Epistle to the Romans, and departure from its doctrine and precepts.

2 CORINTHIANS, AS A WHOLE

```
A | i    1, 2. Salutation.
   B | a | 3-11. Thanksgiving.
       |   b |  12. His Ministry.
       |       C | i. 13-ii. 13. Epistolary.
   B | a | ii. 14-17. Thanksgiving.
       |   b | iii, 1-vi. 10. His Ministry.
               C | vi. 11-xiii. 10. Epistolary.
A | xiii. 11-14. Salutations.
```

It will be seen from this that considerably more than half the Epistle is occupied with Epistolary reproof; and a comparison of this with the Epistle to the Romans will bring out the same features as those seen in the First Epistle.

It is evident from the above structure that the two important members are C and C, which occupy eight chapters out of the thirteen into which the Epistle is divided.

We must, therefore, set these two members out in greater detail; and it will be seen that, though they are separated in the general structure, there is a perfect design and correspondence between them.

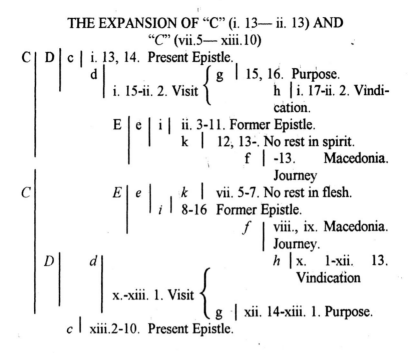

THE EXPANSION OF "C" (i. 13— ii. 13) AND
"*C*" (vii.5— xiii.10)

C | D | c | i. 13, 14. Present Epistle.
        d |
        i. 15-ii. 2. Visit { g | 15, 16. Purpose.
                            h | i. 17-ii. 2. Vindi-
                                  cation.
                E | e | i | ii. 3-11. Former Epistle.
                        k | 12, 13-. No rest in spirit.
                                f | -13.   Macedonia.
                                            Journey
C
                E | e | k | vii. 5-7. No rest in flesh.
                    i | 8-16 Former Epistle.
                                f | viii., ix. Macedonia.
                                      Journey.
    D | d | h | x. 1-xii. 13.
                                              Vindication
        x.-xiii. 1. Visit {
                            g | xii. 14-xiii. 1. Purpose.
    c | xiii.2-10. Present Epistle.

The more the above structure is examined, the more will its
perfection and beauty be seen. Member answers to member with
perfect correspondence. Nothing is wanting in any part. There is,
first, the main introversion of D, E, *E*, *D*. Then there are the sub-
introversions of c, d, *d*, *c*; i, k, *k*, *i*; and g, h, *h*, *g*. Between all these
introversions there comes one alternation, e, f, *e*, *f*.

If the scope of this epistle is to be understood, its structure must
be studied. Then, we must remember that the portions marked by the
corresponding letters read on from one to the other, and must be
taken together; all between them being regarded as in a parenthesis.
Mental confusion must result if this be not observed.

Then there is the same reference to Romans as we saw in the
first epistle; and these references have the same character.

In Romans we have the frequent mention of "the righteousness
of God," as a matter of doctrine and instruction. We have the same
in 2 Cor.: but introduced not as a revelation, but in the course of
argument, and given as a reason; *e.g.*, 2 Cor. v. 21, "that we might

87

be made the righteousness of God in Him."

In Rom. v. 13, we learn directly that "sin is not imputed where there is no law" (So iv. 15). In 2 Cor. v. 19 it comes in as part of another argument, "that God was in Christ, reconciling the world unto himself, not imputing their trespasses unto them."

In Rom. v. 15, the vicarious death of others in Adam is stated, and all are said to have "died" through the one offence of that one man (Adam). In 2 Cor. v. 14, the same fact that "all died" comes out indirectly, and as part of an argument, to show the love of Christ as a power constraining the apostle in his devotion to their cause (verse 13). "For, whether we were beside ourselves, *it was* for God *(i.e. for His glory):* or are sober-minded, *it is* for you *(i.e., for your good).* For the love of Christ *(to us)* constraineth us; having judged this—because One died for all, then all died[40] (in Him); and He died for all, that they that live should no longer live to themselves, but to Him that died for them and was raised again." The argument being, to show, that he, in view of this love of Christ as manifested to him, was constrained to labour for them to such a degree as for them to think him beside himself. Thus the great truth of our death in Adam, and our death in Christ comes out indirectly, whereas in Rom. v. 15 it is stated dogmatically: as is also the truth that we, having died with Christ, should henceforth "walk in newness of life" (Rom. vi. 4, and xiv. 7, 8).

In Rom. viii, 3, we are taught as a matter of doctrine that God sent His own Son in the likeness of sinful flesh; and, by His sacrifice for sin. He condemned sin (*i.e.*, the old nature) in the flesh. But in 2 Cor. v. 21 it is given as a reason why in acting as ambassadors for God, God exhorted by them, and they besought on behalf of Christ— "Be reconciled to God, for He hath made him that knew no sin, to be sin (*i.e.*, a sin-offering) for us."

In Rom. viii. 18, we are taught that "the sufferings of this present time are not worth to be compared with the glory which shall be revealed in us." But, in 2 Cor. iv. 17, precisely the same truth is introduced as a reason why he fainted not (ver. 16) at all the

---

40. Aorist tense, as referring to a past definite act.

persecutions and tribulations he underwent for their sakes, as detailed in verses 8-16. "For which cause we faint not;..for the momentary lightness of our tribulation worketh out for us in ever surpassing measure an eternal weight of glory; we, considering not the things that are seen, but the things that are not seen: for the things that are seen *are* for a time (or temporary), but the things that are not seen are eternal."

Closely connected with this is Rom. viii. 23. We are taught as a matter of fact that, like the whole creation, we who have the first fruits of the Spirit, "groan within ourselves waiting for our sonship *(manifestation) that is to say*, the redemption of our body *(in a glorious resurrection and transformation)*." But, in 2 Cor. v. 2, this same groaning for the same object is introduced, indirectly, as a further reason why the apostle fainted not at the persecutions and afflictions which he endured for their sakes; and why we consider the things which are unseen, and desire that resurrection body— "the building we shall have from God— a house not made with hands, eternal, in the heavens. For indeed, in this we ardently groan, longing to be clothed upon (or, to get put on us) our house which is from heaven."[41] Resurrection is the one great theme of this passage. It commences with resurrection in Chap. iv. 14, "knowing that He that raised up the Lord Jesus will raise up us also with[42] Jesus, and will present us with you." Then it goes on to give three reasons for this assurance: "for" (iv. 15), "for" (iv. 17), "for" (v. 1). This is why we groan, earnestly desiring our resurrection body, knowing that, while we dwell here in this body, we must continue to be absent from the Lord. And therefore we are always of good courage, and

---

41. ἐξ οὐρανοῦ (*ex ouranou*) *out of heaven, or heavenly.* The word rendered "house," is οἰκητήριον (*oikeeteerion*): it is used only here and in Jude 6 of that *body* which angels have and which some who fell, left (and were thus able to commit the sin referred to in Gen. vi.; 1 Pet. iii. 19, 20; 2 Pet. ii. 4, 5; Jude 6). Hence we ardently long "to be clothed upon with our spiritual heavenly body," which we shall have at our resurrection.

42. Tregelles and the best texts and R.V. read *with* Jesus, not "by" Him.

knowing[43] that , while we dwell here in this body, we are away from our home with the Lord. (v. 6,8).

We have no right whatever to introduce the thought of death into this passage. There is no reference whatever to it, except in verse 3, as the one condition in which he would "not be found."

Resurrection is the one great thought and subject of the whole passage. And death would never have been introduced by interpreters if the blessed hope of resurrection had not been well-nigh lost by the churches.

In Rom. xi. 25 we have the dogmatic explanation of Israel's present "unbelief" and "blindness": and the definite promise that it was to be only temporary and partial; because "there will come out of Zion the Deliverer, and will turn away ungodliness from Jacob" (ver. 26). But in 2 Cor. iii. All this is referred to as part of another argument, and as flowing from the *reproof* with which the chapter commences. "Do we begin again to commend ourselves? Or need we, as some other, epistles of commendation to you, or letters of commendation from you. . . .Ye are our epistle, etc. Christ's Epistle ministered by us, written not with ink, but with the Spirit of the living God, not in tablets of stone, but in fleshy table of the heart."

Then he goes on to explain this ministration of the Spirit (ver. 8), and contrasts it with the writing on the table of stone given by Moses. This latter was glorious, but it was done away. This ministration of the Spirit (Christ's epistles in your hearts) is glorious, and it shall never be done away as that was. "For, (ver. 11) if that which is done away [*was done away*] by glory (διὰ δόξης, *dia doxees)* much more that which remaineth [*remaineth*] in glory (ἐν δόξῃ, *en doxee).* Seeing, then, that we have such a hope (*i.e.,* of our work's remaining in glory), we use great plainness of speech, and *are* not as Moses who put a vail over his face to check the children of Israel gazing too intently at the end (or eclipse) of that which was being done away." *i.e.,* We are not as Moses. He gave the law, and though it ministered death, it was glorious; so glorious that even his face shone with such glory that the people could not

---

43. θαρροῦντες . . *καὶ εἰδότες (tharrountes. . . kai eidotes),* these words refer to their state and condition.

look on it, and he had to put a vail over it; which (glory) is done away, as is the Law which he ministered. The People could not look on Moses' face, neither could they see that the Law was to be done away. Nor can they see now: but the illustration is now reversed. It is they who now have a vail on their heart, their minds are blinded, and they cannot understand the "reading of the old covenant, which old covenant is done away with in Christ." They could not look on the glory of Moses' face (which was afterward done away) because of his vail; and they cannot see now the glory of the Gospel (though it remains in glory) because of a similar vail; but that vail is not on Christ or the Gospel, but on their own hearts. And then comes in, incidentally, the blessed fact which is a matter of doctrine and revelation in Rom. xi. 23, 26, that that vail is to be taken away from their heart: for, when their heart shall have turned to the Lord, that vail will be taken away" (2 Cor. iii. 16), *i.e.*, their heart shall have turned because that vail will be already previously taken away.

In Rom. xiv., 10 the *Beema*[44] or "judgment seat" of Christ is spoken of directly in connection with a definite precept in the practical portion of the epistle. "We must all stand before the *Beema* of Christ." This is the reason why we are to deal considerably with those who are weak in the faith, and who have a tender conscience. In 2 Cor. v. 10 a similar statement is made.

Except that in Romans it is παραστησόμεθα (*parasteeso-metha*), "we shall stand before," and in Corinthians it is φανερωθῆναι (*phanerotheenai*), "we shall be manifested." But in 2 Cor. v. 10 it is introduced, not in connection with a direct precept, but indirectly, as a consideration why the apostle labored with and suffered among the Corinthian saints, endeavouring that, whether present or absent, he might be acceptable to God (ver. 9): and he

---

44. The word *Beema* means literally *a step* or *pace* (Acts vii. 5); hence, any raised platform about a *step* high (*i.e.*, about 2 ½ feet). Among the Greeks it was used of any raised place, rostrum, or tribune for speakers in public assembly (Acts xii. 21). Law Courts had three: one for the judge, and one each for the plaintiff and defendant. Thus it was used also of the raised dais from which prizes were given away to those to whom they had been awarded; and not the bench from which a judge gave sentence upon prisoners who might be brought before it.

goes on to add another reason: "For we commend not ourselves again unto you, but give you occasion to glory on our behalf, that ye may have somewhat to answer them which glory in appearance and not in heart. For whether we be beside ourselves, it is to God: or whether we be sober, it is for your cause."

In Rom. xv. 20 he states a definite fact, and says: "Yea, so have I strived to preach the Gospel, not where Christ is named lest I should build upon another man's foundation." But in 2 Cor. x. 13-16 this is introduced in self-defence as will be seen by reading from verse 8.

In Rom. xv. 30, so simple a thought as to their striving together in prayer for him, is a direct request. Whereas, in 2 Cor. i. 11, it is introduced indirectly: God had delivered him, and would yet deliver him, they also "helping together by prayer."

From all these examples (and there may be several others), it is clear that there is a close connection between these two Epistles to the Corinthians and the Epistle to the Romans.

We do not mean that the Corinthians had read the epistle to the Romans[45] and then departed from its teaching. But that, as a church, they had received the same or similar instruction as the Romans through his ministry, and had failed to give a practical manifestation of it, individually, socially, and ecclesiastically.

Unless we learn the teaching contained and given in the Epistle to the Romans we too shall fail in like manner.

---

45. For Romans was not written till afterwards.

The Epistle to the Galatians
Its Structure and its Scope.

We now come to the last Epistle of the first group of three Epistles (which we may call the Romans group)—the Epistle to the Galatians. It has the same relation to Romans that Colossians has to Ephesians. Both relate to doctrinal failure, and are characterised by "correction."

The Epistle addressed to the churches of Galatia stands out very distinctly from all the others; and yet every one can see its link with the Epistle to the Romans. Commentators never fail to call attention to this likeness. But what has not yet been noticed is the *nature* of that relation and the *character* of that likeness.

The structure gives us the scope of the Epistle and the key to its design. In one point it differs from the Epistles to the Corinthians, in that it is mainly occupied with *doctrinal* matters, rather than *practical;* but it is like the Corinthians, in that, when these are mentioned, it is to correct a departure from the teaching of the Epistle to the *Romans:*

Notice the commencements of the two Epistles: the point of each will be at once seen.

Rom. i. 1.	Gal. i. 6.
"Paul, a servant of Jesus Christ, by divine calling an apostle, separated **unto God's Gospel.**"	"I marvel that ye are so soon removing from him that called you in the grace of Christ, **unto a different[46] Gospel.**"

---

46. The word is ἕτερος *(heteros)*, *another* of a *different* kind; hence, here *a rival* gospel. And so the verse goes on to say: "which is not another (ἄλλος, *allos, another* of the *same* kind), but there be some that trouble you and would pervert the gospel of Christ."

Here we have the key to the Epistle as a whole; we are thus prepared for its structure, and expect to see this opening theme enlarged and developed; the departure proved, and the evil corrected. This is exactly what we do see.

First the Apostle has to show at some length the nature of his Gospel, and how he obtained it and his apostleship; then, he proceeds to show why he thus marvelled at their doubt of his authority and their removal from his teaching.

The Epistle was written before the Epistle to the Romans in point of time, (see Appendix), but it is clear that he had taught these Galatians the same truth and the same Gospel which he soon after records in that Epistle to the Romans. It is also clear that the churched of Galatia had soon departed from his teaching.

The Structure of the Epistle to the Galatians.
A | i. 1-5. Epistolary; and Salutation.
    B¹| a¹| i. 6—ii. 14. Paul's solicitude for them. "I marvel" (i. 6), and Defence of his Apostleship and Gospel.
          b¹| ii. 15—iv. 10. Doctrinal correction.
    B²| a²| iv. 11-20. Paul's solicitude for them. "I am afraid" (iv. 11). "I stand in doubt of you" (iv. 20).
          b²| iv. 21—vi. 10. Doctrinal correction.
    B³| a³| vi. 11-14. Paul's solicitude and only ground of joy.
          b³| vi.15. Doctrinal correction. Concluding summary.
A | vi. 16-18. Epistolary; and Salutation.

The whole scope of the Epistle lies before us in this structure. Beyond the very brief Epistolary portions (i. 1-5 and vi. 16-18), the whole Epistle is taken up with alternate expressions of anxious *solicitude* on their account, and the *correction* of their doctrinal departure from the truth as it is set forth in the Epistle to the Romans.

In this Epistle there is an alternation of solicitude and correction just as there is in the Epistle to the Colossians, which is also taken up with doctrinal failure.

On the other hand, it differs from the structure of the two Epistles to the Corinthians, in that the Epistolary portion occupies only as many verses in Galatians as it occupies chapters in Corinthians.

94

This likeness to Colossians in what is *doctrinal correction,* and this contrast with Corinthians in what is *practical reproof* is remarkable, and settles for us what is the true scope and object of the Epistle to the Galatians.

This is seen still further, when we compare the correspondence between the two principal doctrinal portions "b¹" (ii. 15-iv. 10), and "b²" (iv. 21-vi. 10).[47]

The Expansion of "b¹" (ii. 15—iv. 10) and "b²"
(iv. 21—vi. 10):
Doctrinal Correction.

b¹ | c | e | ii. 15-21. Justification.
          f | iii. 1-5. Expostulation.
              d | iii. 6—iv. 11. Illustration (Abraham and his one Seed).
b² | d | iv. 21-31. Illustration (Abraham and his two sons).
     c | e | v. 1-6. Justification.
          f | v. 7—vi. 10. Epostulation.

The minor members are also constructed perfectly: as note this.

Illustration. "d" (iii. 6—iv. 11). "Abraham."

d | g | iii. 6-9. The Promise.
        h | 10-12. The Curse of the Law.
            i | 13,14. Redemption through Christ.
    g | 15-18. Promises.
        h | 19-25. The use of the Law.
            i | 26—iv. 11. Sonship in Christ.

---

47. The third "b³" (vi. 15) is merely a condensed concluding summary of the whole.

95

Similarly we may expand this last member "*i.*"

"*i.*" (iii. 26—iv. 11).
Sonship in Christ.

i | *j* | iii. 26-29. Sons and heirs.
    | | k | iv. 1-6. Illustration.
    | *j* | 7. Son and heir.
    | | k | 8-11. Application.

Likewise we may expand the above member "k" (iv. 1-6).

Illustration.

k | l | iv. 1. The Child.
  | | m | -1. The Servant.
  | | | n | 2-. The Tutors and Governors.
  | | | | o | -2-. The appointed Time.
  | | | | | p | -2. The action of the Father.
  | *l* | 3-. Children.
  | | m | -3-. The Servitude.
  | | | n | -3-. The Tutors (Elements: "Stoicheia").
  | | | | o | -3. The appointed time.
  | | | | | p | 4-6. The action of the Father.

It is hardly necessary for us here to enlarge further on and exhibit all the minutes of the various structures of the Epistle. We could not do so without greatly impeding the course of our study and interfering with our design, which is to show the object and aim of the Epistle as a whole.

Now, having discovered its scope, we may proceed to develope it; and show its bearing on the likeness between this Epistle and that to the Romans.

What is stated plainly and as direct teaching in Romans, was departed from very soon after it had been taught to the Galatians. The same objects necessarily arise, therefore, but in a different form and connection.

There was nothing that called forth the teaching in Romans beyond the good-pleasure of God to instruct us. But in Galatians, after that instruction had been received and departed from, it was necessary to re-state many of the subjects by way of "correction."

So that the similar statements and references which we find in the two Epistles are approached from two different points of view. For example:

In Rom. i. 2 we have the direct statement that the Gospel of God's Grace was "promised afore" by His prophets in the holy Scriptures. In Gal. iii. 8 it is introduced as part of an argument:—foreseeing that God would justify the Gentiles through faith, preached before the Gospel unto Abraham, saying, In thee shall all nations be blessed."

The fulfilment of the promise, predestined and made "afore," was accomplished at the time appointed in the counsels of God. In Rom. v. 6 it is solemnly declared that "in due time Christ died for the ungodly." But, in Gal. iv. 4 it is introduced as part of an argument that "when the fulness of the time was come, God sent forth his Son."

The natural depravity of man and the degradation of the Old nature, the flesh, in man, is set forth clearly in Rom. i. 18-32. But, in Gal. v. 19-21 it is introduced in connection with the opposition of this flesh (the Old nature) to the spirit (*i.e.*, the New nature), and in contrast with "the fruit of the Spirit."

The futility of privilege is set forth in Rom. ii. 17-29, where it is shown what true circumcision is, and how it must be that of the heart, and spiritual, and is not "outward in the flesh." Whereas, in Gal. v. 6 it is given as a reason why Christian believers should not be circumcised, because, in that case, Christ would profit them nothing and they would be debtors to do the whole law.

"The just shall live by faith." This, in Rom. i. 17, is set forth as the foundation of God's Gospel of grace, in which the righteousness of God is revealed; while in Gal. iii. 11 the very same words are quoted (from Hab. ii. 4) as the correction of the departure from the teaching of the Epistle to the Romans: thus: "But that no man is justified by the law in the sight of God it is evident: for, The just shall live by faith. And the law is not of faith: but, The man that doeth them shall live in (or better, *by*) them."

Deliverance from the Law is the great subject of Rom. vi. 1—vii. 6, where this blessed fact is stated, proved, and illustrated, first by the case of master and servant, and then by that of husband and wife. But, in Galatians ii. 19, the fact is brought in incidentally: "For I through (or by means of) law died to law, that I might live unto God." And (in chap. v. 18) to show one the results of being led by the New nature: "but if ye be led by the spirit (i.e., the New nature) ye are not under the law."

The aim, object, end, and use of the Law is set forth in Rom. v. 20, "that the offence might abound": and, in vii. 7, that it might convict of sin. In Gal. iii. 19 its use is mentioned in connection with the fulfilment of God's promise to Abraham: "It was added for the sake of (i.e., to bring out and make manifest) transgressions, till the seed should come to whom the promise was made."

The conflict between the two natures, "flesh" and "spirit," is fully defined and explained at length in Rom. vii. 17-25, as a matter of *instruction;* while, in Gal. v. 17-26, it is introduced as a motive for Christian walk in service to one another (see verses 13-15), and the reason and exhortation is added: "This I say then, Walk according to spirit (i.e., the New nature), and ye will in no way (then) fulfill the flesh's desires (the Old nature's); for the flesh (the Old nature) desires against the spirit (the New nature), and the spirit (the New nature) [*desires*] against the flesh (the Old nature); and these are opposed one to another, in order that ye should not do whatsoever things ye may wish." And then, at the end of this reference to Rom. vii., the correction is again introduced, in verse 26. "If we live [*according to*] spirit (the New nature) we should walk also [*according to*] spirit (the New nature). We should not become vain-glorious, provoking one another, envying one another." Thus a practical use is made of the doctrine of Rom. vii., and the correction is administered, showing how it is only sound doctrine that leads to a sound life and walk.

Sonship and heirship are explained and set forth in Rom. viii. 14-17, showing that as many as are led by Divine spirit (i.e., the New nature from God) are sons of God, having received a sonship spirit, whereby they cry Abba: i.e., Father. But in Gal. iv. 5-7, similar words are used in connect with quite another subject, *viz:* that being made sons of God, we are no longer children (like bond-servants) under tutors and governors, but in the Father's appointed time have been set free form the bond-service which is connected with the observance of "days and months and times and years." These have to do with *religion*, not with Christ, and those who are "in Christ" are freed from the bondage of Religious ordinances.[48]

The names for the two natures, "flesh" and "spirit" are used in Galatians as in Romans; and the same care has to be taken as to whether it should be written or printed *spirit* or *Spirit*. The section in Galatians which treats of the two natures opens with the correction and question (iii. 1-3): "O foolish Galatians, who hath bewitched you[49] . . . .before whose eyes Jesus Christ was openly set forth *as* crucified.[50] This only I wish to learn from you. Was it on the principle of the works of the law that ye received the spirit (*i.e.*, the New nature), or by the hearing of faith (*i.e.*, the report which ye believed)? Are ye so senseless? Having begun in spirit (*i.e.*, the New nature), are ye now going to be made perfect in the flesh (the Old nature's) ye will certainly not fulfil."

In both Epistles the fundamental truth is maintained that "there is no difference" between men (Jew or Gentile) before God; but, in Romans, this is taught as a positive truth: (See iii. 22; x. 12; xi. 32): while, in Galatians it forms part of an argument as to the promise of life in Christ being given apart from the Law. See Gal. iii. 22.

The same references are made to Abraham and his Seed. In Rom. iv., the teaching is positive and dogmatic as to justification now by the same faith as that of Abraham. While, in Gal. iii., the consequences of this, and the connection between the Promise and the Law are worked out so as further to show and make clear the logical results of this great truth.

As to baptism, there is the same remarkable reference to "as many as (ὅσοι, *hosoi*) were baptised," &c.; and while in Romans we are taught the dogmatic truth as to our death with Christ, expressed "in the likeness of His death." the old man being put off having been "crucified with Christ"; here (in Gal. iii. 27) the baptism with the Spirit is referred to whereby Christ, the New Man

---

48. See *Figures of Speech,* under the Figure of "repetition."

49. The words "that ye should not obey the truth" must go out according to the Textual Critics: Griesbach, Lachmann, Tischendorf, Tregelles, Alford, and R.V.

50.. The words "among you" must go out also, according to the above authorities.

is put on,[51] *i.e.*, that those, who are risen with Christ "in the likeness of His resurrection," wherein they are to exist (Rom. vi. 5) stand covered with Him and His righteousness as with a garment. No longer reckoned as being in the first Adam, but standing before God on new ground, resurrection ground, "in Christ," having thus "put on Christ" not by baptism in water, but by burial and resurrection with Christ. When the exhortation is given to "put on Christ" it can mean only that we are to reckon ourselves as having died and risen in Christ. How else can it be done? Truth, to be *practical*, must be *practicable*. In what way can we mortify the flesh? Not by controlling it. Controlling is not killing, and the word rendered "mortify" means to put to death. By what act, then, can we put the flesh to death, except by reckoning ourselves as having died, according to Rom. vi. 11, and by knowing that our old man was crucified with Him (Rom. vi. 6)? This is the knowledge which is given in Romans and the practical outcome of it is seen in Gal. ii. 20. "Christ, I have been crucified-together-with; yet I live; and yet it is no longer that I live, but in me Christ."[52]

Gal. v. 24: "They that are Christ's have crucified the flesh with its affections and desires." But how? Only by the reckoning of Rom. vi. 6, 11.

So in Gal. vi. 14. It is the cross of Christ which has this meaning now for all who were crucified with Him by God, and in God's sight.

In like manner we may ask: In what way are we to "put on Christ," except by faith, reckoning that we have risen with Christ, and are walking on resurrection-ground in resurrection life?

Thus we have shown, and have seen, the intimate relation

---

51. The context "there is neither Jew nor Greek," shews that the baptism here named, whereby Christ is put on, is that with the Holy Spirit administered by the Lord Jesus, as in 1 Cor. xii. 13 and Coloss. iii. 10, 11. The Spirit of Sonship, the power whereby the Lord Jesus was proved to be the Son of God, Rom. i. 4. Where the Spirit of the Lord is there is liberty, 2 Cor. iii. 17; Gal. v. 1.

52. This is emphasised by the figure of *Epanadiplosis* (in the Greek), by which the sentence is made to begin and end with the same all-important word, "Christ," as shown above.

between Romans and Galatians, and the nature and character of that relation.

This completes the first group of (three) Epistles; or rather the first great text-book—*Romans*, with its two subsidiary books (Corinthians and Galatians) supplementing it by bringing out and developing still further its wondrous teaching. This is done two ways: (1) by showing the bearing of Romans teaching on the mistakes of *practical* life by the *reproof* conveyed in the Epistles to the Corinthians; and (2) by showing its bearing on various errors of *doctrine*, which come from not heeding its teaching, as shown by the *correction* given in the Epistle to the Galatians.

The Epistle to the Ephesians.

I. *Its* Structure *and Scope.*

We now come to the second part of the great Text book of the Holy Spirit, which is His special instruction for the churches, and His special lessons written, not only *for* them (like all other Scriptures) but *about* them.

As in Romans we get all the truth concerning the standing of the sinner in Christ as having died and risen with Him, so, now, we are taken on to a further stage of direct, positive doctrinal teaching, showing how the sinner not only died and rose again in Christ, but is now, in God's sight and purpose, *seated* in Christ in the heavenlies.

But, before we take up its special teaching, as shown by its structure and its scope, we must first notice a remarkable circumstance connected with its title.

The facts are as follows:—

1. The titles of the books of the New Testament are the subject of such variations in the ancient manuscripts that they cannot be regarded as fixed, or altogether genuine.

2. The Revised Version puts the following note in the margin against the words "at Ephesus," in verse 1: "Some very ancient authorities omit '*at Ephesus.*'"

3. Among these authorites are B and ℵ: *i.e.,* the Vatican and Sinaitic, two of the most ancient manuscripts. The words, "at Ephesus," however, are written in the margin by a later hand. And a corrector of the Cursive MS., known as No. 67, has marked the words, in that MS., as suspicious.

4. ORIGEN (who died 253 A.D.) wrote a commentary on this Epistle, and it is certain that the words "at Ephesus" were not in the MS. he had before him.

5. The same may be said of BASIL (who died 379 A.D.) See

Contra Eun. 11,19.

6. MARCION, an early Christian writer, believed that this epistle was written to the Laodiceans.

7. The explanation of all this, probably, is that the epistle, was *Encyclical*, and that the space now occupied by the words ἐν Ἐφέσῳ *(en Phes ō) at Ephesus,* was originally left blank, so that the name of the various churches to which it was sent could be filled in.

8. It is certain from Col. iv. 16, that Paul *did* write an Epistle to the Laodiceans: therefore, either an epistle has been lost, or this is the one so written. We prefer to believe that the latter is the case.

The Epistle to the Colossians appears to have been a similar epistle, to be sent round and read by other churches. For Col. iv. 16 says: "And when this epistle has been read among you, cause that it be read in the church of the Laodiceans also, and that ye likewise read the epistle from Laodicea." This latter would be the epistle now known by us as, addressed "to the Ephesians," which, being Encyclical, would reach the Colossians "from Laodicea."

The interest of all this to us is— (1) no epistle has been lost! and (2) that this epistle to the Saints "at Ephesus" *was addressed to them,* but was addressed also to other churches as well, besides Ephesus, and therefore in a very special manner to us, though we shall continue to speak of it as, and to call it, "the Epistle to the Ephesians."

It comes to us therefore as the second great Text-Book of Church Doctrine, and cannot be understood until we have mastered the lessons taught us in the Epistle to the Romans. It follows that Epistle, and carries on its teaching.

Romans ends with a reference to the revelation of the mystery. Ephesians takes up that subject and unfolds it to us. The Doctrinal portion of Romans ends with the eighth chapter, and that chapter is the foundation on which the Ephesian truth is built. It is more like a treatise than an epistle.

The scope of the epistle will be seen from its structure:—

103

EPHESIANS AS A WHOLE.

A | i. 1, 2. Epistolary. Salutation.
> B | i. 3-iii. 21. Doctrinal, as to our standing.
> B | iv.-vi. 20. Doctrinal, as to our state.
A | vi. 21-24. Epistolary. Salutation.

From this it will be seen how large a portion—nearly the whole—is occupied with doctrine; one half as it concerns our standing, and the other half as it affects our state; thus showing that sound doctrine is the foundation and source of correct practice; while true practice is the outcome of sound doctrine.

The key to the whole epistle is contained in its opening words (as we saw was the case with Galatians). "Blessed be the God and Father of our Lord Jesus Christ, who hath blessed us with every spiritual blessing, in the heavenlies, in Christ or, "heavenly places," as in the A.V. and R.V.

The sphere of these blessings, therefore, is heavenly, for they are "in Christ." He has entered into "heavenly places," and we are there in Him; for God "when we were dead in sins, quickened us together with Christ, and hath raised us up together, and made us sit down together in heavenly *places* in Christ Jesus" (ii- 5, 6).

So that we have here, as the scope of the epistle, a distinct advance on the teaching of the Epistle to the Romans.

But we must show the structure of some of these larger and more important members, in order to see the special points to which our attention is directed thereby.

THE EXPANSION OF "B" (i. 3—iii. 21).

Doctrinal.

B | a | c | i. 3-14. The PURPOSE of God (i. 9) in Himself (i. 9) concerning Christ Personal. "The Mystery of God."

d | i. 15-23. PRAYER to "the God of our Lord Jesus Christ," as to " c."

b | ii. OURSELVES. The object of these purposes and these prayers.

a | c | iii. 1-13. The PURPOSE of God in Christ (iii. 11) concerning Christ Mystical. "The Mystery of Christ" (iii. 4).

d | iii. 14-21. PRAYER to "the Father of our Lord Jesus Christ" as to "c."

Here we have three great members "a," "b," and "a." In "a" and "a" we have that which relates to God; in "b" that which relates to ourselves.

In the first member, "a" (i- 3-23), we have the purpose of God which He hater purposed in Himself concerning Christ Personal, and all that He has made Christ to be unto His People.

In the third, "a" (iii. 1-21), we have the same purpose revealed concerning the Christ Mystical, and what God has made His People to be in Him.

Thus in these two members we have the expansion of the opening words in i. 3.

Then in the second and fourth members ("d" and "d" we have two prayers. The first prayer (i. 15-23) is based on and refers to what goes before—the purpose of God, and what He has made Christ to be unto us: while the second prayer (iii. 14-21) is based on and refers to the Revelation of the Mystery, and what we are made to be in Christ.

A comparison of these two prayers will show this, as we shall see later. But note, now, that, in between these purposes and these prayers, right in the centre of all these blessings, we have *ourselves* described, who are the objects of both, and the recipients of all this wondrous grace.

We are described in our *past* and in our *present* condition, individually and collectively:

THE EXPANSION OF "b" (chapter ii).

```
b | e |  ii.  1-3.  Past.
                          ⎧  g |  4, 5-.  Quickened.
          f |  4-10.  Present.  ⎨     h |  -5.  By Grace.
                          ⎩  g |  6, 7.  Raised and Seated.
                                h |  8-10.  By Grace.
      e |  11, 12.  Past.
                          ⎧  i |  13.  Nearness in Christ.
          f |  13-22.  Present.  ⎨     k |  14-17.  Results.
                          ⎩  i |  18.  Access through Christ.
                                k |  18-22.  Results.
```

This expansion shows the wondrous workmanship (ii. 10) put forth in us and upon us, in God's purpose, and by God's grace.

We must, however, return now, to see what that "Purpose" is: though we can do no more than point out the *scope* of the member which sets it forth.

EXPANSION OF "c" (i. 3-14), (page 105).
The Purpose of God in Himself.

```
c | g¹ |    3.  Blessing.  "All spiritual blessings."
      h¹ |    4.  Measure.  "According as he hath chosen us" in
                  Christ.
    g² |    5-.  Blessing.  Sonship.
      h² |    -5, 6.  Measure.  "According to the good pleasure
                  of his will."
    g³ |    7-.  Blessing.  Redemption.
      h³ |    -7.  Measure.  "According to the riches of his
                  grace."
    g⁴ |    8, 9-.  Blessing.  Wisdom, even the Mystery.
      h⁴ |    -9, 10.  Measure.  "According to his good
                  pleasure."
    g⁵ |    11-.  Blessing.  Inheritance.
      h⁵ |    -11-14.  Measure.  "According to his purpose."
```

106

From this it will be seen that the foundation of all blessing is in "the purpose of God" Himself. No sinfulness on our part hindered its outflow, and no merit on our part called it forth. The will of God is the source of all our blessing. The work of Christ is the channel of it. And the witness of the Holy Ghost is the power of it. (Heb. x.)

There is no reason for our blessing except in the spontaneous, free, eternal, everlasting, inexhaustible grace of God. It is this side of it which is further brought out in chapter ii. in connection with ourselves; but here (in chapter i.) it is God's side which is presented to us: and His "eternal purpose which He has purposed in Christ." It is the mystery (or secret) of His will" (i. 9) which is here made known.

This is a peculiar expression; and, with the word μυστήριον *(mysteerion)* untranslated, it conveys little or no sense. The word translated (or rather transliterated) "mystery" means *a secret.*[53] We have a very similar expression in Judith ii. 2, where Nebuchodonosor, when about to set out on a great campaign, "called together all his servants and all his great men and communicated to them the mystery of his will": *i.e.,* his *secret plan* of campaign, which no one knew but himself.

This expression is very interesting; not only because of the Word *secret,* but because of the word used for "will." It is not the same word as in Eph. i. 9. Both words mean will: the one *to will* or *determine*; the other *to will* or *desire.*

With Nebuchodonosor it was what he willed, because he had *determined* to do it (it may be he had no choice): while with God (Eph. i. 9) it means that He willed it because he *desired it.*

In both cases it means[54] *secret purpose* or *counsel.*

This is what God is making known in this Epistle to the Ephesians. Romans was concerning the knowledge of *Man* and how he is justified. Ephesians is concerning the knowledge of *God* and what He has done, in blessing, for those whom He has justified.

---

53. See *The Mystery,* by Dr. Bullinger, price sixpence.

54. By the figure *Hypallage.* See *Figures of Speech,* by the same author. Page 535.

This purpose (in chapter i.) is seen to be concerning Christ. All the blessings are in Christ ("g^1" i- 3). We are "predestinated unto sonship through Jesus Christ to Himself ("g^2" i.5). This secret counsel is concerning Christ ("g^3" i. 9) given to the church and made the Head over all things—all things being headed-up in Him.

Hence the prayer which follows ("d" i. 15-23) is that we may have given unto us "the spirit of wisdom and revelation in the knowledge of HIM," and of "HIS calling," and of "HIS inheritance in the saints," and of "HIS power to us-ward who believe.

Having entered the school of Grace where the Holy Spirit is the teacher, the first lesson we have to learn is about ourselves, in the Epistle to the Romans. We are reproved and corrected as to this great lesson (in Corinthians and Galatians) until we have thoroughly mastered it.

Then we are moved up into a higher class; and our first lesson here is to learn God, and to have spiritual wisdom imparted to us. Having been taught that we died and have risen in and with Christ; and learned, not merely how He was substituted for us, but how we are identified with Him, we are then prepared to learn how God has not only raised us up together with Him, but made us sit together in Him in heavenly places in Christ. The first part of this "purpose" ("c" i. 3-14) is what He has made Christ to be unto us. While the second part of it ("c" iii. 1-13) is what He has made us to be in Christ.

In the real Divine order, of course, and as regards God, Ephesians comes before Romans: for it records God's eternal purpose "before the foundation of the world" (i- 4). But, as regards ourselves, in point of order and apprehension, Romans comes first. We approach these great truths from our own standpoint and must learn the lessons taught in Romans before we can understand the truths revealed in Ephesians.[55]

---

55. Just as with the great *Offerings* in Leviticus. The Revelation begins, from God's side, with the burnt offering. But we begin, in our experience, with the sin offering, and learn their truths in the reverse order.

So also with the *Tabernacle;* God, in describing its construction, commences with the "Ark of the Covenant," and proceeds outward to the "Court" (Exodus

The Epistle to the Ephesians.
The Purpose of God in Christ.

In connection with what God has "purposed in Himself" concerning Christ (i. 3-14), we will consider what He has "purposed in Christ Jesus" concerning the Church (iii. 1-13); leaving the two Prayers ("d," i. 15-23, and "d," iii. 14-21) to be considered together in our next paper.

In speaking of the "purpose" of God it is important that we should distinguish between His "purpose" and His "counsel."

The two words are quite different, in Greek as in English. "Counsel" βουλή, which means, *will, determination;* also *counsel* in the sense of conference or *advice:* while "purpose" is πρόθεσις *(prothesis) a setting before;* hence, that which a person *sets before* his mind or *proposes to* himself; *ie., purpose, deliberate resolution,* or *plan.*

"Counsel," therefore implies the deliberation of distinct persons. See Gen. i. 26, which contains the first statement of God's revealed counsel: "Let us make man in our image and let him have dominion . . . over all the earth," etc. (Ps. viii.). It relates to man and his dominion over the earth, as distinct from the "purpose" of God which was eternal (Eph. iii. 11) "before the foundation of the world" (Eph. i. 4), and therefore outside of and prior to the "counsel" of Gen. i. 26. "Purpose" is thus associated with Deity in *Unity,* while "counsel" is associated with Deity in *Trinity.*

"Counsel" is distinguished from "purpose" in Eph. i. 11. The former has to do with *plan;* while the latter has to do with the *working out* of that plan.

---

xxv. -xxvii.): but, it is through the "Court" that the worshippers enter, and learn the lessons, and all the blessed truths which are to be taught within.

"Counsel" has to do with *man*, and the Son of Man, and His dominion in the earth; and hence is equivalent to the Kingdom as distinct from the Church (see Acts xx. 25-27). While "purpose" has to do with the Church of God, the Mystery or secret as distinct from the Kingdom.

The Apostle expounded to the Elders of Ephesus "the whole counsel of God" as it related to the Kingdom (Acts xx. 25-27), and he names the fact which was the basis of his further teaching; but, whether he went on to explain to the "Elders of Ephesus" the truth afterwards written to the Church in his Epistle we are not informed. It is outside the subject of the Acts of the Apostles to inform us; and there is no intimation in the Epistle that the "Mystery" had been the subject of his teaching to them before that epistle was written.

The distinction between the "counsel" of God and His "purpose" is important; because it constitutes the difference between Paul's *preaching* "according to the Scriptures," and his *teaching* as recorded in his Epistle concerning the Mystery which had been "hidden from ages and generations."

It is this teaching which we are now to consider as set forth in these two chapters (Eph. i. and iii.).

This "purpose" of God was twofold. It was (chap. i.) concerning "Christ," as made the Head over all things: all things in heaven and earth being ultimately headed-up in one under Him. It was (chap. iii.) concerning the "Church," as the Spiritual Body of Christ, made one in Him.

We have seen the structure and therefore the scope of the first part of this wondrous purpose (chap. i. 3-14, see page 33) and now we have to see the structure of the second part.

"*C*". iii. 1-13.

The purpose of God in Christ.

C | i | iii. 1. Paul. His imprisonment for their sakes.

    j | k | 2-4. The Mystery revealed and committed *to* Paul's stewardship *(οἰκονομία*)*.

        l | 5-. The Mystery hidden before.

           m | -5, 6. The Mystery revealed to the Church through Apostles and Prophets by the Spirit.

    j | k | 7-9-. The Mystery made known *by* Paul, according to the stewardship *(οἰκονομία*[56]*)* committed to him.

        l | -9. The Mystery hidden before.

           m | 10-12. The mystery made known to principalities and powers through the Church by God.

  i | 13. Paul. His tribulations for their sakes.

It is perfectly clear from this that God's purpose in Christ was a great *secret* (for this, as we have seen, is the meaning of the word "mystery") hidden in Himself, and never revealed or made known until it was specially revealed to the Apostle Paul, and by him to the "holy apostles and prophets" of the new dispensation.

That these apostles are not necessarily the Twelve Apostles, and that these prophets are not of the prophets of the Old Testament dispensation is clear. For there were Apostles quite apart from the Twelve. PAUL himself was one. BARNABAS is included among the Apostles (Acts xiv- 4, 14). ANDRONICUS and JUNIAS are said to be conspicuous or "of note" among the Apostles (Rom. xvi. 7). From 1 Cor. iv. 9 it would seem that he called APOLLOS and himself "the last apostles" (see margin). 1 Cor. ix. 5 and 2 Cor. xi. 5; xii. 11, 12, seem to imply the existence of more than twelve. But Eph. iv. 8, 11, is conclusive; for there it is distinctly affirmed that

---

56. οἰκονομία *(oikonomia) administration, or stewardship,* is the correct reading according to Griesbach, Lachmann, Tischendorf, Tregelles, Alford, and R.V., instead of κοινωνία *(koinonia) fellowship.*

111

after Christ "ascended up on high. . . . He gave gifts unto men . . . and He gave some apostles,and some prophets," etc. SILVANUS and TIMOTHY are included among the apostles (1 Thess. ii. 6, compare with i. 1). We find "Apostles of churches" in 2 Cor. viii. 23.

The New Testament Prophets are also clearly distinguished from those of the Old Testament in 1 Cor. xii. 28 and Eph. iv. 11. The existence of such an order of ministry is shown by those who formed part of it, *eg.,* BARNABAS (Acts xiii. 1), AGABUS (Acts xi. 28; xxi. 10), SILAS and JUDUS (Acts xv. 32), MANAEN and Lucius of Cyrene (Acts xiii. 1).; TIMOTHY (a man of God, *ie.,* a prophet), 1 Tim. vi. 11 and 2 Tim. iii. 17); the DAUGHTERS of Philip the Evangelist (Acts xxi. 8) and others, not named (Acts viii. 17, and 44-46; xix. 6).

In Rom. xvi. 26 we are told that this Mystery was made manifest "by prophetic writings." There is no article here, either with the word "writings," or "prophets." Indeed the word is not a noun, but an adjective *προφητικόν (propheeticon),* as in 2 Pet. i. 19 (in contrast with the Old Testament prophets and their prophecy in verse 21).

Let us set forth this member (iii. 1-13) more accurately, word by word:

"i" (iii. 1). *Paul. His imprisonment for their sakes*
For this cause, Paul, the prisoner of the Lord for you Gentiles.

"k" (2-4). *Paul's stewardship of the Mystery to the Church.*
If, at least, ye have heard of the stewardship of the grace of God, grace that has been given to me for you, how that by revelation was made known to me the Mystery (or Secret) according as I wrote before, briefly; with an eye to which secret, in reading, ye can perceive my understanding in the Mystery (or Secret) of the Christ.

"l" (5-). *The Mystery hidden before.*
a secret which in the other generations never was made known to the sons of men.

112

"m" (-5, 6). *The Mystery revealed to the Church through Apostles and Prophets by the Spirit.*

as lately it was revealed to His holy apostles and prophets by the Spirit—that the Gentiles should be joint heired, joint bodied,[57] and joint shared of the promise In Christ Jesus[58] through the Gospel.

"k" (7-9-). Paul's stewardship of the mystery.

of which Gospel I was made a minister according to the gift of the grace of God, the gift given to me according to the working of His power: unto me—the less than the least of all the saints—was given this grace, to announce the glad tidings among the Gentiles, the untrackable riches (or wealth) of the Christ, and enlightening all as to what is the stewardship[59] of the mystery (or secret).

"l" (- 9). The Mystery hidden before.

that has been hidden, from eternity (or the ages) in God[60] who created all things.

---

57. σύσσωμα *(sussoma)*. This word occurs only here. It does not mean that there was a Body already or previously in existence, to which others were afterwards added, and became members; but, that Gentile and Jewish believers (ii. 14, 15) should now form one *jointbody,* being made "of twain, one new man" (Eph. ii. 15).

58. The word "Jesus" is to be added here according to Lachmann, Tischendorf, Tregelles, Alford and the R.V.

59. According to the above authories (Lachmann, Tregelles, Tischendorf, Alford, and R.V.) The word here should be οίκονομία *(oikonomia) administration,* or *stewardship,* and not κοινωνία *(koinonia) fellowship.*

60. "By Jesus Christ." These words are omitted by all the Critical Greek Texts and the R.V.

"m" (10-12). *The Mystery made known to angelic beings, through the Church, byGod.*

in (or that) now, to the principalities and the authorities in the heavenlies might be made known through (*i.e.*, by means of) the Church, the manifold[61] wisdom of God, according to the eternal purpose (or purpose of the ages) which (purpose) He made in Christ Jesus our Lord, in whom we have boldness and access, with assurance through the faith of (or, relating to) Him.

"i" (13)- *Paul. His tribulations for their sakes.*
Wherefore, I beg you not to faint at my tribulations on your behalf, which is your glory.

This structure gives the scope of the whole passage which is, clearly, the "Mystery"; or, the eternal purpose of God as to what He has made His People to be in Christ.

The common interpretation wholly disregards this point, which, as we have shown, is the scope of the passage. It treats it as though this were merely a reference to the fact that the Gentiles were to be brought into blessing in connection with Christ.

But this was never a secret "hid in God," and "not made known unto the sons of men," and "now revealed" for the first time (Eph. iii. 9, 5). This was never "kept secret since the world began," and only "now made manifest" (Rom. xvi. 25, 26). This was never "hid from ages and from generations," and "now is made manifest to the saints" (Col. i. 26).

If Eph. iii. merely relates to the Gospel, then, language is useless for the purposes of revelation.

If there is one thing clear in Scripture it is this, that the Gospel, or Salvation through Christ alone, and justification by faith, was the subject of Divine revelation all through the ages and generations. That Gospel, it is expressly declared, "was preached before unto Abraham" (Gal. iii. 8). That good news was not "hid in God," but was "promised afore by His prophets in the holy Scriptures" (Rom.

---

61. The word is πολυποίκιλος *(polupoikilos)* many-coloured or much-variegated.

114

i. 2). That Gospel was never "kept secret since the world began," but it was "witnessed by the law and the prophets" (Rom. iii. 21) and preached to Israel (Heb. iv. 2).

And that Gentiles, as such, were to be blessed with Israel was never "kept secret." It was "made known to the sons of men." It was made known to Abraham in the very first promise made to him—"in thee shall all families of the earth be blessed" (Gen. xii. 3). This promise was often repeated; and over and over again it was made to Abraham and the Patriarchs (Gen. xviii. 18; xxii. 18; xxvi. 4, etc.); and made the subject of prayer and praise. See Ps. lxxii. 17; xviii. 49; Deut. xxxii. 43; Isa. xi. 10; Luke ii. 32 ; Isa. xlix. 6, etc., etc.

No! the secret was: that, a people should be taken out from among both Jews and Gentiles, who should with Christ be made σύσσωμα (sussoma) a joint-body in Christ (Eph. iii. 9); a Body of which Christ should be the glorious Head in heaven, and His People—the members of that body on the earth— "one new man."

This was the secret which was revealed to God's "holy apostles and prophets by the Spirit," and which had never entered into the heart or mind of mortal man,—CHRIST MYSTICAL.

The members of the Body of Christ are those who have believed God's testimony, (as Abraham believed it), as to their lost condition as sinners, and as to the great salvation which is in Christ the Saviour; and who have reckoned themselves as having died when He died, and risen again when He rose: thus identified with Christ (not in His incarnation, which is a modern heresy, but) in His death and resurrection. This is the truth which is bound up with the meaning of "the Body of Christ."

When He, the Head, died; then we, the members, in the eternal purpose and judgment of God, died in Him.

When He, the Head, rose again; then we, the members, must be risen in Him (Romans).

If He, the Head, is in Heaven; then we, the members, are seated in the heavenlies in Him (Ephesians).

When He, the Head, shall appear; then shall we appear with Him in glory.

When He shall come to be glorified in His saints, His saints shall be "caught up to meet the Lord in the air, and so shall we ever be with the Lord" (1 and 2 Thessalonians).

This is the subject of Eph. iii. 1-13: the "eternal purpose" of God "which he purposed in Christ Jesus our Lord." This is what was kept secret, and never revealed until it was made known to the Apostle Paul, and committed to him and to his *stewardship (οἰκονομία) oikonomia* as he so clearly states in verses 2 and 9.[62]

This is the second great lesson for the Church of God to learn concerning its standing in Christ. This is the second Text-book which it is to master. Having learned the truth as it is set forth in Romans, the next great truth is revealed in Ephesians. Having been taught (in Romans) that the members of Christ's Body died with Christ, and rose with Christ, the next revelation (in Ephesians) is that we are now seated in the heavenlies in Christ, and are waiting to be received up into glory by Him (1 Tim. iii. 16), and to be glorified together with Him.

Seeing that the members of Christ's Spiritual Body died with Christ, there is no reason now why they should ever die at all! No, not even though it is "appointed unto men once to die" (Heb. ix. 27). Hence another part of this great secret is given in 1 Cor xv. 51. "Behold I shew you a mystery," i.e.,

"BEHOLD, I TELL YOU A SECRET!"

What is it? "We shall not all sleep." What? Not though it is appointed to men once to die, and after this judgment (Heb. ix. 27)? Must we not die? No! blessed be God. It is not necessary! The members of the Body were judged with the Head, and were "crucified with Christ"; and therefore there is no reason why they should ever die at all, and no reason why they should ever come into judgment (Rom. viii. 1). They may "fall asleep," but "not all."But, whether alive or asleep, "we shall all be changed; in a moment, in the twinkling of an eye, at the last trump: for the trumpet shall sound, and the dead shall be raised incorruptible, and we shall be changed" (1 Cor. xv. 51-57).

---

62. For a fuller treatment of the whole subject, see *The Mystery,* by the same author and publisher, price 6d. and 1s.

This is one of the things of which it is specially said, "I would not have you ignorant."

Oh! what a blessed truth to be initiated into. Well, may he say, "Behold, I tell you a secret." "I would not have you ignorant" of it.

This, then, is to be the end of Christ *mystical,* as it was of Christ *personal.* The members are waiting to be "received up in Glory," as the Head was. This is our hope, our "blessed hope."

So that "waiting for God's Son from heaven" is part of our Christian position. It enters into the very foundation of our standing in Christ.

It is not the mere study of prophecy as such which may, or may not, be taken up by Christians, as an "extra subject":but it forms the warp and woof of our Christian standing. It is our "blessed hope;" waiting to be

"RECEIVED UP IN GLORY."

The Epistle to the Ephesians.
THE TWO PRAYERS: (i.17-23 and iii. 14-19).

Each of the two great declarations (in chaps. i. 3-14 and iii. 1-13) concerning "the purpose of God" is followed by a prayer (as we have seen from the structure on page 105).

The subject is so vast and so full of grace and glory that the mind is lost in wonder, and can only go forth in prayer to Him Who has purposed such things for us as pass man's understanding.

The two declarations of God's purpose are (as we have seen), His purpose "in Himself" concerning Christ (i. 3-14), and His purpose "in Christ Jesus" concerning His Church (iii. 31-12).

The two prayers follow these two purposes respectively: the second ending in a doxology which very emphatically separates, into two parts, the Doctrinal portion of the Epistle; the first of which relates to our standing in the heavenlies, and the second to our state on the earth.

The scope of these two prayers, therefore, can be understood only as we refer them to the teaching concerning God's special purpose, which precedes them.

The first words of any book or special passage always give the key to its object. It is so here. The Doctrine commences (after the Epistolary opening) with verse 3, "Blessed be the God and Father of our Lord Jesus Christ, who hath blessed us with all spiritual blessings in the heavenlies in Christ."

The rest of the Epistle is the development and expansion of these words.

Two relationships are announced at the outset: "God" and "Father." "God" has reference to *creation*-power and glory, while "Father" has reference to *covenant*-relationship and grace.

These two titles, which are here combined together, are afterwards separated in these two prayers.

The title "God" has respect to the first revelation of His purpose

118

(i. 3-14). "Father" has respect to the second (iii. 1-13).

"God," has reference to what He has purposed in Himself concerning Christ in making Him the Head of all creation, **"with a view to the administration of the fullness of the times, to head up (or re-unite under one head) for Himself all things in the Christ: both the things in the heavens and the things on the earth, in Him."**

"Father," has reference to what He has purposed in Christ concerning us in making us one "family" in Him, members of His body, sons and heirs in Christ, one with Him in all His glory.

Hence the two prayers commence respectively with these titles. The first prayer is addressed to "the GOD of our Lord Jesus Christ" (i. 11), while the second is addressed to "the FATHER of our Lord Jesus Christ" (iii. 14).

The contrast will be better seen if we exhibit them thus:

THE FIRST PRAYER. (1. 17-23).	THE SECOND PRAYER. (iii. 14-19).

Addressed to

"The GOD of our Lord Jesus Christ, the Father of glory,"	"The FATHER of our Lord Jesus Christ," the Father of the family,

that He might give (δῴη)

"The Spirit of wisdom and revelation. The eyes of the heart enlightened." (*The enlightenment* of the inner man).	"With power to be strengthened by His Spirit in the inner man." (*The strengthening* of the inner man).

the knowledge

of GOD The hope of HIS calling. The riches of the glory of HIS inheritance in the saints. The surpassing (ὑπερβάλλον) greatness of HIS power.	of CHRIST. The breadth of Christ's love. The length of it. The depth of it. The height of it. The knowledge-surpassing (ὑπερβάλλουσαν) LOVE of Christ.

The means.

We in Christ	Christ in us.

The measure.

"According to the working of His mighty power, which He wrought IN CHRIST."	"According to the power that worketh IN US.."

The end.

"The Church, which is His Body, the fulness (πλήρωμα) of Christ who filleth all."	"That ye may be filled with all the fulness (πλήρωμα) of God."

120

It will thus be seen that the great subject of the first prayer is *Power*—the surpassing power of God in carrying out His purpose in setting Christ to be the Head of the Body, and over all things for the Body. The great subject of the second prayer is *Love:* the love of Christ.

We in Christ, is the subject of the first prayer: while, in the second prayer, it is *Christ in us,* and the surpassing love of Christ dwelling in our hearts through faith.

This is the subjective truth of the Mystery, apart from which the mere doctrinal knowledge of it is as nothing.

This is the power of the great Secret; not when we hold it, but when it holds us.

These prayers are not given to us to expound, but they are for us *to pray;* and to pray until we understand all that they mean in a blessed and happy experience.

They are the prayers of the Holy Spirit (through Paul) for us. He it is who here "maketh intercession for us," and these are His intercessions referred to and promised in Rom. viii. 26, 27.

If we could live in the spirit of these prayers, and realize the wondrous standing which God has given us in Christ, and know something of "the riches of His grace" (i. 7) and "the riches of His glory" (i. 18; iii. 16) which are here displayed before our eyes and our hearts, our walk would be more worthy of it.

In chapter iv. 1 we are exhorted to "walk worthy of the calling wherewith we are called." But how can we do so unless we know what that calling is? How can we take that calling as the measure and standard of our "walk" unless we know what it is? Surely, the more we know of that wondrous standing which God has given to the members of Christ's Body, in Him, of the power and love which placed us there, and of the grace which keeps us there, the more will our walk be worthy of it.

Instead of this, we see, on every hand, thousands of Christians who are wholly ignorant of their standing in Christ (through not having studied the Epistle to the Ephesians). They look at their walk; and, seeing that it is not what it ought to be, and not what they would have it to be, they set themselves to work to mend it, and improve it; and by every kind of artifice—from Romish methods like those of Thomas à Kempis to Protestant methods like those of recent times imported from America—they seek to acquire a standing in the flesh.

They are so "foolish" that, having begun in spirit, they now seek to be made perfect by the flesh (Gal. iii. 3). The new Gospel of "surrender" has been substituted for the Gospel of the grace of God. The sinner is told to "surrender." The saint is taught to "surrender." And they are to "let God" do this, and "allow God" to do that (as though He had no "purpose" at all), until God Himself is practically shut out and self is (unconsciously) deified! So opposite are man's thoughts and ways to God's, that God's way of salvation and sanctification is turned upside down through ignorance of that which He has specially written and given for our instruction.

Into no other profession would any one be allowed to enter, as people enter on the profession of Christianity. Every other profession has its text books for study: and no one is allowed to enter it until an examination can be passed in those text books. No one can enter the army, or the law, or the medical profession—no one can be a "professor" in any art or science—until he is proficient in the knowledge of all that pertains to it. No one can obtain the humblest situation in life without being asked for some evidence as to his knowledge of or proficiency for such a position.

But the Christian profession is treated very differently. Any one is supposed to be qualified to be a "professor" of Christianity, whether he knows little or nothing. Whether the conversion be wrought by God, or whether, by man, a person is said to be "converted to God," the result is much the same; man's books are studied, and God's Book is neglected. The Epistles, which are given as the Christian's Text-Books, are not used as such. If read at all, they are treated as consisting of so many "portions" to be read through in so many days, or as so many texts to be printed on a card to be hung upon a wall or sent through the post. And, even if studied, they are not studied contextually; but treated apart from their scope and context; and scrappy collections are made of the four "buts," or the five "therefores," or the six "whys"; and, by a system of text-garbling, the design and object and scope of the various books of the Bible are altogether lost, while the reader is deceived into thinking that he is a Bible student.

No other book is treated in this way. No other book *could* be understood or learned if studied in such a way.

No wonder that such ignorance of God and of His Word prevails. No wonder that such a low standard of walk is manifest. The means which God has provided in order to impart knowledge of such truth, in order to secure true holiness, are set aside; while man's books and man's methods are resorted to—but in vain.

In these prayers the great burden is that we may know "what is the hope of HIS calling" wherewith He has called us. But Christians want to know *their* calling.

And what are "the riches of the glory of HIS inheritance in the saints"; but the saints, in their selfishness, want to know about *their* inheritance.

And "what is the exceeding greatness of HIS power to usward who believe"; but Christians to-day want to know about *their* power, and where to get it, and how to find it and how to get what is called "Enduement"! It is all *self* from beginning to end: and Christ is brought in as a mere makeweight and partner. They talk and sing about being "nothing;" while all the time the one aim and object is to be *something!*

Not until we know Christ as He is revealed in the Epistles, and understand "the things of Christ," which the Holy Spirit there shows us, shall we know ourselves: and not until we know the calling and standing which God has given us in Christ shall we ever be able to "walk worthy" of it.

The Epistle to the Ephesians.
PRACTICAL CONCLUSION (Chap. iv. to end).

Having considered the first great doctrinal portion of this Epistle, which concerns our standing in Christ, it now only remains to conclude our notes by giving the structure of the second portion of it, which has to do with our walk, and is the practical working out of the Doctrine and of the truth received within.

It is made up of four large members, thus:

"B" (iv. 1—vi. 20).
Practical.
Their walk among themselves and others.

B | n | iv. 1-16. Their walk among themselves as worthy of their calling; being members of one Body. *(Ecclesiastical).*
o | iv. 17-v. 21. Their walk among others. *(Spiritual).*
n | v. 22-vi. 9. Their walk among themselves. *(Domestic).*
o | vi. 10-20. Their walk among others. *(Spiritual).*

These four members are capable of further development, thus: The first member, "n" (iv. 1-16), defines the nature and measure of their walk, and shows how it can be worthy of their "calling" only by a correct understanding of what that calling involves, ecclesiastically. Thus:—

"n" (iv. 1-16).
Their walk among themselves.
(Ecclesiastical).

n | p | 1-3. Exhortation.
q | 4-6. The unity of the Body itself.
q | 7-13. The diversity of gifts to the Body.
p | 14-16. Exhortation.

This structure shows us that verses 4-13 ("q" and *"q"*) are practically in a parenthesis, setting forth the unity of the Body and the diversity of the gifts for building it up: while verse 3 reads on to verse 14, and shows that this knowledge of "His calling" is the only source of power for a walk worthy of it; and our only security against being "carried about with every wind of doctrine," which is fatal to such a walk.

Only by "holding the truth in love" is it possible to "grow up into Him in all things, who is the Head—even Christ."

The thought here is not merely individual. It is collective also: for we are led on to consider (in verse 16) and instructed as to the growth of the Body of Christ, by the physiological illustration of the human body.

Christ is the head; and from Him "**the whole body continually fitted together and compacted** (or, ever fitting together and compacting) **by every sensation**[63] **of the supply, according to a working corresponding to the measure of each individual part** (or, according to the proportional energy of each single part), **brings about the growth of the body with a view to the building up of itself in love.**"

This is the growth of the Body, and this is the security for a walk in worthiness and holiness. This wondrous truth, which we are to hold in love, is at once the source and the security of both. How different from the modern, miserable Gospel of "surrender"; which not only obtrudes "self" where God is all in all, but shuts out the very power which it professes to seek. How it brings us down from

---

63. The word ἀφή (haphee), a touching, Lat., junctura, occurs only here and in the other parallel passage (Col. ii. 19). It is not a "joint," but a nexus, or connection, by which supply is passed on from one organ to another: and not so much the corresponding parts in contact, not so much the actual touching of the parts, as the mutual relation between them. Galen (second cent. A.D.) says the body "owes its compactness partly to the articulation (arthron), and partly to the attachment (sumphusis) Aristotle (B.C. 356) speaks of two kinds of union, contact and (symphusis) cohesion. So that it is the contact between the various parts which conveys the necessary supply, with special reference to the adaptation and mutual sympathy and influence of the parts in contact. Aristotle speaks of this as full of feeling, or sensitive (patheetika), and we have tried to express it by the word "sensation."

heaven to earth! How it occupies us with our wretched selves, instead of with the surpassing greatness of God's power (i. 19), and the surpassing knowledge of Christ's love (iii. 19)!

No wonder that Christian walk is what it is, and should have become lowered to the standard which is presented everywhere today.

We now pass on to the

EXPANSION OF "o" (iv. 17—v. 21).
Their walk among others.
(Spiritual).

o | r | iv. 17-19. The others.
    s | 20-32. Themselves (negative and positive).
    s | v. 1-4. Themselves (positive and negative).
  r | v. 5-21. The others.

This practical portion also is full of teaching and blessed instruction. The contrast between themselves and the others (taking up again the subject of chapter ii.) shows that the walk will be in accordance with the measure in which we learn Christ (iv. 20).

It depends on whether we have "heard Him, and have been taught by Him even as truth is in Jesus" (iv. 21). Not as we have heard this or that teacher *about* Christ; not as we have read this or that writer concerning Him. But as we have "heard HIM"—Christ Himself; for His words which He speaks to us are "spirit and life" (John vi. 63). Note also that it does not say, as these words are continually quoted, "the truth as it is in Jesus." If it said this it would imply that there is some truth which is not in Him: which is not the case. No! the words are, "As the truth is in Jesus"; implying that there is no truth apart from Him. "I am the truth," He declared (John xiv. 6), and the word which testifies of Him is truth (John xvii. 17).

Here is the enabling power for a worthy and holy walk.

We next come to

"n" (v. 22—vi. 9).
Their walk among themselves.
(Domestic).

n | t^1 | v. 22-24. Wives.
u^1 | 25-33. Husbands (masc.)
t^2 | vi. 1-3. Children.
u^2 | 4. Fathers (masc.)
t^3 | 5-8. Servants.
u^3 | 9. Masters (masc.)

This does not call for any extended comment beyond the remark that we have here the outcome of doctrine-an illustration of domestic relationship and social duty as flowing out of the doctrine.

The duty of husband to wife is illustrated by the relation of the head to the body, inasmuch as the husband is the head of the wife (1 Cor. xi. 3, etc.).

Christians, in their usual selfishness, attempt to rob others of their place as the Bride, and thus lose their own still "better" place (Heb. xi. 40) as part of the Bridegroom.

It is clear from all the Scriptures which treat of the Mystery that the Church is the Body of Christ, and that the members of that Body are members of Christ, Who Himself is the Bridegroom.

It is also clear that the Bride is the subject of Old Testament prophecy, and therefore could not form part of the Mystery which was kept secret, and formed no part of Old Testament revelation or prophecy.

Isa. liv. 5-8; ixii. 4.[64] Jer. iii 14. Hos. ii. 16, 19, and other scriptures, speak of the Bride as of Israel. Perhaps an elect remnant. For all through there were those who walked by faith (Heb. xi.) and who were therefore "partakers of a heavenly calling" (Heb. iii. 1; xi. 10, 13-16). If we compare Heb. xi. 10 with Rev. xxi. 9-27, are we not distinctly to infer that the "city" for which Abraham looked was

---

64. In Isa. iv. 5 there is a reference to the *Chuppah*, or *marriage canopy*, still used by the Jews, and mentioned elsewhere only in Ps. xix. 5, and Joel ii. 16; and referring to Isa. lxii. 4.

"the Bride, the Lamb's wife"?

True, the Apostle might address the saints concerning his desire to present them "a chaste virgin to Christ" (2 Cor. xi. 2). But this no more declares that the Church IS the Bride of Christ than that the Apostle himself was their father (1 Cor. iv. 15), or their mother (Gal. iv. 19). It is merely an illustration, to show his jealous care of them as a "friend of the Bridegroom"; as the others showed his painful anxiety as a "mother," and his loving care as a "father."

So in Eph. v. 28, 29, the argument is that "husbands ought to love their wives as their own bodies; for he that loveth his wife loveth himself; for no man ever yet hated his own flesh; but nourisheth and cherisheth it, even as the Lord the Church, for we are members of His Body," *i.e.*, AS Christ loves His own Body, the Church, SO ought husbands to love their own selves, (*i.e.*, their wives), because they and their wives are "one flesh." Thus the great secret is employed as an argument as to the reciprocal duties of husbands and wives. In neither case is it said that the Church IS the wife, or that Christ IS the husband.

But that AS Christ loves His Body (the Church), SO husbands ought to love their own bodies (their wives).

What is clear and certain is that the Church is the Body of Christ Himself, and that the members of that Body being "in Christ" (mystical), are PART OF THE BRIDEGROOM, and cannot possibly, therefore, be the Bride herself.

A remarkable example of the perversity of Expositors, is this; that, while they hold that the Bride is the Church, persist in interpreting the parable of the Ten Virgins, as though the Bride's attendant "Virgins" are also the Church. Though who ever heard of an Eastern Bride going out "to meet" the Bridegroom? The Virgins, "her companions," went, but not the Bride. So our expositors can hold whichever of these two positions they please, but, clearly, they are not entitled to hold them both. The "Bride" *must* be distinct from "the virgins her companions that follow her." If we rightly divide the Word of Truth, we see that the Church is neither the one nor the other, and that the subsequent revelation of the "Mystery" cannot be read into either Ps. xlv. or Matt. xxv.; which are perfectly clear as they stand, and must have been capable of a plain interpretation to the first hearers or readers of those words, quite apart from the truth subsequently revealed.

The mystery was "hid in God." It does not say it was hidden in the Scriptures, but "hid in God" Himself. There can be therefore no *types* of it in the Old Testament, inasmuch as types *teach,* and were meant to teach, doctrines. But, if truths and doctrines, which are elsewhere clearly revealed in the New Testament, can be *illustrated* from the Old Testament, that is quite another matter. The *illustration or application* of Old Testament Scripture to the Church is quite lawful and profitable, so long as it is kept distinct from *interpretation.* It is one thing to see an illustration of the Church in the Old Testament; but it is quite another thing to say that that is there revealed which God distinctly declares *was not revealed* or "made known to the sons of men."

It will be observed that the scope of Eph. v. is *practical:* and therefore this reference to the Mystery in verse 32 is not for *teaching,* doctrinally, but only by way of illustration to enforce the practical precept.

The practical portion concludes with the fourth member which completes its structure:—

"*o*" (vi. 10-20).
Their walk among others.
(Spiritual).

o | v | vi. 10. Exhortation to be strong in the Lord.

     w | x^1 | 11-. The Armour or Panoply of God ($\pi\alpha\nu o\pi\lambda\acute{\iota}\alpha$).

         y | -11, 12. The purpose: "that ye may be able to stand" ($\sigma\tau\tilde{\eta}\nu\alpha\iota$).

     x^2 | 13-. The Armour or Panoply of God ($\pi\alpha\nu o\pi\lambda\acute{\iota}\alpha$).

         y | -13. The purpose: "that ye may be able to withstand" ($\dot{\alpha}\nu\tau\iota\sigma\tau\tilde{\eta}\nu\alpha\iota$), and "stand" ($\sigma\tau\tilde{\eta}\nu\alpha\iota$).

     x^3 | 14-17. The Armour defined and explained.

  v | 18-20. Exhortation to prayer, for all the saints, and for himself.

It will be noted that the two members which refer to their walk among themselves ("n," iv. 1-16 and "*n*," v. 22—vi. 9) are *Ecclesiastical* and *Domestic*: while the two which refer to their walk among *others* ("o," iv. 17—v. 21 and *"o,"* vi. 10-20) are both *Spiritual.*

The scope of these four practical members, therefore, shows us this: that the spiritual doctrine of the Mystery is used as an illustration to enforce domestic duty: while it causes the Epistle to close with a spiritual exhortation suited to the whole of the great truth revealed in the Epistle.

It opens with a declaration of our Blessings which are in the heavenlies, in Christ. We are further shown how the truth of the Mystery reveals our position before God, in Christ, as seated with Him in the heavenlies.

That therefore is exactly where our danger lies. That is the sphere of our conflict. And so the "final" (vi. 10) exhortation has reference to this danger; and shows us what the Divine provision is with reference to it.

As it is so important it is better to set this forth in full:

TRANSLATION OF "w," vi. 11-17.

Put on the panoply of God, that ye may have (inward) power to stand against the strategies of the devil: because our struggle is not against blood and flesh, but against the principalities, against the authorities, against the world-rulers of this darkness,[65] against the spiritual forces of evil In the heavenlies.

For this reason take up the panoply of God, that ye may have Power (or, be inly enabled) to withstand in the evil day, and, having overcome[66] all, to stand.

Stand then, having girt about your loins with truth, and

---

65. "This darkness" (which in the reading of Griesbach, Lachmann, Tischendorf, Tregelles, Alford, and R.V.) applies to all the "principalities" and "authorities," as well as to the "world-rulers."

66. The Greek is κατεργασάμενοι *(katergasamenoi), having worked out:* *i.e.,* having done all that was ordered in spite of the opposition.

having put on the breastplate of righteousness, and having shod your feet with the readiness of the Gospel of Peace: with all these having taken up faith's shield, wherewith ye will have (inward) power to quench all the burning darts of the evil one. The helmet of salvation[67] also receive ye; and the Spirit's sword, which is Gods Word.

The question arises, Why is this beautiful exhortation respecting the Christian's armour introduced here? There must be a good reason why it is here, and not in any other part of the Epistle! The answer is that it is here because our blessings and standing are in the heavenlies; and because our conflict therefore is in the heavenlies also. That is why we need Divine armour. We need the girdle of truth—the truth taught in Ephesians. We need the breastplate of righteousness—God's righteousness as taught in Romans. We need the helmet of salvation combined in these two, as revealed in God's word which is the Spirit's sword.

Faith's shield is Christ. All is contained in Him, and in the grace or favour which gives us our standing in Him: "Blessed with all spiritual blessings in Christ:" and Christ the "shield" which defends us and preserves all these "blessings" to us. And all is of grace or favour, as it is written: "Thou, LORD, wilt bless the righteous: with favour wilt thou compass (marg., crown) him as with a shield" (Ps. v. 12).

So that we come back to the Grace or Favour of which Romans and Ephesians both testify.

In His favour is life (Ps. xxx. 5).
In His favour is mercy Isa. lx. 10).
In His favour is preservation (Ps. lxxxvi. 2, marg.).

---

67. σωτηρίον (soteerion) It is difficult to distinguish this word from σωτηρία (soteeria) which is the ordinary word for *salvation*. But it seems to have the idea of salvation achieved, or accomplished. As distinct from the salvation wrought in Christ's sufferings it denotes the final complete salvation contemplated as complete with reference to the glory. It occurs in Luke ii. 30; iii. 6; Acts xxviii. 28 (compare Isaiah lix. 17); Eph. vi. 17.

In His favour is victory (Ps. xli. 11).

And the prayer of all who are the subjects of this favour is: "Remember me, O LORD, with the favour that Thou bearest unto Thy people" (Ps. cvi. 4).

With Christ for our Shield, faith can quench all the fiery darts of the evil one: for it is by faith we reckon that we died and rose with Him (Rom. vi. 11). It is by faith that we know that we are seated in the heavenlies in Him (Eph. ii. 6-8).

This, then, is our Divine Panoply; to be used against spiritual forces in defence of spiritual blessings; in the use of which we shall be more than conquerors through Him who loved us and gave Himself for us.

The Epistle to the Philippians.
ITS STRUCTURE, SCOPE, AND HISTORICAL SETTING.

The Epistle to the Ephesians, like the Epistle to the Romans, is followed by two Epistles. As Romans is followed by Corinthians and Galatians, so Ephesians is followed by Philippians and Colossians.

And in this case, as in the other—the former of each two (Cor. and Phil.) has. to do with what is *practical* failure, while the latter of each two (Gal. and Col.) has to do with *doctrinal* failure.

There are two little links which unite together the two Epistles which have to do with *practical* failure.

In 1 Cor. iv. 16, and xi. 1, the Apostle twice exhorts the Corinthians, "Be ye followers of me." The same exhortation is twice given in Phil. iii. 17, and iv. 9.

So that, in each of these Epistles he lays the same stress on his own personal, practical example.

In using the word "reproof" of these two Epistles, we have done so merely because it is the A.V. rendering of 2 Tim. iii. 16. But the word means *proof* rather than "reproof." *ἔλεγχος (elengchos)* is used of an axiom or declaration of a self-evident truth; as when we say, "the whole is greater than any of its parts." Josephus uses it in the sense of *clear-proof.*[68] So that in this Epistle we have not reproof, as such; but the *clear proof* or *demonstration* of the failure of these saints, and the demonstration of Ephesian truths practically exhibited; and this is followed by a clear proof or demonstration as to how that teaching should be exemplified.

The great doctrinal teaching of Ephesians is that Christ is the head of that Body of which His people on earth are the members.

---

68. He says *(Ant.* 16, 8) that Herod's slaves said he dyed his hair, so as to hide the *clear proof* of his age.

This wondrous calling implies a corresponding responsibility on the part of the members to walk worthily of it; not only with respect to Christ the Head, in glory, but with respect to the fellow-members of that Body here upon earth. Consequently the more practical part of Ephesians opens with this very exhortation, "I beseech you that ye walk worthily of the calling wherewith ye are called." And what that worthiness is to be is shewn in Eph. iv. 1-16, viz., "With all lowliness and meekness, with long-suffering, forbearing with one another in love, being diligent to keep the oneness of the Spirit in the uniting bond of peace." The rest of the chapter goes on to give the reason for this exhortation. And it is this: because "there is one Body, and one Spirit, even as ye were called also in one hope of your calling." The means and the end are then set forth.

Now it was in the practical exhibition of this precept that there Philippian saints failed. The truth of the "one Body" involves the recognition of it in the walk of the members; and these saints failed in this particular.

The Structure shows how the Holy Spirit deals with the matter; how gently He demonstrates it, and how skilfully He leads up to and brings conviction, in order to secure the remedying of what was wrong.

After the Salutation and Epistolary portion, Phil. i. 1, 2, the Apostle's concern for them is shewn; and an earnest exhortation is given, that they might conduct themselves as it becometh the Gospel of Christ, and "stand fast in one spirit, with one soul labouring together for the faith of the Gospel."

This is followed by *four examples* which practically fill up the rest of the Epistle; the first and fourth being marked off from the other two by being preceded and followed by suitable exhortations.

Example, here, in this practical Epistle, takes the place of precept.

The whole scope of the Epistle is beautifully exhibited by the structure: which is as follows:

The Epistle to the Philippians as a whole.

A | i 1, 2. Epistolary, and Salutation.
  B | i. 3-26. Paul's concern for the Philippians.
    C | i. 27-ii. 18. Exhortation, and Example Of CHRIST.
      D | ii. 19-24. The Example of TIMOTHY..
      D | ii. 25-30. The Example of EPAPHRODITUS.
    C | iii. 1-iv. 9. Exhortation, and Example of PAUL.
  B | iv. 10-20. The Philippians' concern for Paul.
A | iv. 21-23. Epistolary, and Salutation.

We thus have before our eyes the whole aim, object, end, and scope of the Epistle as a whole;[69] which is to enforce the precept of Eph. iv. 1, 2, and to illustrate it by these four beautiful examples.

But before we consider them we must notice the member "B," which gives us the historical setting of the Epistle.

We have elsewhere remarked that in this group the three Epistles (Eph., Phil., and Col.) are linked together by the fact that they were all written from prison.[70] Yet we cannot fail to note that the whole Epistle is characterised and pervaded by joy. Something had recently happened to cause it. He says, in i. 12, "The things which happened unto me have fallen out rather unto the furtherance[71] of the Gospel" and not, as they and he had feared, to the hindrance of it. In i. 7, that they have been sharers with him in grace, "both in my imprisonment, and in the defence and confirmation of the Gospel." The word rendered "confirmation" (*βεβαίωσις bebaiōsis)[72]* is a

---

69. And yet Lightfoot says, "There is an absence of plan in the Epistle."

70. Eph. iii. 1; iv. 1; vi. 20. Phil. i. 7, 13, 14. Col. iv. 3, 16, 18. .

71. The word προκοπή *(prokopee)* occurs only in Phil. i. 12, 25, and 1 Tim. iv. 15, and its verb προκόπτειν *(prokoptein)* only in Lu. ii. 52, Rom. xiii. 12, Gal. i. 14, 2 Tim. ii. 16; iii. 9, 13; refers to such progress by the clearing away of obstacles as can be seen and noted by an observer; and hence, perhaps, to what is regarded as progress by observers. Compare in this connection Lu. ii. 52.

72. The Latin *auctoritas* or *evictio.* See Deismann, *Bibelstudien,* p. 100, &c.

technical legal term, almost answering to our *guarantee* or *security*, and shows that he looked on the favourable turn in his affairs as a guarantee of "the furtherance of the Gospel." Indeed, in i. 19, he says he feels sure it will turn to his deliverance, and to his coming to them again (i. 26; ii. 24). His bonds had been recognised as being for Christ's sake (i. 13) in all the palace; *ie.*, not the "Praetorian Guard," or the "barracks of the guard," as is commonly supposed, but, as Professors Mommsen[73] and Ramsay[74] have strikingly shewn, the *præfecti prætorio*, or the judicial authorities delegated to hear such appeals as that of St. Paul. The greeting sent from those who were of Cæsar's household (iv. 22) confirms this.

His whole position then was one of suspense. He was now a prisoner, awaiting the day fixed for the hearing of his case and the decision of the higher tribunal.

One thing occupied his mind and caused his concern for the Philippian Saints. This is the subject of the whole member, B. ch. i. 3-26 (Page 155), in which, verse 23 comes as a parenthesis. His imprisonment had turned out for "the furtherance of the gospel" *(v.* 12). Many of the brethren had waxed confident, and Christ was preached without fear (*v.* 14).

If *his imprisonment* and the *contention* were such a gain to the cause of Christ, his *death* might prove a still greater gain; and therefore he was willing to live or die, for Christ would be magnified through his body in either case: "**For, to me, living**[75] [*would be*]

---

73. *Sitz-Berichte* of the Berlin Academy, May 30, 1895, p. 498, etc.

74. *St. Paul the Traveller*, p. 357.

75. *Greek "the to live;"* and *"the to die."* It is the article with the Infinitive Mood of the verb, which substantivizes the verb, making it a verbal substantive, and expressing the abstract notion of the verb. The sense varies with the Tense. The Present Infinitive, as in verse 21, marks continuity: τὸ ζῆν *(to zēn)* means *living, or life,* and τὸ ἀποθανεῖν *(to apothanein)* means *dying,* or *death, ie.,* continuance in these states respectively.

On the contrary, in verse 23 it is the Aorist Infinitive, which marks *the single and separate act;* τὸ ἀναλῦσαι *(to analusai)* means *the return: i.e.,* the act of Christ's return from heaven.

Christip; and dying[75] **a gain.** [Not to himself, but to Christ, and the cause of Christ. It was not his own gain, of which he was selfishly thinking, but the furtherance of the gospel for which he was prepared with perfect unselfishness[76] either to live on in prison, or to die.] **But, whether this living in the flesh [will be] the fruit of my labour; and what I shall choose, I do not know.**

(**For I am being pressed** (pres. passive) out of (ἐκ occurs 857 times, and is nowhere else rendered "betwixt," but 165 times *out of)* the two *(ie.,* living or dying), **having** (a third thing) **the earnest desire for the return** (τὸ ἀναλῦσαι *(to analusai)* the return *(i.e.,* of Christ) see Luke xii. 36[77], the only place where

---

76. This *unselfishness* is seen here with regard to himself, as it is seen with regard to the preaching of others in verse 18, with which it corresponds. (See *Things to Come* for June, 1905, page 71).

77. ἀναλύω *(analuo)* means to *return* from another place to here; not from here to another place.

It occurs also in the Apocryphal books: which though valueless for establishing doctrine, are useful for proving meaning and usage of words.

Tob. ii. 9. The same night I *returned* from the burial.

Jud. xiii. 1. Now when the evening was come, his servants made haste *to depart (ie.,* to return to their tents).

1 Esd. iii. 3. Being satisfied, *they went (ie.,* returned) *home.*

Wisd. ii. 1. Neither was there any man known to have *returned from* the grave.

Wisd. v. 12. Like as when an arrow is shot at a mark, it parteth the air, which immediately *cometh together* (returneth) again..

Wisd. xii. 14. The spirit when it is gone forth *returneth not.*

Ecclus. iii. 15. As the ice *melteth away (ie.,* returneth to water).

2 Macc. viii. 25. They pursued them far; but lacking time, they *returned.*

2 Macc. ix. 1. Antiochus *returned* and came away with dishonour from the country of Persia.

2 Macc. xii 7. He went backward, as if *he would return* to root out all them of the country of Joppa.

2 Macc. xv. 28. Now when battle was done, *returning azain* with joy, they knew, &c.

the word occurs in the New Testament except here[78]) **and to be with Christ,** for it is **far, far better** (than either living or dying). Then, resuming from verse 22, "Yet what I shall choose I cannot tell," he goes on to say:)

but to remain in the flesh is more needful for you (*i.e.*, better than dying; not better than "the return of Christ," which is far better than either).

The Apostle does not make the independent statement that Death of itself is a "gain" to anyone; but that if it should prove "a gain" to the furtherance of the gospel, he would be as content to die as to live.

Verse 21, commencing with the word "For," is part of the argument. Verse 23 is an independent parenthetical statement as to the Return of Christ, which will be better than either living or dying.

There is only one way of being "with Christ," and that is the one stated in 1 Thess. iv. 17, *οὕτως (houtōs)*, thus, *"in this manner shall we ever be with the Lord"*: *i.e.*, by being caught up to meet the Lord in the air, on His return. This would be better than either living or dying.

---

78. The noun *ἀνάλυσις (analysis)* occurs only once, in 2 Tim. iv, 6, where it is rendered *departure*— "time of my departure is at hand." But the meaning is the same as the verb, *returning*, viz., the returning of the spirit to God who gave it, and the returning of the body to the dust as it was. The word *dissolution* would exactly suit the Greek, as the apostle is speaking of in event which was to happen to him, and not of a journey which he was to take.

The Epistle to the Philippians.
THE FOUR EXAMPLES.

In turning to the other members of the structure of this Epistle, we do not propose to expand them further, though this might well be done for edification.

But we do not wish to delay our approach to the study of the four great examples which form the main body of the Epistle.

The examples are interspersed with repeated references to the object had in view in introducing them.

The great exhortation is summed up in ii. 5, which introduces the first example.

"Let this mind be in you which was in Christ Jesus also."

Christ is the head of the Body; and, as the body is controlled by the head, so the members are to think the same and to be actuated by the same consideration (i. 27). Hence ii. 1 begins, **"If then there is any comfort (or hortative virtue), in Christ, if aught stimulative of love** *(παραμύθιον, paramuthion,* occurs only here. Plato uses it *of alleviation (Rep.* p. 329 E), and of *stimulant (Critias, p.* 115 B), probably both meanings are true, here), **if any fellowship of spirit (or spiritual fellowship), if any great tender-affection and compassion, make my cup of joy full** *(ie.,* you have sent supplies to me (iv. 10), and your care for me is so great; now, if you want me to be really happy, fill ye up my joy), **that ye may be of the same mind, having the same love, joined in soul, minding the one (and** the same) **thing, doing nothing by way of contention vain-glory; but, in lowliness of mind, each esteeming the others as more excellent than themselves each regarding not his own** (interests, gifts, advantages, etc.), but **each** (regarding) **those of others also. Let this mind be in you which was in Christ Jesus also."**

The First Example. Christ.
ii. 6-11.

This, like the fourth example (Paul), is accompanied by exhortation: and thus the *first* and *fourth* correspond, while the *second* and *third* (Timothy and Epaphroditus) go together as the two minor examples, which are considered more briefly (six verses each):—

C | i. 27—ii. 18. Exhortation, and example of CHRIST.
   D | ii. 19-24. The example of TIMOTHY.
   D | ii. 25-30. The example of EPAPHRODIITUS.
C | iii. 1—iv. 9. Exhortation, and example Of PAUL.

Christ's example and Paul's are further marked off by a setting forth of what each gave up, and of what each gained in consequence. The giving up of what were "gains" but are counted as "loss," and the obtaining of real eternal and glorious gains in God's own way.

These seven stages in Christ's humiliation stand in direct contrast with the seven stages of His exaltation.

We have not put them in parallel columns, as this would have cramped our references to them; but, by their corresponding numbers, they may easily be compared and contrasted.

"Who existing (or subsisting) **in the form of God,**

1. **Did not esteem the being equal with God a usurpation** (or **a** thing to be grasped at by an active effort, as did the first Adam, who, when told "Ye shall be as Elohim," "took of the fruit and did eat" (Gen. iii. 5, 6) in order to obtain the promise. The word ἁρπαγμός *(harpagmos)* denotes the *act of grasping at,* and not the thing grasped).

2. **But emptied himself,**

3. **Taking a servant's form,**

4. **Having become** or taken His place **in men's likeness.**

5. **And, having been found in fashion as a man, He humbled Himself,**

6. **Becoming obedient even unto death** (μέχρι *mechri,*

140

compare verse 30. It denotes *degree*, as it does in 2 Tim. ii. 9. Heb. xii. 4, etc.),

7.   **And the death—that of the cross."**

And now, the depth of His humiliation being reached, the exaltation is described: and, like the other, it begins with God:—

Wherefore God also
1.   **Highly exalted Him** (or uplifted Him far on high),
2.   **And granted to Him** (ie., graced or favoured Him with) **the name that is above every name,**
3.   **In order that at the name of Jesus every knee should bow** (in submission and subjection, and in acknowledgment of His Lordship.   As, when Joseph was exalted, "they cried before him, Bow the knee," when he was made ruler over the land (Gen. xli. 43), so shall the prophecy (Isa. xlv. 23) be fulfilled, "Unto me every knee shall bow, every tongue shall swear [allegiance]." This is referred to Christ in Rom. xiv. 11),
4.   **Of beings** (or knees) in **heaven,**
5.   **And beings on earth,**
6.   **And beings under the earth;**
7.   **And every tongue confess** (Rom. xiv. 11) that **Jesus Christ is Lord, to God the Father's glory.**

Here then was "the mind of Christ." Though he was rich, yet for our sakes He became poor, and is bringing many sons unto glory.

He did "nothing through strife or vain-glory." He did "not look on His own advantages, but on those of others."

This is the example of the Head.   Now look at some of the members.

The Second Example. Timothy.

ii. 19-24.

Timothy had something of "the mind that was in Christ " (ii. 5). He did not act through strife or vainglory.   He, in lowliness of mind, esteemed others better than himself (ii- 3).   He did not look only on his own things, but on the things of others also (ii. 4), for the Apostle says (ii. 20.) **"I have no one like-minded who will** genuinely care for the things that concern you. For all are seeking their own things (or interests), not the things (or interests) of Jesus Christ."

The Third Example. Epaphroditus.
ii. 25-30.

Epaphroditus was another like Timothy. He was more concerned about other saints, the other members of the Body, than about himself. The Apostle says, ii. 26:

"**For he was longing after you all** *(to see you all,* according to L. and WH.), **and was deeply despondent** (because he had been sick? No, but) **because ye had heard that he had been sick** (and well ye might hear of it): **for indeed he was sick** and likely **to die** *(lit.,* like to death), **but God had mercy on him, and not on him alone, but on me also, that I might not have sorrow upon sorrow. I have sent him therefore the more promptly; that seeing him again ye may rejoice, and I may be the less sorrowful. Receive him therefore in the Lord with all joy, and hold such in reputation** (Why? Because, like His Master, he 'made himself of no reputation'): **because for the sake of the work** (some MSS. add 'of Christ,' some 'of God,' others 'of the Lord') **he was nigh unto death, having hazarded his life** (reading παραβολευσάμενος, *paraboleusamenos,* with G.L.T.Tr. A. WH. and R.V.; instead of παραβουλευσάμενος *parabouleusamenos* with A.V.) **that he might fill up** (or supply) **your lack of service toward me."**

So that Epaphroditus was another practical demonstration of how the members of the One body should walk worthily of God's calling.

The Fourth Example. Paul.
iii. 1-iv. 9.

We now come to the fourth great example, which, like the first (Christ's), is preceded and followed by exhortation as to real gains and losses. This marks these two examples off from the two central ones which we have just noticed.

After a brief exhortation, Paul enumerates his gains: at least, the things which he esteemed as such, but which he thankfully gave up for something of far greater value. He was like his Master as to their number, but not as to their nature. Christ's glory, which He laid aside was real. Paul's gains, which he gave up were unreal; they were no gains at all. He thought they were, but he found that they were only losses, and counted them but "dung" compared with the glory of Christ. His supposed gains were seven in number and are soon stated:

1. **Circumcised the eighth day.**
2. **Of the stock of Israel.**
3. **Of the tribe of Benjamin.**
4. **A Hebrew of Hebrews.**
5. **As to law, a Pharisee.**
6. **As to zeal, persecuting the Church.**
7. **As to righteousness, such as is by** (the deeds of the) **law, found blameless.**

He is speaking here, not of his sins, but of his supposed "gains"; of his standing in the flesh, as a man; but he had so learned Christ that he could say, **"What things are gain to me, the same I counted, for Christ's sake loss."**

He thankfully gave them all up, because he had found something better. Seven better things took their place, and he, like his Master, could count up seven stages in his exaltation.

All these blessings were "in Christ,"—"the knowledge of Christ Jesus my Lord." All else was counted as dung that he might gain Christ.

1. **And be found in Him.** That was his standing now. **Not having a righteousness of my own—that which is by** (the deeds of) **the Law, but that which is by faith in Christ. The righteousness which comes of God** (conferred on) **faith."** That was his standing now. A real "gain"; compared with which his former supposed "gain" was "loss," for it consisted of "confidence in the flesh" instead of in God.

2. **That I may know him.** (Greek, τοῦ γνῶναι αὐτὸν, *ton gnōnai auton.* May not this difficult genitive be explained by

143

referring it back to verse 8, "the excellency of the knowledge"—to wit the knowledge or the excellency of knowing Him). This knowledge of Christ was now the one object of his life. Not merely knowing things about Him, but knowing Him in a very special way, which, by the Holy Spirit, he goes on to set forth. It is the figure of *Zeugma* which is employed to do this, and our attention is thus called to the importance of what is about to be unfolded.

By the use of this Figure *one verb* is used of several subjects while it refers strictly and properly to only one of them. The other suitable verbs ("experience"and "share") therefore, have to be supplied, and it is in the supplying of these that the instruction conveyed thereby flows into our hearts and minds. The one verb is "know," and the proper object is "Him"—"That I may know Him."

3. But to know Him in all the glory of His person and in all the perfection of His work, I must know also [or rather **experience**] **the power of His resurrection.**

4. And to experience this, I must first know [what it is to **share**] **the fellowship of His sufferings,** *viz.,* that when He, the Head, "suffered, all the members of His body suffered with Him" (1 Cor. xii. 26).

5. And I can "know Him and experience the power of His resurrection and share the fellowship of His sufferings" only by being made conformable to[79] *(i.e.,* like) **Him in His death** *(i.e.,* by reckoning myself to have died with Him (Rom. vi. 11), and to have been planted with Him in His death: not only having a blessed fellowship in His sufferings, but in God's sight, dying in, and crucified together with Him).

Then we are prepared for the sixth stage of the exaltation.

6. **If by any means I might attain unto the out-resurrection—that one from among the dead.** It is very important for us to observe (from the scope of this Epistle and of this third chapter) that Paul is speaking (by inspiration) in this verse (iii. 11) of his advantages as a Jew. He is counting up, as a Jew, what he

---

79. See note on verse 21.

had gained in Christ, and setting his gains over against his losses. As a Jew he had the hope of resurrection, and not only this but the hope of the "first resurrection" (Rev. xx. 5, 6), the resurrection of "life" (John v. 29. Dan. xii. 2), "the resurrection of the just" (Acts xxiv. 15). All this he had as a pious, religious Jew. But, being in Christ, he had a better hope—that which he had taught "the church of the Thessalonians" (1 Thess. iv. 16, 17)—a resurrection which had nothing to do with "times and seasons" (1 Thess. v. 1), as the "first resurrection" will have.

The "gain" which his standing in Christ gave him was this *ἐξανάστασις (exanastasis), an out-resurrection* from among the dead. He had given up Judaism and all its best hopes that he might attain unto this resurrection.

It was not that Paul as a Christian supposed that he could attain to a higher privilege than that of some other Christians. But that as a Christian he had attained to a higher privilege than he could ever have done as a Jew.

The whole scope of the chapter shows most clearly that Paul is speaking of his advantages as a Jew, which he had given up for the more solid advantages which were his in Christ.

These advantages included not merely this out-resurrection, if he should be called to fall asleep, but there was a *seventh* stage in this exultation, a seventh gain, and that was the blessed hope of not dying at all! This is deferred (by a long parenthesis) to verses 20, 21.

This parenthetical digression extends from verse 12 to verse 19, and is made in order to prevent misapprehension, and to indicate further what he really means. He had just stated what he did mean, and now, to make the matter more clear, he puts it the other way, in order to show what he did not mean.

TRANSLATION OF PHIL. iii. 12-19.

Not that (or, By this I do not mean that; compare iv. 17), **I have yet received** (all these gains. The aorist tense (*ἔλαβον, elabon)* is significant, and points to a past act and epoch when he began to receive them in exchange for his losses), **or have already reached the end** (of my gains. The 6th and 7th of my gains I still wait for. I have not yet received them all. I suffered with Christ. I died with Him. I am risen in Him. But for this my actual "out-resurrection" (of which I have just spoken) and the coming of the Lord (which is my seventh gain) I am waiting, that my gains may be completed and perfected). **But I am pressing** (or following) **on, if I may get possession also of that** *(ie.,* the whole of my gains), **for which I have been taken possession of by Christ** (when He—Christ—revealed Himself to me and in me. The correct reading is "Christ," not "Jesus Christ" So the critical Greek texts, G. L. Tr. A. & WHb). **Brethren** (with the view of arresting their attention), **I** (very emphatic) **do not reckon myself** (emphatic, in contrast, not with what others think of him, but with others' estimate of themselves) **to have got possession of** (all my gains yet. These are the scope of and key to the whole passage); **but one thing** (the *Ellipsis* must here be supplied: either *"I do,"* as in A.V. and R.V., or "I *reckon;"* or *"I have received."* What follows refers to *action,* so that "I do" seems to be the most appropriate), **the things behind me, indeed, forgetting** *(ie.,* the things I formerly thought to be gains, but now count as losses, and only things to be forgotten), **but eagerly reaching myself** (middle voice) **forth** (my expectant gaze) **to the things before me** *(ie.,* these last two of his gains—the out-resurrection and the coming of the Lord, *v.* 20, 21), **I am pressing forward** (looking) **toward the goal** (σκοπός *skopos,* only here in N.T. It is the goal *as looked at,* rather than reached. Used by the Greeks as a target for aiming at), with a view to εἰς *eis,* with L. T. Tr. A. WH. and R.V., not ἐπί *epi upon* or *for, i.e.,* with my mind looking forward to) **the prize** (only here and 1 Cor. ix. 24: he goes on to tell us what this prize is) **of my** (or our) **calling on high by God, in Christ Jesus** (κλῆσις, *kleesis; calling* is always used *of the act of calling, in* N.T. God will be the Caller, and He will call us up on high by Christ Jesus, "the Lord Himself." All our gains centre in Him (verses 7, 8). He Himself is "the great gain." He includes all other gains. This calling is upward, on high. The word is not ἄνωθεν, *anōthen, from above, but* ἄνω, *anō' to above, ie.,* heavenward). This calling includes the out-resurrection from among the dead, if called to fall asleep (v. 11), or change and rapture if we are "alive and remain" (verses 20, 21). This we have not yet received. For this, therefore, we wait and look forward with outstretched gaze.

As many of us **therefore as** would be thus **completed** (those who are "grown up," full grown, as opposed to children. Those who have got beyond the bondage of ordinances (Gal. iv. 3, 4), and know that they have all in Christ. The τέλειοι *(teleioi)* are those who have reached the τέλος *(telos) or end;* those who have passed through all the various stages (as in the Pagan mysteries, and in modern Freemasonry, which is their survival, and have *been initiated* into the last and highest "degree"). To all such there is nothing more beyond. *Τέλος (telos), end,* was the word at the end of Greek books, answering to *"Finis,"* which is the Latin word. Those who know the truth of the great Mystery, as revealed in Ephesians, have reached the last revealed truth (1 Cor. ii. 6, 7). As many as have learned this, and are thus perfect, *i.e.*, have thus reached their *telos,* and are "perfect" as to what there is to be learned. All they have to do now is to live it out, as to practice (Philippians) and as to doctrine (Colossians): holding the *members,* as to the true practice, and "holding the Head" as to true doctrine. Hence the exhortation follows) **let us set our mind on** this (as to our wondrous "gains" in Christ as described in verses 7-14). **And if as to anything ye think somewhat** *(τι, ti)* **differently among yourselves** *i.e.*, if you do not all see exactly alike, do not let this affect your love one toward another), **this** (great truth respecting which you think differently, i.e., the Mystery) **also** as well as the other truths He has revealed) **will God reveal to you. Nevertheless** (do not let any diversity of thought produce dissension, or hinder your union or unity) **as far as we have attained** (or advanced, i.e., in Ephesian teaching, and in this initiation into all the truth) **walk** ye **in the same,** i.e., walk according to your attainment. The verb "walk" here, *(στοιχεῖν, stoichein,* implies especially ecclesiastical walk. The words "rule, and let us mind the same thing," are to be omitted from the text according to L. T. Tr. A. WH. & R.V., *i.e.,* let us, as members of the Body of Christ, walk according to the truth to which we have attained, looking for God to reveal further truth to us, and exercising forbearance and love to one another).

Become followers together of me, my brethren (Only here in

N.T. the word rendered "follower" meaning not imitators of Christ in common with me; but, imitators of me in common with each other; joint imitators) **and observe** (and look steadily on them, so as to follow; not mark, so as to avoid) **those who walk in such manner as ye have us for an example** (such as Timothy and Epaphroditus in chap. ii. The walk here is not the same as in verse 16, but is the ordinary word for walking, i.e., living). **For many are walking, whom I often mentioned to you** (in time past), **but now** (again; for the evil is growing) **even weeping,** I tell you they are the **enemies of the cross of Christ.** (Not only are they ignorant of what that cross means for those who are in Christ, *viz.*, the crucifixion of the Old Man, and our having died and risen in Christ; but they oppose this great and blessed teaching). **Whose end** (for they have a $\tau\acute{\epsilon}\lambda o\varsigma$ *(telos)*, an end, as well as we) is **destruction, whose God is their belly** (*i.e.*, their flesh, the part being put for the whole, by the Figure *Synecdoche)* **and whose glory** is (subjective; *i.e.*, they glory in **their shame, they, namely, that mind earthly things.** (Not seeing or knowing the truth concerning those who died with Christ (Col. ii. 20), and are risen with Christ (Col. iii. 1), they do not "seek the things that are above," and "set their affections on them" (Col. iii. 2), but mind earthly things. Those, on the other hand, who are expecting their calling on high shortly will have their minds "set on the things which are above," and not on earthly things. Our calling will be "upward," to meet the Lord in the air; hence, our look is upward, and we have our hearts and minds set on the things which are upward and "above," $\check{\alpha}\nu\omega$, *anō,* Col. iii. 1, 2, the same word as that rendered "high" in Phil. iii. 14).

We thus come to the end of the Apostle's *sixth* gain: which has been dwelt upon by him, and thus enlarged upon because of its vast importance. The first five gains are enjoyed now by faith; but the remaining two (Resurrection and Advent) are still future, and remain to be enjoyed by sight.

This is the reason for the apparent digression. It is not really a digression; but it is combined instruction and exhortation called forth by the need that existed for it. It existed then, and exists still more now. How few know about the gains which they have in Christ. How many are still looking for some ground of confidence in the flesh; and hence do not understand the true nature of spiritual worship, and do not find Christ Jesus all they have to glory in. This is what all this *fourth* example starts from (iii. 3). Not knowing this, they still feel they have some, "gains" as to their standing in the flesh; and have not yet learned to count them all "loss," and to find all their "gain" in Christ. They are "found in Him," as their righteousness (iii. 9), but they do not "know Him" as their sanctification.

The *first* gain is Christ our Righteousness.

The *second, third, fourth,* and *fifth* gains have respect to knowing Christ as our Sanctification.

The *sixth* and *seventh* gains set Christ as "the hope of glory" before our hearts and minds.

Having thus come to the end of the *sixth* gain, we now approach the seventh and last.

7. **"For our politeuma exists in heaven** (we purposely leave the Greek word untranslated, because of the difficulty arising out of the fulness of its meaning. Πολίτευμα occurs only here in the New Testament. The A.V. "conversation," *i.e.,* manner of life, is in harmony with the only two occurrences of the verb πολιτεύω *(politeuō),* Phil. i. 27, and Acts xxiii. 1. According to these it would mean *a conducting of one's self according to the seat of government to which one belongs.* The R.V. "citizenship" (margin, *commonwealth)* does not quite satisfy it. The word means the *seat of government* to which we belong as citizens; and the functions which we perform, and the privileges which we enjoy as citizens. The singular verb points to the former. In either case the words **from which** (seat of government, ἐξ οὗ *(ex hou)* being singular *refers to politeuma,* and not to *heaven* which is plural in the Greek. The word ὑπάρχει *(huparchei)* is also very emphatic. It is not the ordinary verb "is," but points backward. It *exists* even now. It is there, in heaven. That is why we **are eagerly awaiting** (only here and in Rom. viii. 19, 23, 25; 1 Cor. i. 7; Gal. v. 5; and Heb. ix. 28) the **Saviour also,** viz., **the Lord Jesus Christ.** (We do not mind earthly things therefore, for we are looking for the Lord Jesus to come and save us *(i.e.,* deliver us out of them. The word Saviour

being put out of its usual place by the Figure *Hyperbaton* is very emphatic: *i.e.*, we look not only for the Lord Jesus, but we look for Him as a Saviour, *i.e.*, in the character of, and to do the work of, a great Deliverer by completing His great work of salvation, 1Pet. i. 5). **Who will refashion** *(ie., change the fashion of)* **the body of our humiliation** (*i.e.*, of our present low estate), **in order that** (we must omit the words "that it may be" G. L. T. Tr. A. WH. and R.V.) **it may become of like form with** (*i.e.*, be conformed to. The two words "fashion," σχῆμα *(schema)*, and "form," μορθή *(morphee)* must be distinguished. The former relates to the world and the old man, which are *changeable as to fashion,* fictitious, and illusory (1 Cor. vii. 31; Rom. xii. 2; 1 Pet. i. 14; 2 Cor. xi. 13, 14, 15). The latter relates to the new man, and what is *fixed as to form* (Rom. viii. 29; Phil. ii. 6, 7; iii. 10; 2 Cor. iii. 18; Gal. iv.19). In Rom. xii. 2 we have both words, "Do not follow the changing *fashion* of this world, but act according to the new *form*—the renewal of your mind." So here in Phil. iii. 21, "Who will change the *fashion* of the body of our humiliation, and *fix* it in the *form of)* **His glorious body** (the body of His glory with the emphasis on "glorious," and thus pointing to the glory of His body, with which He is now clothed in His glorified estate) **according to** (after the analogy of the **putting forth of the power which He** (inherently) **possesses to subject also** (not merely change and transform the body, but to subject) **all things to Himself** *(i.e.,* to Christ)."

All this is bound up in "the excellency of the knowledge" of Christ Jesus our Lord, for which great gain (ver. 8) he counted all things "loss."

Thus is the counting up of the apostle's real "gains" completed. Seven is their number, and their division is into four and three. His greatest gain, his great desire, was three-fold. It was all CHRIST, and that he might

"BE FOUND IN HIM" as to his *standing (one* gain),
"KNOW HIM" as his *object (four* gains), and
"BE LIKE" HIM, as his *hope (two* gains).

To "know Him" in all the glory of His person, and all the

150

perfection of His work, is now the true Christian's one object, carrying out practically Eph. iv. 21. Apart from this there can be no real Christianity: for true Christianity is Christ. How many professing Christians make sad failure in this, through ignorance of the teaching of the Epistle to the Ephesians, is painfully evident on all hands. But the only remedy lies here: in the doctrine of that Epistle. That it is which, being planted within, can alone enable us to grow up into, Christ.

Well might the apostle say, "Brethren, become followers together of me" (iii. 17). "Those things which ye have both learned, and received, and heard, and seen in me, do, and the God of peace will be with you" (iv. 9).

Well might he urge, in view of this example, that they should all "walk by the same rule, and mind the same thing" (iii. 16).

Well might he beseech Euodia and Syntyche to be "of the same mind in the Lord" (iv. 2).

Would that we could see among Christians to-day even the Philippian measure of this walk! But with the practical loss of Ephesian truth; with the reviling of, and sneering at, those like ourselves who are doing what we can to recover it; What can we expect? These who act as "monitors," and arrogate to themselves the authority of judges, these are the ones who fail most of all in exhibiting this love, which should animate all the members of the One Body; and maintain that what God declares to have been "hid" in Himself and never before revealed, He had not hidden at all and had revealed all along to the Old Testament saints. What can we expect, but the saying with the same breath, "my lord delayeth his coming," and the smiting of the fellow-servants, which always follows such a saying; instead of exhibiting "the mind of Christ" as inculcated in this Epistle, and following the wondrous examples of Christ; and of His servants, Timothy. Epaphroditus, and Paul; here so strikingly set before us?

The rest of the Epistle consists of the members *B* (iv. 10-20), *the Philippians' care of Paul;* and *A* (iv. 21-23), which is *Epistolary,* local and ephemeral. As these do not effect the one great scope of the Epistle, we leave them for our readers to study for themselves, and pass on to the Epistle to the Colossians.

The Epistle to the Colossians.
ITS SCOPE AND CHARACTER.

CHAPTERS i. 1—2. 7.

Like the Epistle to the Galatians, the Epistle to the Colossians has to do more with doctrine than with practice; and it stands in the same relation to Ephesians as Galatians stands in relation to Romans.

The subject of Galatians is "correction" for failure as to the doctrine and instruction contained in Romans: while the subject of Colossians is correction for failure as to the doctrine and instruction contained in Ephesians.

The likeness between Colossians and Ephesians is as marked as that between Romans and Galatians, if not more so. For, out of 95 verses in Colossians, 78 have a marked resemblance to Ephesians (*i.e.,* more than three quarters of the whole). While out of the 155 verses in Ephesians, one half (or 78) resemble Colossians.

But it is the nature of this resemblance which is so significant. What is stated by way of teaching in Ephesians comes up again in Colossians by way of correction for departure from that teaching.

There is also another and peculiar link which binds this group of three Epistles together. Ephesians, Philippians, and Colossians were all written during Paul's first imprisonment in Rome. All three mention the fact. (Eph. iii. 1; iv. 1; vi. 20. Phil. i. 7, 13, 14, 16, 25, 26; ii. 24. Col. iv. 3, 10, 18.)

Then, like the other Epistles (Corinthians, Galatians, Philippians), it was called forth by some special circumstances. But nothing appears to have called forth the other three (Romans, Ephesians, and Thessalonians, or at any rate Romans and Ephesians). What Ellicott says of Ephesians is equally true of Romans and 1 Thessalonians: "It does not appear to have been called forth by any particular circumstances . . . . but was designed to set forth the origin and development of the Church of Christ."

The structure of Colossians will show us that there is the same manifestation of *solicitude,* as there is in the epistle to the Galatians. This is most marked. The same care and fear and anxiety are observable in both.

But now, to see the scope of the Epistle, we must look at

Colossians as a whole.

A | i. 1, 2. Epistolary: and Salutation.

   B | i. 3-8. Mutual reports and messages by Epaphras, our dear fellow-servant and your faithful minister.

      C | i. 9—ii. 7. Paul's solicitude for the Colossian saints, and his prayer for them ("We pray for you"), and that concerning their holding the Mystery.

         D | ii. 8-23. Doctrinal correction for failure as to Instruction in Ephesian truth—having, "died with Christ."

         D | iii. 1—iv. 1. Doctrinal correction for failure as to Instruction in Ephesian truth—having "risen with Christ."

      C | iv. 2-6. Paul's solicitude for the Colossian saints; and their prayers for him ("praying also for us"), and that concerning his preaching the Mystery.

   B | iv. 7-9. Mutual reports and messages by Tychicus and Onesimus, "beloved brethren."

A | iv. 10-18. Epistolary: and Salutation.

In this beautiful Introversion we have the whole scope and design of the Epistle.

The Colossian saints had been taught concerning the Mystery as set forth in Ephesians, *viz.*: that Christ is the Head of the Body, and His People the members of that Body upon earth.

The Philippian saints failed practically in *not holding the members;* and the Colossian saints failed doctrinally "not holding the head" (ii. 19): these are the key-notes of the two Epistles.

In the one case the failure led to various practical evils–strife and contention and vain-glory: while, in the other, it led to various doctrinal errors which necessarily arose out of it.

153

As Romans' truth was practically recovered at the Reformation, so the evils of Galatian departure and failure are not so manifest as they were before the Reformation.

But, as Ephesian truth has never been really or properly recovered, it is clear that we have in the present departure from it, and in the present failure with regard to it, the source and fountain-head of all the abounding uncharitableness, and of all the errors and "winds of doctrine" which characterise the present day.

No Epistle has such a warning voice for us as the Epistle to the Colossians. None is so practical or so timely in the correction it contains for us.

To learn its lessons with the view of getting back to Ephesian truth is the first step in that great Reformation which the churches stand in such need of at the present moment. The evils and errors are seen by many. But all do not see the root-cause of them in the departure from Ephesian teaching.

This is the cause of all the want of union and unity of Christians in the present day. They do not realise their union in Christ, as having died and risen again in Him. Hence, they are betrayed into various vain methods of seeking union—from the schemer for the re-union of Christendom to the smaller evangelical alliances and associations.

The same cause produces all that we call Ritualism; which is the embodiment of an evil principle, which pervades all the churches in the magnifying and resorting to ordinances of all kinds—making them the centre of union because of "not holding the head" (ii. 19).

Hence, the solicitude shown and the correction ministered.

The expansion of C (i. 9—ii. 7) will bring this out and exhibit it more clearly. It consists of seven members, in repeated alternation, as follows:—

THE EXPANSION OF C (i. 9—ii. 7).
Solicitude for the Colossian Saints.

C | a¹ | i. 9-11. Solicitude as to their faith, and a walk worthy of it. Prayer that they might be filled with the knowledge of God's will.
| | b¹ | i. 12-22. This knowledge imparted, concerning Christ "the Head of the Body." The Mystery revealed.
| a² | i. 23-25. Solicitude as to their continuing in the faith.
| | b² | i. 26, 27. The Faith stated. The Mystery declared.
| a³ | i. 28-ii. 2-. Solicitude, warning, teaching, and conflict, as to their growth and assurance.
| | b³ | ii. -2, 3. The Mystery acknowledged.
| a⁴ | ii. 4-7. Solicitude as to their steadfastness and stablishment in "the faith."

Here, again, the seven is divided into *four* and *three*. Four members are occupied with *solicitude;* while three are occupied with the re-statement of the Mystery.

The solicitude as to their standing fast in the truth, and the faith, which they had learned as written in the Epistle to the Ephesians, will be better seen if we give a translation of C (i. 9-ii. 7) in accordance with the scope of the passage:

a¹ (i. 9-11).
Solicitude as to their faith, and a walk worthy of it.

i. 9-11. **On this account** (referring to verses 3 and 4) **we also** (on our part), **from the day when we heard** (the happy tidings; see verses 4, 6, 8), **have not ceased** (to pray) **on your behalf, praying and desiring** (this is the figure *Hendiadys:* "praying, yes, and that with desire too") **that ye may be filled with a fuller knowledge** (ἐπίγνωσις, *epignosis,* as in Eph. i. 17; iv 13) **of His will in all wisdom and spiritual discernment** *(Hendiadys* again: "Wisdom–yes, not like that of the false teachers, ii. 23, but a spiritual discerning wisdom too. The two words go together in Ex. xxxi, 3. Deut. iv. 6. 1 Chron. xxii. 12. 2 Chron. i. 10. Isa. xi. 2; xxix. 14. Dan. (Theod.) ii. 20. 1 Cor. i. 19. In Eph. i. 8 it is "wisdom and φρόνησις," *phroneesis,* which is practical: while here

155

it is wisdom and σύνεσις, *sunesis*, which apprehends the bearing of things, as in 2 Tim. ii. 7), **so as to walk worthily** (Eph. iv. 1. Phil. i. 27. 1 Thess. ii. 12, as the consequence, not the purpose) **of the Lord** (*i.e.*, of the Lord Christ) **in all ways well-pleasing** (to Him, not men, compare iii. 22) **in every good work bringing forth fruit and growing** (as in Eph. iv. 13) **by means of the full** (or true) **knowledge of God** (The best texts read "by or by means of the knowledge of God." So R.V. marg.), **being strengthened** (δυναμ ούμ ε νοι, *dunamoumenoi*, occurs only here in N.T.) **with all strength according to His glorious might** (κράτος, *kratos*, *might*, is in N.T. ascribed solely to God (Heb. ii. 14), but the emphasis is on the word "glorious" **unto all patient endurance and long-suffering with joyfulness** (such is the power of this wondrous truth of the Mystery, that by means of its knowledge we may have joyful endurance, and joyful suffering, which finds its expression in thanksgiving; compare Rom. v. 3).

We next take the member b[1], (i. 12-22), but must first show its beautiful sub structure, before we give our translation of it.

It is the knowledge of the Mystery imparted, so far as it first concerns "the Head of the Body," Christ Jesus the Lord.

The Colossian saints failed in *doctrine* in consequence of "not holding the Head[80] (ii. 19). Therefore the glory of "the Head" is the first part of the Mystery which is here developed, in order to show His fulness and His glory.

---

80. As the Philippian saints failed from *not holding the members.*

b¹ (i. 12-22).

The Mystery revealed, as to "the Head."

```
b¹ | E | i. 12-14. You Gentiles, made meet to be partakers of the
   |   | Inheritance with us (13, 14) Jews.
   |     F | c | 15. Who is. Christ's essential glory.
   |       | d | 16. For. Reason: Creation of all things.
   |           G | 17. And He is. (Symbol. As tronomy.)
   |           G | 18-. And He is. (Symbol. Anatomy.)
   |     F | c | -18. Who is. Christ's acquired glory.
   |       | d | 19, 20. For. Reason: Reconciliation of all
   |       |    | things.
   | E | 2I, 22. And you Gentiles, reconciled and presented perfect
   |   | before God.
```

We have printed the key-words in thicker type so as to enable the eye to catch and see the Correspondence, which, in the Greek, is still more marked.

We wish we could print the translation of this, setting it out according to the above structure, but the exigencies of space and type forbid it. It will amply repay our readers for any amount of time spent in writing out the following translation in full for themselves, exactly according to the sub-structure of b¹.

THE TRANSLATION OF b¹ (i. 12-22).

The Mystery revealed, as to the Head.

i. 12-22. **Giving thanks** (this thanksgiving follows the prayer in verses 9-11) **to the Father** (there is some doubt as to what the words "in the light" refer. Some connect them with "saints," others with "the Father," but we prefer to take them with the inheritance) **that hath made you** (Lachmann, Tischendorf, Tregelles margin, Westcott and Hort, Alford, and R.V. margin read "you" and not "us," as in A.V. The pronouns seem to have been tampered with by some scribe who did not grasp the scope of the passage. The correspondence, moreover, requires it. See member *E*, verses 21, 22) **meet** (*i.e.,* called and qualified you, once Gentiles), **for a part and lot** (see Deut. xxxii. 9 and Job xxxi. 2, and compare Acts viii. 21) **of** (or among) **the saints** (or separated ones, who were once

157

Israelites, as you were once Gentiles) in (the kingdom of) **the light** (compare Acts xxvi. 18). **Who delivered us** (once Israelites) **out of the authority of** (the power of) **darkness** (or Him who has authority in this dark world), **and transferred us** (the word μετέστησεν, *metesteesen,* occurs only five times in N.T., and each time a complete change or transfer is indicated; Luke xvi. 4. Acts xiii. 22; xix. 26. 1 Cor. xiii. 2) **into the kingdom of His beloved Son** (Again a reference to Acts xxvi. 18), **in whom we have redemption** (We must omit "through His blood" with Griesbach, Lachmann, Tischendorf, Tregelles, Alford, Westcott & Hort, and R.V.): *i.e.,* **the remission of** our **sins** (Eph. i. 7), **who is the image** (the manifested representation) **of God—the invisible One** (not Adam, Gen. i. 26, 27, but Psalm viii.), **the heir** (*lit.,* first-born) **of the whole creation: because by** (or in relation to) **Him all things** (or beings) **were created in the heavens and on the earth, visible and invisible; whether Thrones, or Dominions, or Principalities, or Authorities** (compare Eph. i. 21) **the whole** (whatever they may be, or may be called) **have been created through Him and for Him: and He is** (both words are emphatic, "He emphasises the *personality,* "is," the *pre-existence) before all* (in time, John i. 1-4), **and by Him all consist** (*i.e.,* He holds the universe together: He it is who holds all in the unity of harmonious order and law). **And** (not only is this so as regards the Old creation, but it is the same with regard to the New creation, His Church, which is His Body) **He is** (the same emphasis as in the corresponding member above) **the head of the Body—the Church** (1 Cor. xii. 12-27. Rom. xii. 4, etc.); **who is the Beginning** (Prov. viii. 25-31), as being **the first-born** (Deut. xxi. 17) **from the dead** (Rev. i. 5. For it is as risen that He becomes the Head of the Church. Phil. iii. 10. Rom. vi.), **in order that He Himself, amid all, might have the pre-eminence** (not Reuben, Gen. xlix. 3: "The excellency," see Septuagint): **for God was well pleased that all the fulness should dwell in Him** (*i.e.,* in Christ's person): **and through Him (having made peace by the blood of His cross)—to reconcile all to Himself, through Him** (I say) **whether** they be **things on earth or things in the heavens; and you being in time past alienated in your minds** (Passive) **and enemies by your evil works** (Active), **yet now ye have been**

158

reconciled (so Lachmann, Tregelles marg., W. H. marg., and R.V. marg.) **by the body of His flesh through His death** (this *pleonasm* is used in order to distinguish Christ's human body of flesh from the Mystical and glorious Body which is the subject of this section, verse 18, as it is in Eph. ii. 15, 16) **to present you (I say) holy, without blemish, unimpeachable, before Him.**

We now come to the second expression of *solicitude* in

a^2 **(i. 23-25).**
Solicitude as to their continuing in this faith.

i. 23-25. **If indeed ye continue in the faith** (thus delivered to you), **built on the foundation** (Eph. ii. 20), **and (therefore) firm** (1 Tim. iii. 15), **and (be) not moved away from the hope of** (*i.e.*, and made known by and revealed in) **the Gospel which ye heard** (from me), **and which has been preached in all the creation** (*i.e.*, to every one without distinction) **under heaven, of which, I Paul** (weak and unworthy as I am) **have become a minister. Now do I rejoice in my sufferings on your behalf, and I am filling up** (on my part) **that which is lacking of the tribulations of the Christ** (*i.e.*, Christ Mystical, the tribulations of the members of the Body of Christ, as he goes on to explain) **in my flesh, on behalf of His Body, which Body is the Church, of which Church I myself have become a minister, according to the dispensation of God given to me for you fully to preach** (and completely develope) **the word of God:**

b^2 **(i. 26, 27).**
The Faith stated. The Mystery declared.

namely, the Mystery (*i.e.*, the secret concerning the Body of Christ) **hidden from the ages and from the generations, but it is now made manifest to His saints, to whom God did will** (or was pleased) **to make known the glorious riches of this mystery among the Gentiles, which is, Christ, (as) the glorious hope, in you.**

a³ (i. 28-ii. 2-).

Solicitude, warning, teaching, and conflict as to their growth and assurance.

Whom we preach, admonishing every man and teaching every man in all wisdom, in order that we may present every man complete in Christ; for which end I toil also, striving according to the (or His) working that worketh in me with power. For I would have you know how great conflict I have concerning you, and those in Laodicea, and as many as have not seen my face in the flesh, that their hearts may be encouraged, being knit together in love, and unto all richness of the full assurance of understanding:

b³ (ii. -2, 3).

The Mystery acknowledged.

with a view to the full knowledge of the mystery of God:—viz: **Christ, in whom all the treasures of wisdom and knowledge** (*i.e.,* all knowledge to be gained by us by way of learning) **are hid.**

a⁴ (ii. 4-7).

Solicitude as to their steadfastness and stablishment in "the faith."

And this I say, that no one may lead you astray with persuasive words. For, if even I am absent in the flesh, yet I am with you in my spirit, rejoicing, and seeing (*i.e.,* rejoicing to behold) **your order, and the steadfastness of your faith in Christ. As therefore ye have received Christ Jesus as your Lord** (so) **walk ye in Him, firmly rooted** (once for all), **and getting built up in** (*i.e.* built, not on Him, as a building is built up, but as a body grows, *v.* 19, and Eph. iv. 13) **Him, and established in the Faith, according as ye have been taught, abounding in that Faith with thanksgiving.**

The solicitude is very marked in all this large member: and the way in which it is alternated with the Mystery shows us that it is all in connection with that: in its revelation (in b¹), its declaration (in b²), and its acknowledgment (in b³).

The holding of this is the important matter; and, just as the

160

solicitude in Galatians was concerning their departure from the doctrine and instruction of Romans, so here it is concerning departure from the doctrine and instruction of Ephesians.

What that was we have seen in our examination of that Epistle.

The solicitude is as to their standing fast in the truth and, "the faith" which they had learned; while the truth and the faith are declared to be concerning the Mystery which is the great subject of Ephesian teaching.

The solicitude is further seen in the expansion of the members D (ii. 8-23) and D (iii. 1-iv. 1), which consist of Doctrinal correction for failure.

As this is the great scope and the main object of the Epistle as a whole, it is necessary that we should carefully note and study the special scope of these two members. This can be done only by exhibiting their structure, which we must leave for our next chapter.

The Epistle to the Colossians.

CHAP. ii. 8-23.

Doctrinal Correction: we having died witk Christ.

The Structure of the Epistle as a whole (see page 153) reveals the fact that, with the exception of the Solicitude (in C and *C*), the great bulk of the Epistle is made up of Doctrinal Correction (in D and *D*).

It will, therefore, be necessary for us to get the scope of these two main portions, in order that we may be able to understand and gather the design and import of the words.

First, therefore, let us give

THE EXPANSION OF D. (ii. 8-23).

Doctrinal correction: we having died with Christ.

D | c | ii. 8. Caution. "Let no man *deceive* you."
   d | ii. 9, 10. Christ the Head: and the Body complete in Him.
     e | ii. 11-15. Ordinances, therefore, done away in Christ.
  c | ii. 16-18. Caution. "Let no man *judge* you."
   d | ii. 19. Christ the Head: and the Body nourished by Him.
     e | ii. 20-23. Ordinances, therefore, done away in Christ.

Having thus got the scope of the first of these two great central members of the Epistle, we are now in a position to apply it to the interpretation of the words and expressions employed; for we thus hold the key in our hands, without which it is impossible to give a true exegesis.

We see at once that in the one we have correction for doctrinal failure with regard to Ephesian teaching as to our having "DIED

WITH CHRIST" (D, ii. 8-23); while, in the other, we shall see that we have correction for doctrinal failure with regard to Ephesian teaching as to our being "RISEN WITH CHRIST" (D, iii. i–iv. 1.

It is interesting to notice that the *caution* given in "c" (verse 8) corresponds with that given in *"c"* (verse 16); and how our completeness in Christ is brought out in the other two members respectively.

We now give our translation of

D. (ii. 8-23).
Correction of doctrine: we having died with Christ.
c. (ii. 8). *Caution:* not to be *deceived.*

See to it, lest (The indicative fut. after βλέπετε μή, instead of the usual subjunctive (Luke xxi. 8), shows that the danger is real and present; compare Heb. iii. 12 and Mark xiv. 2) **there shall be anyone who secures you as his prey** (you who have such a perfection and completeness of standing in Christ. The verb συλαγωγέω, *sulagōgeō, to carry off prey,* occurs only here in N.T.) **through his philosophy**–yes, his **vain, deceitful philosophy** (This is the force of the figure *Hendiadys* here) **according to the tradition of men, according to the stoicheia** (*i.e.,* the religious ordinances and rites) **of the world and not according to Christ."**

The warning is heightened, by first stating the danger *positively* (twice), and then repeating it negatively, so that there may be no mistake about the matter. It is the figure *Pleonasm;* used here to give great emphasis.

We have here, also, in this chapter a wonderful link which unites Galatians and Colossians, and confirms our statement as to the object of these two epistles.

It is very remarkable that the word στοιχεῖον[81] *(stoicheion)* occurs only in two of these seven epistles, *viz.,* Galatians and Colossians—the two epistles which are corrective of errors of doctrine. And it occurs twice in each epistle, thus linking them

---

81. The verb στοιχέω *(stoicheō), to walk,* occurs five times (Acts xxi. 24. Rom. iv. 12. Gal. v. 25; vi. 16. Phil. iii. 16), and means to walk according to religious observances.

together (Gal. iv. 3, 9 and Col. ii. 8, 20). The word occurs seven times in all in the N.T.; and, as usual the *seven* is divided into *four* and *three*, the other three occurrences being outside these epistles to the churches (Heb. v. 12 and 2 Pet. iii. 10, 12).

It is curious also that, in Galatians, the A.V. translates the word twice "elements," with *rudiments* in the margin; and in Colossians, twice "rudiments," with *elements* in the margin. The R.V. renders the word alike in all four passages, *viz:* "rudiments" in the text and *elements* in the margin.

The word refers to *ceremonialism,* whether pagan or Jewish; whether the Essenic asceticism; Heathen mysteries; or Jewish meats, drinks, washings; days and months, seasons and years, etc., etc. (Gal. iv. 10).

Three times out of its four occurrences in these two epistles, the word is connected with the "world" *(κόσμος, cosmos),* and refers to what is material as opposed to what is spiritual.

In Gal. iv. 8, these *stoicheia* are referred to thus:—

"When ye knew not God, ye did service" (or "were in bondage," the same word as in verses 3 and 9) "to them which by nature are no gods." The *stoicheia* were the religious rites and ceremonies of heathen idolatry.

In Greece to-day every mountain, tree, grove, and fountain, has its *stoicheion* or divinity, who has to be appeased and propitiated.

These Galatians had been such idolaters (verse 8); but they had abandoned these rites and ceremonies for Christianity, and yet wanted to bring in the *stoicheia,* or the rites and ceremonies of Judaism, into the Church.

The same term is thus applied both to Paganism and Judaism; and, from the standpoint of being "all one in Christ Jesus" (iii. 28), the Jewish rites of circumcision, purification, and the observance of "days and months and times and years," etc., are put upon the same level as the worship and propitiation of spirits in trees and mountains, etc. And the Holy Spirit asks by the Apostle, "When ye knew not God ye did bond-service to them which by nature are no gods: but now having known God, ... how turn ye **again** to the weak and beggarly *stoicheia* whereto ye desire **again**[82] to do bond service? Ye observe[83] days and months and times and years. I am afraid of you, lest I have bestowed upon you labour in vain" (Gal. iv. 8-11).

So here, in Col. ii. 8, 20, we have exactly the same thought and argument.

Here, then, we have the source of all the errors of doctrine. Four distinct warnings are given (*viz.,* ii. 4, 8, 16, 18), lest the saints should fail to hold fast the truth (contained in the Epistle to the Ephesians) concerning Christ as the Head of the Spiritual Body, and the individual perfection of the members in Him, as regards their standing before God, with its consequent result as regards their position among men.

All the danger consists in "not holding the Head" (ii. 19). Therefore it is that the saints are exhorted, in verse 6: "As ye have received Christ Jesus as the Lord, so walk ye IN HIM," etc. Their safety lies in holding fast what they have received concerning HIM, giving no heed to enticing or persuasive words.

To preserve them from man's vain deceitful philosophy (so-called), the Deity of Christ is set before them, and the fact of their spiritual perfection and completeness in Him is emphasised.

This is the subject of

d. (ii. 9, 10).
Christ the Head: and we, complete in Him.
For in Him dwelleth (mark the present tense) all the fulness[84]

---

82. The figure of *Rebetition*

83. The force of the preposition $\pi\alpha\rho\acute{a}$ *(para)* in composition with the ,verb, gives it the force of our "mis-." And the middle voice suggests a personal application. In no instance in the N.T. is it used without a sinister reference. "Ye observe," but *ye* really *mis-observe.*

84. $\pi\lambda\acute{\eta}\rho\omega\mu\alpha$ *(pleerōma)* is the result or product or act of the verb: *complement* or *filling up: fulness* in exchange for emptiness. We, *the filling up* of the Body, completing it as to its members: and Christ the Head, *the filler up* of the members with all spiritual blessings, gifts, and graces (Eph. i. 3, 23).

of the Godhead (θεότης, *theotees*, only here in N.T., not θειότης, *theiotees*, as in Rom. i. 20, which only means *divinity*, and rightly so. But, here, it is *Godhead* as to essence, not merely *Divinity* as to character) **bodily** (*i.e.*, corporately. Or, "For in His person God dwells amid all His possessions in bodily form"). **And in Him ye are made complete** (R.V., "made full;" what a wondrous fact! How calculated to make all ceremonial ordinances appear to be the weak and beggarly things they really are), **who is the head of all government and authority** (The two words ἀρχή, *archee*, and ἐξουσία, *exousia*, occur together frequently, as in Eph. i. 21. Sometimes they are human (Luke xii. 11. Tit. iii. 1); and, sometimes spiritual, either good (Eph. iii. 10) or evil (Col. ii. 15), or both (1 Cor. xv. 24). In Rom. viii. 38, we have ἀρχαί *(principalities)* without ἐξουσίαι *(authorities);* and in 1 Pet. iii. 22 the reverse).

e. (ii. 11-15).
Ordinances therefore done away in Christ.
in whom ye were circumcised also (the aorist here marks a definite time when this was done, viz., at Christ's burial) **with a circumcision** (three-fold in nature, viz., 1st, its *character)* **not done by hand** (i.e., spiritual, not material; not a ceremony performed on the eighth day (Phil. iii. 3, 5); 2nd, its *extent* and completeness, having reference not merely to a part of the flesh, but to the old man himself) **in the putting off of the** (whole) **body** (that is to say) **the flesh**[85] (by reckoning ourselves as having died with Christ (Rom. vi. 6, 11) and 3rdly, its *author;* it is not the circumcision of Abraham or Moses, but) **In the circumcision of Christ** (*i.e.*, accomplished by Christ. Gen. of origin or instrument); **having been buried together with Him in** His **baptism** (*lit.*, the baptism of Him, in His baptism unto death; *i.e.*, in His burial. Mark x. 38; Lu. xii. 50. Compare

---

Compare Eph. iv. 13 and Ps. xxiv. 1, 2.

85. The words τῶν ἁμαρτιῶν *(tōn hamartiōn), the sins of,* must be omitted with all the Textual critics and the R.V.

166

Rom. vi. 3-5).[86] The aorist tense puts the burial as being contemporaneous with the circumcision; *i.e.*, ye were circumcised when ye were buried with Christ. Thus far we have the end of the Old Man; Now we come to the origin of the New Man), **wherein** (in His burial) **ye were raised with him also through faith** (that is to say through the superhuman) **power of God** (who did not leave Christ in the tomb, but) **who raised Him from the dead.**

And you (Gentiles: compare iii. 7, 8; Eph. i. 13, ii. 1, &c., 11, 13, 17, 22; iii. 2; iv. 17), **being** (*ὄντας, (ontas), being,* as marking the state, *i.e.,* being judicially viewed as) **dead as regards your sins** (the preposition *ἐν (en)* in, goes out according to Tischendorf, Tregelles, Westcott and Hort, and R.V.) **and the uncircumcision of your flesh** (*i.e.,* your uncircumcised state as Gentiles) **He quickened, even you** (these two words must be added according to Lachmann, Tischendorf, Tregelles, Alford and R.V.[87] Even you, I say), **together with Him** (Eph.ii. *5),* **having graciously treated us** (*i.e.,* both you and us) **as to all our transgressions,** (and) **by cancelling the bond** (*χειρόγραφον, cheirographon* is the idiomatic legal term for a note-of-hand, Juvenal xiii. 187; xvi. 14) **standing against us with its demands** (Eph. ii. 15, "the law of commandments contained in ordinances." This is the force of the word *δόγμασιν,* here, as in Luke ii. 1. Acts xvi. 4; xvii. 7. Eph. ii. 15, and here. The word occurs nowhere else in N.T.), **which** (bond) **was directly opposed to us** (referring to its active hostility rather than to its valid claim in the previous clause). **He hath**[88] **taken it** (*i.e.,* the bond) **also** (as well as the body of flesh, though this latter is at present in abeyance until the time for our resurrection shall have come. This is what is implied in the word "also") **right away, having nailed it** (the bond) **to** (His) **cross** (and) **having despoiled** (*ἀπεκδυσάμενος, apekdusamenos,* a word never before used) **the**

---

86. See *Figures of Speech,* Ellipsis, pages 18, 19..

87. The Vatican MS. (B) reads "us" instead of you.

88. This perfect, standing in the midst of aorists, is very emphatic. It denotes finality, meaning: "He hath finally taken it right away and for ever."

governments and the authorities (see above under verse 10, and compare Luke xxii. 53. Heb. ii. 14, 15). **He exhibited openly** the spoil (as trophies) **making them** (you and us) **triumphant in Himself** (compare the only other occurrence of the word, θριαμβεύω *thriambeuō,* in 2 Cor. ii. 14. Observe there the "us," and the "you"; and, "us" in this context. Christ is the "head of all principalities and power' (verse 10), and having despoiled these, He makes you and us to triumph in Himself—the Head.)

The ordinances referred to here belonged to the rites and ceremonies of Religion as distinct from Christianity. In Christ they are done away. The Holy Spirit teaches us here, through Paul, that for those who are in union with Christ the Head, as members of His Body, these ordinances have been fulfilled, and are ended and done away in the body of His flesh through His death.

To return to them, therefore, in any way, is to deny our completeness and perfection in Christ. It is practically to say that He is not sufficient, that something further is necessary to be added to Him, that in spite of all He has done and notwithstanding all His merits, we are incomplete, and need some ordinance to make us quite complete.

If believers died with Christ and were buried with Him, there is an end of the whole matter. What has a dead person to do with ordinances? They were perfectly useless to us when we were dead *in sins;* and now, since we died with Christ, we are useless for them. The bond which stood against us in all its valid claim consisted of ordinances (ver. 14). This bond He has taken away and abolished (Eph. ii. 15). The Second Man bore the sentence passed upon the first man, and endured the curse of the law given through Moses (Gal. iii. 13). By His burial He returned to the ground whence man was taken (Gen. iii. 19), and put off all that belonged to Him in relation to Israel and to the earth. His Divine glory was veiled when the Living One became dead, and was laid in the grave. But that which seemed like defeat was really victory (Heb. ii. 14); for God raised Him from the dead, and in His resurrection He led captivity captive. He triumphed over all principalities and powers that were opposed to Him. His triumph was shown openly in heaven above, and on earth in the power that accompanied the preaching of Christ crucified and risen.

This being so, another warning becomes necessary, and we have it in

c. (ii. 16-18).
Caution: not to be judged.

Let no one therefore judge you in the matter of eating or drinking (*i.e.*, seeing that the bond of ordinances is cancelled, beware of subjecting yourselves to man. Suffer no man to call you to account in the matter of eating or drinking) **or in the matter of a feast or new moon or of a Sabbath day** (the three words go together as embracing all the sacred seasons. 1 Chron. xxiii. 31. 2 Chron. ii. 4; xxxi, 3. Ezek. xlv. 17. Hos. ii. 11), **which things are a shadow of the things** (realities) **to come, but the Body** (which is the real substance) **is Christ's.** (These things were the shadows of *the future Millennial Kingdom,* and do not now concern those who have been crucified and buried with Christ. We are the Body of Christ, and therefore hold quite a unique position with regard to that kingdom. Being risen with Christ already *(de jure),* we are to be judged and esteemed as such. Resurrection places us beyond all earthly judgments.

Now, we have a double caution. The first as to the ordinances of Judaism (verse 16), "Let no man call you to account." The second as to the ordinances and dangers of heathen Gnosticism (verse 18), **"Let no man defraud you of your prize, exercising his [own] will in [his] humility**[89] **and [his] religion**[90] **of angels, intruding into things which he has not seen.**[91] **vainly puffed up by his fleshy**

---

89. The word is always used in a bad sense in heathen writers. Here it is the false humility, which implied that God was inaccessible except through aeons, or angels, or spirits.

90. *Threskeia* is elsewhere rendered religion (Jas. i, 26, 27. Acts xxvi. 5). See *Things to Come,* Nov., 1903, and April, 1904.

91. Or dwelling on the things which he hath seen. There is question as to the reading here. If the negative goes out (as in R.V.) it means dwelling on the things he has seen, and admits what they allege. If it be retained (as in A.V.) it

mind, and not holding fast the Head."

To hold fast to Christ as the Head of the one spiritual body is to keep us from being defrauded of that wondrous possession and prize.

Then we come to the other word in verse 23.

"Which sort of things [namely, the forbidding ordin ances—Touch not, taste not, handle not] **having a reputation for wisdom in will-religion, and in lowering the mind** (referring to the same two things mentioned in verse 18), **and in discipline of the body, and** [yet] **not** [really], **of any value to remedy indul-gence of the flesh."**

The danger to these Colossian saints was the religion which had to do with the will, thus making them an easy prey to "the willers" or familiar spirits, who would defraud them of their prize. We have the same danger to-day, and need the same caution.

The exhortation here is plural: but the warning is directed against some individual who, puffed up and led by his old nature, would fain lead them astray to rest in the outward ordinances of Religion. These were the only things that the fleshly mind could see. This was the only standing that the flesh could comprehend. But these Colossian saints were not to be defrauded of that high standing which they had in Christ, which enabled them to come with boldness to the throne of grace.

There is nothing here to lead us to suppose that these saints had fallen so low as to worship angels. There is no historical basis for such a tradition. It is evolved wholly from this passage, by those who fail to see its true scope, which is far too high to warrant us in believing that these saints needed a warning against angel-worship!

Not only is Christ the head, and we are *complete* in Him, as in d. (ii. 9, 10); but He is the Head, and we are *nourished* by and built up in Him.

This is the statement in

---

is the denial of what they allege.

d. (ii. 19).

And not (*oὐ*, ou, not, *μή mee*, denying it as an absolute matter of fact. He may think he holds it, but he does not) **holding fast the Head, from whom the whole Body, by means of the junctures** (*i.e.*, the points of contact) **and ligaments** (Galen uses the word *συνδέσμων sundesmōn*, of muscles or tendons, etc.), being **bountifully supplied** (with all necessary nutriment), **and knit together, increaseth with the increase of God** (*i.e.*, wrought by God).

It is not merely *unity* which is taught here (as in Ephesians), but *growth*. This is the ultimate result of the intermediate processes. The origin of all is God: who hath given Christ to be the Head over all things to this wondrous Body. Christ, the Head, is the *source of all*; but the members of the Body are made and used as the *channels* of communication in their mutual relation to Him and to one another.

To cease "holding the Head," therefore, is to lose, practically, all our special privileges as members of His Body. It is to take up an attitude before God in our access to Him below that in which His love and grace has set us. It is to take the place of humility as the angels, as servants instead of sons, even the sons of God. It is to worship with veiled faces at a distance, instead of "with unveiled face, beholding the glory of the Lord" in the face of the glorified Lord Jesus. It is a feigned humility, not apprehending the exceeding riches of the grace of God toward us in Christ Jesus, which is sure to issue in a regard for visible things and religious ordinances, which are the natural objects of the fleshly mind (the Old nature), the only things which it can comprehend or understand.

All this is the sure result of "not holding the Head."

Hence, the theme of ordinances being done away in Christ is again taken up in *"e"* (as in "e," ii. 11- 15).

e. (ii. 20-23).

If then ye died[92]**with Christ from the Stoicheia** *(i.e.*, the rites

---

92. This is the *Aorist* tense, to mark the one definite crisis in Christ's death: never *the perfect* tense in this connection.

and ceremonies of religion as such, see the note above) **of the world, why, as living in the world** (as though you had not died with Christ) **do ye subject yourselves to ordinances:** (as when they wickedly say) **'Touch not (this), Taste not (that), Handle not** (the other)'—**which things are all** (destined) **for corruption in the using** (of them)—**according to the precepts and teachings of men** (Is. xxix. 13)—**precepts which have indeed a reputation for wisdom in observances and humiliation** (of mind) **and discipline of (the) body; yet not really of any value to remedy indulgence of the flesh**[93] (the Old nature).

Those who are reckoned as having died with Christ, and have the Spirit of God dwelling within them, and therefore are "not in the flesh" (Rom. viii. 9), are "set free from all those restraints which were enjoined by God upon those who were in covenant with Him by an ordinance in their flesh" (Gen. xvii. 13). The law of commandments in ordinances, which has been abolished by the Lord Jesus in His death and burial, includes not only the ordinances of the Mosaic Law, but extends to all enjoined by men. They are "*the stoicheia* of the world" (Col. ii. 8, 20); the observances, rites, and ceremonies of Religion, as distinct from Christianity. They may be taught with a show of wisdom of words, as a self-devised religion of man's will, with feigned humility, and abstinence, and discipline.

This is the present teaching of Christendom; but the result of that teaching, as seen in the present state of the religious world, shows that these things are, of no value against the indulgence of the flesh " (R.V.).

---

93. See R.V. and Lightfoot, *Com.* in loco, for this beautiful and happy rendering.

172

The Epistle to the Colossians.

Chap. iii. i—iv. 1.

Doctrinal Correction: as having risen with Christ.

Having thus received the solemn and important doctrinal correction contained in D (ii. 8-23), showing the wondrous consequences which come from our having *died with Christ,* we are now, in the corresponding portion, *D* (iii. 1—iv. 1), led on to see the blessed consequences of our having *risen with Christ.*

Many call these two portions "practical." But practice, to be real, must, and can only be the spontaneous outcome of belief of the truth; otherwise it is merely "works without faith," and is "dead." Anyone can practise, but practise *what?* That is the question. The flesh can practise. All false religions have plenty of practice. But only that practice can be acceptable with God that is the result of His revealed truth received and believed; for "whatsoever is not of faith is sin."

So that it is, from one point of view, quite true that these portions are practical; but more truly, they are *doctrinal.* That is to say, true doctrine is laid down, and then the errors of faith and life which come from not seeing and holding this truth are pointed out and corrected. This is the practical part of the truth here enforced. This second great portion is, like the first, an *extended alternation,*[94] and its scope may be seen from its expansion.

---

94. See *Figures of Speech,* under, "Correspondence," by the same author and publisher.

THE EXPANSION OF *D*. (iii. 1—iv. 1).
Doctrinal Correction: as having risen with Christ.

D | *f* | iii. 1-9. Our calling, as risen with Christ, the rule of the old man ended and put off.
| | *g* | iii. 10-11. The new man put on.
| | | h | iii. 12-14. The effects seen, in the exercise of charity as "the bond of perfectness."
| *f* | iii. 15. Our calling in the one body: the rule of God's peace begun.
| | *g* | iii. 16. The word of Christ put within.
| | | *h* | iii. 17-iv. 1. The effects manifested, in the exercise of charity as the bond of all domestic relations.

All true practical holiness is here shown to spring from the holding of true doctrine; and it cannot be procured in any other way. All is based here on the fact that the saints, being "in Christ," were raised with Him, and now stand on resurrection ground in Him. This comes out in the first member.

f (iii. 1-9).
Our calling as risen with Christ.

If therefore (if this be so: if) **ye were raised** with **Christ** (not *have been* raised. This is the fundamental condition and basis of the whole. To interpret this of infant water baptism, as ecclesiastical commentators for the most part do, is error of the very worst kind: so flagrant and gross and fatal that we need not pause to controvert it here) **seek the things which are above, where Christ is at the right hand of God** (now) **seated** (Eph. 1. 20). **Set your mind on the things that are above, not on the things connected with the earth** (This is wider than seeking, and includes the whole region of mental and spiritual occupation), **for ye died** (as in ii. 12. Rom. vi-4-7: here again, as always, the *Aorist;* for a definite act and event is spoken of, not a (condition or state), **and your** (new) **life** (which is in the risen Christ, the Head) **has been** (or lies) **hidden** (now we have the *perfect* tense, κέκρυπται *(kekruptai)*, because the permanent effect is spoken of) **with Christ in God. When Christ** (a fourth time mentioned for emphasis, otherwise a pronoun would

174

have done) **shall be manifested, who is our life, then shall ye also** (as well as us and all who are Christ's), **together with Him, be manifested in glory.** Put to death therefore your members that are on the earth.

Now, note that this injunction is in the *Aorist* tense, and that shows that a *definite act,* and not a state or condition, is here contemplated. It is not a continuous action or practice, but a definite act.

But truth, to be practical, must be *practicable.* How are we to put our members to death? If we did so physically, it would be suicide. It must be a possible act. What is it? It surely can be no other than what we have in Rom. vi. 11. "Reckon ye yourselves to be dead." It is an act of faith in the one act of Christ on the Cross, when "our old man was crucified with Him" (Rom. vi. 6)

"They that are Christ's crucified *(Aorist* tense again) the flesh with its affections and lusts" (Gal. v. 24) When did they do this? When they, by faith, made this blessed reckoning once for all, and learnt the wondrous truth of what God had done for them on Calvary! "If by (the) spirit (the new nature) ye put to death the deeds of the body, ye will live" (Rom. viii. 13).

In these passages we have the same reference: "They that are Christ's did crucify the flesh." It is one past definite act; and, if any are now complaining of the lowness of their life and walk, then it is for them now to, do what they have never yet done, and reckon themselves to have died when Christ died, and thus, practically, obey the injunction of Col. iii. 5. "If ye were raised with Christ" .. *ye must have died with Him;* put yourselves therefore to death, reckoning by faith that *ye did thus die.* Occupy your mind and activities in seeking the things which are above, as risen ones. Thus, and thus only, will you truly live; and will find that your members which are upon the earth are dead, practically, having no sphere for their activities as long as your heart and mind are in the heavenlies. While, by faith, you dwell there, all will be heavenly: occupation with heavenly things will produce a heavenly walk on earth. Nothing else will really accomplish this. Other plans and devices may appear to do so, but the result is only artificial and temporary. It will not last. It is like tying paper flowers on to a plant. It is an attempt to produce holiness of life in a way *other than that which God has revealed.*

Just as Cain attempted to procure justification (and therefore "righteousness") by a way of his own, instead of taking God's way, so do those who are in the modern movement of the present day attempt to procure a "progressive sanctification" by means and methods, arts and artifices, which are other than God has revealed in these epistles.

In Christ we are complete. We are justified, and we are sanctified, "in Him." This is our *standing* which God has given us in Christ. We cannot grow in this. We can never grow in relationship. We may and can grow in our knowledge of it, in our experience of it, and in our enjoyment of it; but not in the thing itself. And we can grow in all this only by learning and resting in what God has done, and not by continually trying to do it ourselves!

If we learn the blessed fact that the Lord's people died and rose again with Christ, by and in His one definite act which can never be undone, then, the more we realize this, the more shall we walk worthy of such a wondrous calling.

Hence this member f. (iii. 1-9) ends with another *aorist* participle (verse 9) : not "seeing ye have put oft the old man," but **"seeing ye did put off the old man with his deeds,"** when ye reckoned yourselves to have died with Christ, and thus put yourself—the old man-to death.

When Christ died and was buried, as we are taught in ii. 11, His people were crucified with Him; hence the reality of this wondrous reckoning when they, by faith, put off the old man.

When Christ was raised from the dead, those who were then "quickened together with Him" (ii. 13) "put on the new man," the Head of a new creation. His members are one with Him..

Now, this is the blessed standpoint of every believer. It is now made known among the Gentiles, now made manifest to His saints, "to whom God would make known what is the riches of the glory of this mystery: which is Christ—the hope of glory—in you. It is not the possession of those well-instructed in Scripture, or advanced in knowledge; but it belongs to children, still in their parents' homes, and to slaves still in bondage to their masters. This is shown in *h*

(iii. 17-iv. 1).

The prayer of Epaphras, in iv. 12, is **"that ye may stand fast perfected and fully assured in the whole will of God"** (see Eph. i. 9: *i.e.,* fully persuaded, or convinced, and satisfied, in all this truth which has its foundation and source in the will of God).

This prayer is similar to the two prayers of Paul in Eph. i. and iii. These prayers are that the saints may live in the experimental enjoyment, and in the practical manifestation, of the grace revealed in "the mystery" of the gospel.

Thus the Epistle to the Colossians completes the word of God to the Gentile believers, in making known "the riches of the glory of the mystery" which hath been "hid from ages and from generations, but now is made manifest to His saints" (Col. i. 26-27).

The Epistle to the Colossians stands side by side, as we have shown, with the Epistle to the Galatians. Both are marked by "correction." Both are concerning failure, and in both that failure is with respect to doctrine. Both churches had been instructed in the doctrine and truths contained in the Epistle to the Romans. Both had therefore received "the beginning of the gospel:" and now further truth was communicated to them.

But in Colossians the correction is in advance of that in Galatians; inasmuch as the Colossians had received the further truth as it affects the subject of ordinances, for those who have Christ for their sanctification (as well as their righteousness), and who know their perfection and completeness in Him. Those who died with Christ, and are *justified* in Him, need no law of works for justification. In like manner, those who are risen with Christ are *sanctified* in Him, and need no rules and regulations, or ordinances, for their sanctification.

That this is the case is now to be shown in the epistles to "the Church of the Thessalonians," This is a model or typical church: and in it we shall see what a church was like which was built up in the church teaching and church truth revealed in these epistles.

177

The Epistle to the Thessalonians.
Introductory.

We come, now, to the last of the seven Text-books prepared and provided for our instruction by the Holy Spirit. And before we have done we shall see why, though written earlier than those to any of the other six churches, it is placed last in order.

It stands out by itself. There is no other Epistle which answers to it. The other two primary Epistles (Romans and Ephesians), written for "doctrine and instruction," are each followed by two others, one for "reproof" as to practical failure, and the other for "correction" as to doctrinal departure, with respect to the special teaching of each respectively. But Thessalonians is followed by no other church-epistles. The other six epistles make two perfect and complete sets of three each;[95] but Thessalonians stands alone. It is full of doctrine, as are the other two but, unlike the two pairs (Cor. and Gal. on the one hand, and Phil. and Col. on the other), there is an entire absence of reproof and correction, both as to practice and doctrine. There are a few exhortations, it is true, but there is no blame: nothing but unqualified thanksgiving and praise for their faith and love and hope from beginning to end. Indeed, we have here

A MODEL CHURCH

—the only one of all the seven which is specially spoken of as a church—"the Church of the Thessalonians," as though it were the only one worthy of the name; the only one which exhibits the full results of having learnt the lessons taught in Romans and Ephesians.

---

95. The number *seven* is generally divided into *four* and *three;* but sometimes (as in the Golden Candlestick) into *six* and *one.* In these seven epistles we have both these arrangements.

The saints of "the Church of the Thessalonians" could have passed an examination in the doctrines taught in those two Epistles. Hence, their wonderful character; individually and collectively.

The Apostle had no occasion to say, as he said to the Corinthians, "I fear when I come I shall not find you such as I would . . . and lest when I come again my God will humble me among you, and I shall bewail many which have sinned already, and have not repented of the uncleanness and fornication and lasciviousness which they have committed" (2 Cor. xii. 20, 21).

There was no need to say, as he said to the Galatians, "I marvel that ye are so soon removed from him that called you into the grace of Christ unto another Gospel" (Gal. i. 6), or, "O foolish Galatians, who hath bewitched you, that ye should not obey the truth?" (Gal. iii. 1).

There was no occasion to say to the Thessalonians as he said to the Philippians, "Many walk, of whom I have told you often, and now tell you, even weeping, that they are the enemies of the cross of Christ; whose end is destruction, whose God is their belly, and whose glory is in their shame, who mind earthly things" (Phil. iii. 18, 19).

There was no need to say to the Thessalonians, as he said to the Colossians, "Beware lest any man spoil you through vain deceitful philosophy" (Col. ii. 8).

All these four epistles contain reproof and correction: but in those to the Thessalonians, we find the very opposite. Not only no blame, but continuous praise.

The first epistle is stamped (after the epistolary portion) by the opening words, "We give thanks to God always for you all, making mention of you in our prayers; remembering without ceasing your work of faith, and labour of love, and patience of hope in our Lord Jesus Christ, in the sight of God, even our Father; knowing, brethren beloved, your election of God" (i. 2-4).

This is followed by "Ye were ensamples to all that believe in Macedonia and Achaia" (i. 7).

"For this cause also thank we God without ceasing, because, when ye received the word of God which ye heard of us, ye received it not as the word of men, but as it is in truth, the word of God,

179

which effectually worketh also in you that believe" (ii. 13).

"For what thanks can we render to God again for you, for all the joy wherewith we joy for your sakes before our God?" (iii. 9).

The second epistle is characterised in the same way. It opens with the words, "We are bound to thank God always tor you, brethren, as it is meet, because that your faith groweth exceedingly, and the charity of every one of you all toward each other aboundeth; so that we ourselves glory in you in the churches of God for your patience and faith in all your persecutions and tribulations that ye endure" (2 Thess. i. 3, 4).

"We are bound to give thanks alway to God for you, brethren beloved of the Lord, because God hath from the beginning chosen you to salvation through sanctification of the Spirit and belief of the truth" (ii. 13).

The epistle closes with the expression of the assurance: "We have confidence in the Lord touching you, that ye both do and will do the things which we command you" (iii. 4).

There was no need of laboured argument to prove the fundamental doctrine of resurrection, as in 1 Cor. xv.

No fear lest he had bestowed upon them labour in vain, as in Gal. iv. 11.

No tearful warnings against strife and vain-glory, as in Phil. i. 15, 16; ii. 3; iii. 18, 19.

No need of asking, "if ye be dead with Christ from the rudiments of the world, why, as though living in the world, are ye subject to ordinances?" as in Col. ii. 20.

True, in one place, and only one, he has to say "We hear that there are some which walk among you disorderly, working not at all, but are busybodies. Now them that are such we command and exhort by our Lord Jesus Christ, that with quietness they work and eat their own bread (2 Thess. iii. 11).

With this single exception—which is all the stronger, not merely because it is the only one, but because of its character when compared with the reproofs and corrections of the four other epistles—with this single exception, there is one devout note of praise and thanksgiving throughout the two epistles.

But not only is "the Church of the Thessalonians" a model

church in this respect; it is a model also in that it was most remarkable for its missionary activity. Sound doctrine produced fruitful service for God.

From this assembly in Thessalonica sounded forth the word of God throughout Macedonia and Achaia (1 Thess. i. 8). A tract of country as large as Great Britain was evangelised by this little flock. How they did it we do not know: for they had no railways, no printing-presses, no great missionary societies; but all we know is that in some way they sounded forth the word of God throughout that vast region.

And we know also that this is what other churches then and since have not been remarkable for, and for which they are not noted in our own day.

There must be therefore some cause for this great difference: some secret, of which other churches were, and are not, possessed.

What that secret was we learn through a fact which is strongly emphasised. Three times the Apostle calls attention to it; and lays stress upon "the manner of his entering into" Thessalonica. In 1 Thess. i. 5, he says, "Ye know what manner of men we were among you for your sake." In verse 9, "They themselves show of us what manner of entering in we had unto you." And in chap. ii. 1, he says, "For yourselves know, brethren, that our entrance in unto you was not in vain."

The question arises, What was there so peculiar or remarkable in that "manner" to which he thus three times so pointedly refers? The answer is given in Acts xvii., where we have the historic record of his arrival at Thessalonica: and we read, "Paul, as his manner was, went in unto them, and three sabbath days reasoned with them out of the Scriptures."

How refreshing it is to read these simple words! Here was Thessalonica, a city of some 70,000 inhabitants, far worse than any city with which we are acquainted to-day. The Gentiles sunk in all the awful abominations of heathen idolatry, and the Jews hating the very name of Christ, and persecuting the saints of God (2 Thess. ii. 14-16). Some were religious, some were profane; some were moral, some were vicious; but all alike were ignorant of Christ, and all alike sinners and transgressors before God.

181

Yet the Apostle had no need of bands of music, sensational announcements, musical services, or solo singers; none of the tricks or contrivances of the present day; none of the modern methods or new fashions of the nineteenth century! Why? *Because he had not lost faith in the power of God's Word!* And this, because he had not lost faith in its *truth!* He believed that the word of God was able to accomplish all God's purposes of grace: that it must prosper in the thing whereto God sent it, and accomplish that which He pleases (Isa. lv. 11).

He believed that the Gospel was "the power of God unto salvation" and, therefore, needed no "handmaids" or "helpmeets." His one aim was not to "get the people in," but to *get the Word of God in,* and leave that to work effectually by the Holy Ghost in the hearts of those whom He had gathered together by His almighty power.

We are already arriving at the secret of the vast difference between the purity, holiness, and zeal of that model church, which makes it stand out in such marked contrast with the corruption, error, and worldliness of modern churches. But there was more than this.

Not only did the apostle reason with them out of the written Word, but he preached the Living Word—the Lord Jesus Christ,— "opening and alleging that Christ must needs have suffered, and risen again from the dead; and that this Jesus whom I preach unto you is the Messiah" (verse 3). This, we learn from verse 7, meant that He was coming again, "another King." Thus He proclaimed a complete Saviour:— *a suffering* Saviour, a *risen* Saviour, and a *coming* Saviour. In a word, he preached Christ to them, and did not separate Christ and the Scriptures. He had one Gospel. Not one for Gentile idolators and another for religious Jews; not one for "men" and another for "women only," but a gospel for *sinners.* For all alike are under sin, whatever may be the natural privileges of birth or education.

It is most important, in learning the secret which produced this model church, to note that the apostle did not go to Thessalonica with religious ordinances, ecclesiastical ceremonies, or sacraments: not with plans for self-improvement, called "Christian science," secular education, social reform, the sanitation of Thessalonica, or the "duties of citizenship." He did not aim at making "reformed characters," but at converting sinners by the power of the Holy Ghost. Still less did he go to amuse the ungodly, or to provide entertainments for the goats. He went to seek out lost sinners, to lead them to the knowledge of the Saviour.

He laid his axe at the root of the tree. He planted the cross of Christ before them. He proved that they were lost, and needed a Saviour: and not that they could do something themselves, and needed only a helper. He taught them that Christ had died for His People, and that they had died in Him (Romans); that Christ had risen again, and that they had risen in Him, and were "seated in the Heavenlies in Him" (Ephesians); that Christ was coming again, and they were coming with Him (Thessalonians). Hence their *faith* was in Christ; their *love* was rooted and grounded in Him; and their *hope* was anchored within the veil. All their Christian graces were in fullest exercise, and were all developed and increased in due proportion. The reason of the thanksgiving is given and shown by a comparison of 1 Thess. i. 3 with verses 9 and 10:—

Their "work of faith" (verse 3) was seen in that they had "turned to God" from every idol (verse 9).

Their "labour of love" (verse 3) was seen in that they now served the living and true God (verse 9).

Their "patience of hope" (verse 3) was seen in that they waited for God's Son from heaven (v. 10).

Their Christian character was complete: and no Christian character can be complete unless these three Christian graces are present in due and proper proportion.

But the majority of Christians to-day are practically destitute of these three Christian graces. Their *faith* in the *truth*, of God's Word is going, and therefore their faith in *its power* is waning.

Their *love* is not "the love of God shed abroad in the heart;" and therefore it is of self: and, not knowing the truth as to the members of the one body in Christ, love as expressed in true Christian charity is almost unknown, and though admired as "the greatest thing in *the world"* is the *least* of all things *in the Church*.

And as to *hope;* well, the majority of Christians are waiting for many things which God has not given as objects of hope; while the one thing which He has definitely given as the object they not only are not waiting for themselves, but condemn those who are!

Some are waiting for *death*, which is not an object of hope, for people die without waiting for it.

Some are waiting for an outpouring of the Spirit of God, and not for the Son of God.

Some are waiting for the world to be converted, and not for it to be judged by the Son of Man at His coming.

Some are waiting for the return of God's ancient People to their land, instead of the return of God's Son to this world.

Some are waiting for the revelation of Antichrist, instead of the revelation of Christ.

While others tell us that the Lord's coming was fulfilled at the destruction of Jerusalem, in spite of the fact here stated that these saints at Thessalonica were not waiting for Titus to come with his armies from Rome, but for God's Son to come with His holy angels from heaven.

Some are content with Christ crucified; and, though knowing and rejoicing in the benefits of His death and passion, are ignorant of the truths connected with a Risen Christ, and our new resurrection life and walk in Him.

Still more ignorant are the great mass of Christians as to His coming again, and the fact that this is the great and "blessed hope" which is the portion of all who are in Christ.

So great and general is the ignorance that, when professing Christians boldly avow that they "take no interest in the coming of Christ," they do not even know enough to see that they are exposing their ignorance as to their very *standing*, which God has given His people in Christ.

No wonder, then, that there is this difference between the Church of the Thessalonians and the churches of this day!

No wonder that, being ignorant of the great Mystery of the "one Body" in Christ, they are taken up with their own and other so-called "bodies," and are striving in controversy about them, as the Corinthians.

No wonder that, having begun in the spirits they are seeking to be made perfect in the flesh, as the Galatians.

No wonder that, losing sight of the fact that the members are "all one in Christ Jesus," they are not striving together for the faith of the Gospel with one mind and one spirit, but doing many things from "strife and vainglory," as were the Philippians.

No wonder that, "not holding the head," they are not increasing, "with the increase of God;" and are "subject to ordinances . . . after the commandments and doctrines of men," as were the Colossians.

Such was not the condition of the Church of the Thessalonians: and the secret is laid open before our eyes.

The Epistle to the Thessalonians.
II.—THE FIRST EPISTLE (i. 2—iii. 13)

This model Church— "the Church of the Thessalonians"—was now in a position to receive further detailed "doctrine" and "instruction" respecting the Lord's coming again, as none of the other churches had been).

Not until we know subjectively all the blessings which God has given His People in Christ dead and risen again, in and with Him, and seated in the Heavenlies, not only in Christ personal, but in "the Christ" Mystical or "Spiritual," can Christians be in a position to learn further details concerning His return from heaven.

True, they had been taught "to wait for God's Son from heaven," and they waited. That formed their character; that satisfied and increased their hope; that influenced their walk; that purified their life as nothing else in this world could do.

But note: all this was the action of the *heart,* not of the *head;* and by *faith* they reckoned themselves to have died with Christ, and risen to a walk in newness of life in Christ, and to be seated in heavenly places in Christ; hence their *love* was drawn out to Him who had done such great and wondrous things for them, while their *hope* was set upon Him (1 John iii. 3 R.V.), and they waited for God's Son from heaven. This, therefore, was part of their standing as Christians. And this completeness of Christian character was the secret of their holiness of life and of their missionary activity.

The reason why we see so little of either in the present day is that Christian character is not thus complete, through ignorance of what the Holy Spirit has written for our instruction. And the sad result is, that false and vain methods are resorted to in order to procure both holiness of life and missionary zeal.

The new gospel of "consecration" and "surrender" has been vainly invented to supply one defect while all sorts of devices are resorted to in order to supply the other.

A missionary spirit is supposed to be produced by fictitious methods, by exhibiting to the eye in some of many ways the proportion of Christians to heathen; by working on the feelings and exciting compassion; "missionary missions," and "missionary exhibitions," in which sometimes "living pictures" are introduced, and modest English girls are stared at while they are dressed up so as to represent an Eastern Zenana (otherwise known as a "Harem"!); these are among the modern inventions, the result of which is supposed to create what is called a "missionary spirit"!

Not so was the missionary zeal of the Thessalonians produced. Not in this way were they made to sound forth the word of God through Macedonia and Achaia. Not by *sentiment*, but by *truth*, was all their "labour of love" produced, by which they served the living and true God; and this was the spontaneous outcome of their complete Christian character, which no barriers could hinder, and no artificial devices create.

Some Christians already see these evils, and think the remedy is to be found in witnessing more faithfully to the neglected truth of the Lord's second coming. But this is really only another attempt to remove the effects without touching the cause.

What is the cause of this truth being neglected? We reply, Ignorance as to the teaching which the Holy Spirit has given to us in the Church Epistles through Paul! Ignorance, therefore, as to our standing in Christ!

What is needed then is to return to "the old paths" which have been forsaken; to study subjectively, and learn spiritually, and understand experimentally, the text-books of the Christian profession: to know first of all the Epistle to the Romans, to master the fundamental teaching of the first eight chapters, and to go on through the other Epistles.

What would be the result? Why, that holiness of life, and true missionary zeal, would be seen in blessed activity as *the spontaneous outcome* of true doctrine; and this without an effort; without aiming at it, without trying to be, or to do, or to accomplish this or that.

The *walk* would be holy, without vows and resolutions, and surrenderings and "re-consecrations;" and the *service* would be according to knowledge, and full of holy zeal, without the "urgent appeals" to the feelings or the pocket.

This, we repeat, was the position attained by this model church, as the irrepressible result of the Spirit's teaching. To-day, Christians are seeking for the Spirit's power and "enduement," not knowing that it is not to be obtained in this way, or out of the Divine order in which alone it can come.

The first work of the Holy Spirit is declared to be, "He shall guide you unto all the *truth.*" And it is not until after this that the promise is given, "Ye shall be endued with Power from on high."

Christians want to have *the power* without the *truth*; and in seeking for the one apart from the other, they lose both. Hence it is that we see to-day what we do see—confusion, darkness, and misdirected zeal, both in the teachers and the taught; for when the blind lead the blind, both fall into the ditch.

The Thessalonian saints had other teachers; and they had " not so learned Christ."

They had "learned HIM:" and hence they waited for Him—a crucified, risen, and coming Saviour, because of all that that meant for Him and for them.

Now, therefore, the Holy Spirit can proceed to instruct them in further detail as to the coming of Him for whom they waited.

This brings us to consider these two Epistles in order; and first we have to look at each, as a whole, in order to earn the scope. We are at once struck with the same phenomena that we noticed in the structure of Romans and Ephesians, as contrasted with the four other Epistles viz., the large portion occupied with doctrine. And, in this case, it is doctrine concerning the Lord's coming again.

More than a quarter of the whole is taken up with this one subject. Twelve separate references to it in these two brief Epistles which occupy about two leaves of an ordinary Bible. More than in whole volumes of modern sermons or religious periodicals. These for the most part are taken up with man, and self, in some of the ten thousand forms in which self shows itself. Man's "great thoughts"; man's service for man; man's controversies with man; man's plans for raising the masses; man's schemes for making the ungodly temperate or pure, and yet leaving them still "far off" from God;

man's methods for making reformed characters, etc. But there is one thing we do not see: and that is man's concern to know God, and to know and teach God's Word and God's Truth.

Let us now look at

The First Epistle as a whole.

A| i. 1.   Epistolary (Introduction).

   B | a | i. 2-iii. 10 Thanksgiving, Narration, and Appeal: in four members, alternate. (See expansion of "a" below).

        b| iii. 11-13. Prayer, in view of the Lord's coming,

   B | a | iv. 1-v.22. Instruction and Exhortation: in four members, introverted. (See page 195).

        b | v. 23-35. Prayer, in view of the Lord' coming.

A | v. 26-28. Epistolary (Conclusion).

It will be at once noticed that, as in Romans and Ephesians, by far the larger portion of the Epistle is occupied with "Doctrine" and "Instruction." And, though this is more like an Epistle than those, yet how small a portion is epistolary: one verse at the beginning, and three verses at the end!

It will now be necessary for us to examine the details of this structure more closely, and first the

THE EXPANSION OF "a" (i. 2—iii. 10).
Thanksgiving, Narration, and Appeal.

a | c | i. 2-10. Paul and the Thessalonians: concerning their spiritual welfare and condition.

      d | ii. 1-12. Paul and his Brethren. Their teaching and conduct while present; referring to time past.

    c | ii. 13-16. Paul and the Thessalonians: concerning their spiritual welfare and condition.

      d | ii. 17-iii.10. Paul and his Brethren. Their feelings while absent; referring to time present.

Of these four alternate members, "c" and "*c*" are the most important (though "d" and "*d*" are beautifully constructed). We will first exhibit them in brief, and then in full, with our own translations.

"c" (i. 2—10) AND "c" (ii. 13—16) IN BRIEF.
Paul and the Thessalonians: concerning their Spiritual Welfare and Condition.

c | e | i. 2-4. Thanksgiving.
    f | 5. Reason: Reception of the Gospel in the power of God.
      g | 6-9. The effect of the Gospel thus received.
        h | 10-. Believing Thessalonians "wait" for God's Son.
          i | -10. Delivered *from* the wrath to come.

c | e | ii. 13-. Thanksgiving.
    f | -13. Reason: Reception of the Gospel in the power of God.
      g | 14. The effect of the Gospel thus received.
        h | 15, 16-. Unbelieving Jews "killed" God's Son.
          i | -16. Delivered *to* the wrath to come.

Now we will present these two corresponding members in full:

(e). Chap. i. 2-4. **We give thanks to God always concerning you all, making mention of you in our prayers, remembering unceasingly your work of faith** (*i.e.* the work which was the product of faith shown in turning from idols, v. 9), **and labour of love** (in serving the living and true God, v. 9), **and patient endurance of hope** (in waiting for God's Son from heaven, *v.* 10) **of our Lord Jesus Christ before** (*i.e*, making mention before) **God, even our Father knowing** (in that we know or for we know), **brethren beloved** (as in 2 Thess. ii. 13), **your election by God.**

(f) Ver. 5. **Because our Gospel came not unto you in word only, but in power also, and in the Holy Spirit, and in much full assurance** (in our preaching); **even as ye know what manner of men we were among you for your sakes.**

(g). Vers. 6-9. **And ye became imitators** (2 Thess. iii. 7) **of us**

190

and of the Lord, having received the word in much tribulation (see Acts xvii. 5-10; chap. ii. 14 ; and iii. 2, 3, 5), with joy of *(i.e.,* wrought by) the Holy Spirit. So that ye became a type (of what a church should be, a typical or model[96] church) to all that believe in Macedonia and Achaia. For from you sounded out the word of the Lord, not only in Macedonia and Achaia, but in every place your faith which is toward God has gone abroad, so that we have no need to say anything: for they themselves do report concerning us what manner of entering in we had, and how ye turned to God from idols (the work of faith, v. 2) to serve a living and true God (the labour of love, v. 2).

(h.) Ver. 10-. And to wait for his Son from heaven (the patience of hope, *v.* 2); whom he raised from among the dead, even Jesus (in apposition, as in the corresponding member, ii. 15).

(i). Ver. -10. That rescueth us *(i.e.,* our Deliverer) from the wrath that is coming.

(*e*). Chap. ii. 13-. For this cause we too give thanks to God unceasingly:—

(*f*). Ver. -13. Because when ye received the word which ye heard from us—God's (word), ye received not man's word (as having men for its author), but as it is in reality God's word which is made energetic also (*lit.,* energises) in you that believe.

(*g*). Ver. 14. For ye became followers, brethren, of the churches of God that are in Judæa in Christ Jesus, in that ye also suffered the same things from your own countrymen (the Gentiles), as they also from the Jews.

(h). Vers. 15, 16-. Who both killed the Lord—even Jesus, and the prophets (omit "own," G. L. T. Tr. A. and R.),(and drove us out (Paul and Silas, Acts xvii. 5), and do not please God, and are contrary to all men; forbidding us to speak to the Gentiles, that they may be saved.

(*i*). Ver. -16. That they may fill up their sins continually. But (this opposition will not go unpunished, for) the (predicted, Deut. xxxii. 20-39-42) wrath (of God) hath come (was appointed

---

96. L. T. Tr. A. and R.V. read singular instead of plural.

to come) **upon them to the end** (of it : *i.e.*, to the uttermost: *i.e.*, to finality.

The beauty and exact correspondence of these two members, "c" and *"c,"* will be seen the more closely we look into the five ("e," "f," "g," "h," "i," and *"e," "f," "g,' "h," "i"*), of which they are respectfully composed. They ("e" and *"e"* begin with thanksgiving "unceasingly." "In "f" and *"f,"* we have the reason of this thanksgiving: *viz.*, in "f," because, though they received it from men, they received it really from God *("f")*. In "g" and *"g,"* we have the effect of the reception of the Gospel. It brought blessing to the Gentiles *through* them ("g"); and it brought on them persecution from the Jews *("g")*. In " h" and *"h,"* we have God's Son—the Lord, even Jesus, "waited for" by the Christians ("h"), and "killed" by the Jews *("h")*. And then "i" and *"i"* both end with "wrath to come," the one being delivered *from* it ("i"), and the others delivered *to* it *("i")*.

We saw that the sub-member "a" (i. 2-iii. 10) was composed of four members ("c," "d," *"c," "d"*). And these four being arranged alternately, may be so considered in the two pairs of the alternate members. We have seen the structure of the *first* and *third*, which are concerning *Paul and the Thessalonians*. Now we have to do the same with the *second* and *fourth*, which are concerning *Paul and his brethren: viz.*, "d" (ii. 1-12) and *"d"* (ii. 17-iii. 10).

The following is the structure of the two. They are not alike; but, though they are independent as to their separate structure, both are equally beautiful and complete:—

THE EXPANSION OF "d," ii. 1—12.

Paul and his Brethren. Their Teaching and Conduct while
present.

```
d | j |  1¹ | ii. 1, 2.  Their imparting "the Gospel of God:" "Not in
  |   |     | vain."
  |   |  m¹ |3.  Their exhortation: "Not of deceit."
  |   |  1² | 4-.  Their preaching "the Gospel of God."
  |   |  m² |-4-6.  God their witness as to their blamelessness.
  |   |  k  | 7.  Comparison: "As a nurse."
  | j |  1³ | 8.  Their imparting "the Gospel of God," "not only
  |   |     | that," etc.
  |   |  m³ |9-.  Their labour: "Not to be chargeable."
  |   |  1⁴ | -9.  Their preaching "The Gospel of God."
  |   |  m⁴ | 10.  God their witness as to their blamelessness.
  |   |  k  | 11, 12.  Comparison: "As a father."
```

THE EXPANSION OF *"d,"* ii. 17—iii. 10.

Paul and his Brethren. Their Feelings while absent.

```
d | n | p | ii. 17,18.  Their departure.
  |   | q | 19, 20.  Their joy in the Thessalonian saints.
  |   | o | r | iii. 1.  Their solicitude.
  |   |   | s | 2-4.  The mission of Timothy.
  |   | o | r | 5-.  Their solicitude.
  |   |   | s | -5.  The mission of Timothy.
  | n | p | 6-8.  Timothy's return.
  |   | q | 9-10.  Their joy in the Thessalonian saints.
```

These structures do not need much comment. They explain to us the scope of the two passages. But in "n" (ii. 17-20) we have some blessed comfort administered (as we have indeed throughout both Epistles). Paul and his brethren are full of tenderest thoughts and fondest hopes. They grieved at their absence from these pattern saints, from this model church. But the glad thought that there is one day to be a re-union which will know no separation filled their hearts. Distance might divide them now; death might separate them; Satan might hinder re-union here; but it is coming. It is not a matter for speculation. True, we cannot look for it here, while the little flock is scattered and torn; nor in the grave, where all is silent; nor in some fancied region of "space" (for scientists would rob us of a heaven near at hand); nor in a demoniacal "border-land" of lying spirits; nor in death (according to the theology of hymn-books and tomb-stones). But "IN THE PRESENCE OF OUR LORD JESUS CHRIST AT HIS COMING." That is when this longed-for re-union is to take place. At the *parousia*[97] of our Lord Jesus Christ.

This whole member "a" (i. 2—iii. 10) is followed by a prayer, "b" (iii. 11-13) which divides the Epistle into its two great divisions. This prayer occupies only three verses, but it is full of truth and worthy of our closest study. It follows up and concludes the previous teaching. Its subject shows again that the full and permanent perfection of the saints waits for the *parousia* or presence of Christ (for here the word occurs for the second time). In verse 10 he had prayed to see their face; but this again turns the mind to the truth, that it is only at the coming of Christ that all such longings will be satisfied. Only then shall pardoned sinners and erring saints stand "unblamable in holiness before God." Not in this life, not at death, not in any so called "intermediate state" or Protestant Purgatory. But only with all His saints "at the coming of our Lord Jesus Christ." Then shall we be delivered from secret sins and inward conflicts and open foes. No more failures then. No more waverings and falterings and failings then. No more errings or wanderings then. No more harsh judgments from sinful fellow-servants then. No more broken hearts because we have failed to "judge" this or that, then. But all eternally secure; and His People established before God, unblamable for ever and for ever.

That was another reason why they waited "for God's Son from heaven."

---

97. This is the first time the word παρουσία *(parousia)* occurs in these epistles. It occurs *seven* times in all. And, as usual, this seven is divided into *four* and *three*, for it occurs *four* times in the first Epistle (ii. 19; iii. 13; iv. 15, and v. 23), and three times in the second (ii 1, 8. 9).

The Epistles to the Thessalonians.
III.—THE FIRST EPISTLE, iv. 1—v. 25.

In our last chapter we considered the structure of the member "a" (i. 2—iii. 10) and "b" (iii. 11-13),which form practically the first half of the Epistle.

We now come to chapters iv. and v., which contain the special doctrine and instruction as to the *parousia* or coming of Christ for His saints. This is set forth in *"a"* (iv. 1—v. 22) and *"b"* (v. 23-25), which is again a prayer concluding this second portion, as a prayer ("b," iii. 11-13) closed the first.

The following is the structure of the last half of the Epistle:—

THE EXPANSION OF "a" (iv. 1—v. 22).
Instruction and Exhortation.

a | t | iv. 1-12. Exhortation (Practical and General).

u | iv. 13-18. Instruction as to the Lord's Coming. The ascension of His people, whether *"dead"* or *"alive,"* at His Descension *for* them before that day.

u | v. 1-11 Instruction as to the Lord's Coming. The full salvation of His people, whether *watchful or unwatchful,* before that day.

t | v. 12-22. Exhortation (Practical and Particular).

This gives us the scope of the whole section. But we shall take each of these four members separately; or, at least, the first three:—

THE EXPANSION OF "t" (IV. 1-12).

Exhortation.

```
t | v | x | iv. 1. To walk, as before God.
            y | 2. The commandments given.
        w | z | 3-5. God's will: their sanctification (Pos.
                    & neg.).
               zz | 6. The brethren "not to be defrauded"
                    (neg.).
        w | z | 7, 8. God's call: their sanctification (neg.
                    & pos.).
               zz | 9,10. The brethren to be loved
                    (.pos.).
    v | y | 11. The commandments given.
        x | 12. To walk, as before men.
```

This does not call for any comment; but the great doctrinal portion concerning the Lord's Coming (for twice the word *parousia* occurs in this half of the Epistle) will require some consideration.

We must first give the structure of "u" and *"u."* from which it will be seen that chap. v. 1-11 exactly corresponds in every particular with chap. iv. 13-18.

The beauty of this structure will be at once seen, when iv. 13-18 and v. 1-11 are looked at unmarred by present chapter divisions of the A.V.

The one gives *necessary* instruction; the other refers to what is *unnecessary* for them to be instructed in. This is followed in each case by three reasons which are marked respectively with the same Greek words and in the same order.

The first two *reasons* each begin with γάρ *(gar) for;* the third with ότο *(oti) because.* And in these third members respectively we have the same peculiar Greek word ἅμα *(hama) together* (used of *two* parties).

The fifth member of this *extended* correspondence, each contains an exhortation as to "comfort," and almost in the same words.

196

THE EXPANSION OF "u" (iv. 13-18) and "*u*" (v. 1-11).

Instruction: *Our Resurrection and Ascension before the Day of the Lord.*

u | a | iv. 13. Instruction *necessary* as to "them that fall asleep" *(κοιμημένων.)*[98] R.V.

b | 14. *First* reason (γάρ) : For, those who have fallen asleep *(κοιμηθέντας)* God (by Jesus) will bring again from the dead.

c | 15. *Second* reason (γάρ) : For those who "are alive and remain" shall not precede.

d | 16, 17. *Third* reason *(ὅτι)*: Because both shall be caught up together *(ἅμα)* at the Descension of the Lord into the air.

e | 18. Encouragement: "Wherefore comfort one another with these words."

---

98. κοιμάομαι, *to fall asleep* involuntarily: hence used (in nearly every place) of *death;* but only of saints. See page 205.

197

u | a | v. 1. Instruction *not* necessary as to "the times and seasons" of our Resurrection and Ascension which will take place *before* the Day of the Lord.

   b | 2-6. *First* reason *(γάρ)*: For they already knew the character of "the Day of the Lord." Contrast (vers. 4, 5) and Exhortation (ver. 6): "Therefore let us not sleep" *(καθεύδωμεν)*,[99] but "let us watch" *(γρηγορῶμεν)*.[100]

   c | 7, 8. *Second* reason *(γάρ)*: "For they that sleep *(καθεύδοντες)* sleep *(καθεύδουσι)* in the night." Contrast and Exhortation, "But let us, etc." (ver. 8).

   d | 9, 10. *Third* reason *(ὅτι)*: Because God hath not appointed us to wrath, but to obtain salvation (*viz.*, in Resurrection) whether we watch *(γρηγορῶμεν)* or sleep *(καθεύδωμεν)*, we should together *(ἅμα)* live with Him (as in "d" above).

   e | 11. Encouragement: "Wherefore comfort your-selves together," etc.

From this structure we learn many important truths. We may thus enumerate the several points.

I.   Instruction was necessary as to those who had been taken away by death. The Thessalonian saints were "ignorant" as to what takes place after death, as all would have been had not God, who alone can know, seen fit to reveal it to us.

As formerly heathen, they had been either Platonists or Epicureans; and, if Jews, then either Pharisees or Sadducees.

---

99. *καθεύδω*, *to go to sleep* voluntarily: hence not used of death, but either of taking rest in sleep, or of the opposite of watchfulness. The same as in Matt. xxv. 5. See page 205.

100. *γρηγορέω* is translated "wake" only here. Elsewhere it is "watch," "be watchful," or "vigilant."

The former (Platonists and Pharisees) believed that no one died: death being merely life in another form. Indeed, this is the popular belief of the day: but those who hold it do not see that it does away with, and denies the necessity of resurrection.

The latter (the Epicureans and Sadducees) believed that death was death, and that every one who died had died eternally. These denied the doctrine of the resurrection altogether.

Holding one of these two creeds, these saints were, therefore, "ignorant"[101]; and were, of course, much concerned about their friends who had died; fearing, not that they had gone before, but would be left behind, and have no part with those who were alive and remained to the coming of the Lord. Therefore it is written: **"I would not have you ignorant, brethren, concerning them that are asleep, that ye sorrow not even as the others that have no hope."**

II. All is shown to depend, and to turn, on the resurrection of the Lord Jesus. "If we believe" that, then there is another great truth that we are to believe in consequence. There is something built upon this great foundation: "Even so." But to see what it is we must understand the scope of this fourteenth verse.

It is the hope of Resurrection at the coming of the Lord Jesus Christ.

---

101. The expression, "I would not have you ignorant," is peculiar. It occurs *six* times, all in these church epistles. The study of the expression in the order of its occurrence will well repay care.

Rom. i. 13, of Paul's purpose to prosecute his great mission and ministry to the saints in Rome (See xv. 23).

Rom. xi. 25, of Israel's blindness.

1 Cor. x. 1-11, of the camp in the wilderness as the type of the baptized assembly under the preaching of the kingdom..

1 Cor. xii. 1, of spiritual things connected with the Body of Christ by the baptism with the Holy Spirit.

2 Cor. i. 8, of the trouble it Ephesus (Acts xix.), where his preaching of the kingdom ends, and the revelation of the mystery begins.

1 Thess. iv. 13, of those who have fallen asleep).

STRUCTURE OF "v" (iv. 14).

v | f | *Belief.* "If we believe
    g | *Death.* "that Jesus died,
       h | *Resurrection.* "and rose again."

Now we must have three lines exactly corresponding to these: and we have them"—

v | *f* | *Belief.* "In like manner [*we believe*] also
    g | *Death.* "that those who are fallen asleep
      h | *Resurrection.* "will God, through Jesus, bring with Him" (So R.V. margin).

Thus we are taught that like as "the God of peace brought again from the dead (Heb. xiii. 20) the Lord Jesus," even so we are to believe that God, in like manner, will bring again from the dead those who are fallen asleep in Christ (1 Cor. xv. 23).

Who is it that will bring the sleeping saints again from the dead?
    "God," according to John v. 21.

By what agency will God bring them?
    "Through or by Jesus," according to John v. 25, "the Son of God."

In what manner will God bring them?
    "In resurrection, as He brought again the Lord Jesus from the dead."

III.   But then follows a further revelation as to when this glorious event will take place.

(1) We which are alive "shall in no wise precede them that are fallen asleep" (R.V.).

(2) This must carry with it the correlative fact that those who have fallen asleep can in no wise precede those who are alive and

shall remain to the Lord's coming. Otherwise language for the express purpose of removing ignorance is useless. For the words cannot mean that some shall not precede others who are already there.

IV. Then, if we shall not precede them, nor they precede us, how will that affect the hope of resurrection? The answer given reveals the fact that the first thing that will happen in connection with the realisation of our "blessed hope" is that

(a) The Lord Himself shall descend from heaven with a shout, κέλευσμα (keleusma), an assembling shout of command,[102] and with an archangel's voice, and with a trumpet of God.

(b) The next thing that takes place is "the dead in Christ shall rise first" (i.e., before anything happens to us); and note that they are called the "dead," though "the dead in Christ." And they "rise."

(c) After that, we, the living, who remain, "shall be caught up together with them in clouds to meet the Lord in the air." The word "together" is ἅμα (hama), and is used of two distinct companies, and denotes at the same time.

(d) And thus (οὕτως, houtōs) in this manner, shall we be evermore with the Lord.

And, because they possessed this blessed hope, they "waited for God's Son from heaven."

Now, what we must so particularly notice is that, we have here

---

102. A noticeable instance of κελεύσμασιν is found in Æsch. (Eum 226); where Orestes speaks of himself as come at Apollo's biddings. In Cho. 740 (Paley makes it 738), we have κελευσμάτων of the imperious nightly wails or cries of in infant. In Soph. (Ant. 1204) we find it, again in the plural, of orders issued by a monarch ; and that is the only instance of it, in Soph., which Ellendt's Lex. Soph. gives. In the only instance of it in the singular which Linwood's Lexicon to Aeschylus gives—Pers. 389 (399 Paley);—it is used of the word of command to rowers, and κελευστής seems to have been technically used of the officer whose business it was thus to give the time to the oarsmen. The only instance in the Septuagint is Prov. xxx. 27— "The locusts have no king, and yet march orderly at one word of command" (κελεύσματος).

a new revelation. "By the Word of the Lord" denotes a special prophetic message, the revelation of a truth which had never before been known. The promise of the Lord had been, of the Holy Spirit, "He shall show you things to come." Where has He shown them if not here? The Lord had many things to say, but He could not say them when on earth (John xvi. 25). When, then, has He said them at all, if not in these special revelations of the Holy Spirit to the churches? This is truth affecting only the Church of God. It is church-truth of the highest kind. But the churches to-day do not want it! They can do without it. They are all going to die, and are waiting for death—and singing about it every Sunday in most of their hymns. They have invented their own way of being with the Lord quite apart from resurrection,

They are hoping to be with Him *without rising from the dead:* but the Lord has postponed the fulfilment of all His promises to His people concerning their entrance on the coming glory until He returns and raises His dead, and takes them up with His living saints to Himself. We are expressly told that it is "by patience, and *comfort of the Scriptures* we might have hope" (Rom xv. 4). But this "comfort"is not enough for people to-day: and yet the greatest comfort which the great Comforter Himself gave to two bereaved sisters was—"Thy brother shall rise again." This agrees with the special injunction here added—"Wherefore comfort one another with these words (1 Thess. iv. 18).[103]

"The teaching of Jesus," is the cry of the day, but an essential part of that teaching is rejected, for He held out the blessed hope, "I will come again and receive you to Myself." But the reply is

---

103. Those who differ from us must not say we believe this or that. We must be judged only by what we actually say, not by what we have not said. One writer retorts "Oh, then you believe in the sleep of the soul!" We believe nothing of the kind. The expression is not in scripture, and we know not what it means. Those who differ have got to deal with such passages as Acts ii. 34 (taken with 2 Sam. xii. 23), Ps. cxlvi. 4, &c., &c. It is not for us to cast stones at one another; but for each to explain the passages which the others find difficult; and this, in kindness and with forbearance, not with harshness and in a spirit of judgment. We have dealt with such passages as Phil. i. 23 in *Things to Come,* Vol. VI., pp. 87, 88; and 2 Cor. v. 6 (Vol. VI., 118).

practically "No! Lord, Thou needest not come for me. I will die and come to Thee." And, instead of a belief in Christ's teaching, a new Creed altogether has been formulated. *"I believe in . . . the reception of believers by Jesus in the hour of death."*[104] In this Creed there is no reference beyond this whatsoever, either to *Resurrection,* or to the Lord's coming! So complete is the present apostasy![105]

Of course, all this makes no difference. They will not get this "reception by Jesus" any sooner. Not until the Lord's own time which He has appointed.

But it makes a great difference in another way. It makes a great difference now, and here. For, through this ignorance, which the Lord would not have His People to be in, and which they persist in remaining in, they lose the present power for a holy life, and they lose the present power for diligent service. And this is the true and only explanation of the vast difference between the churches of to-day and this typical, model "church of the Thessalonians."

Christians to-day go even so far as to say that "Paul was mistaken": and this, notwithstanding his inspiration by the Holy Spirit of Truth to record this revelation for us to learn (not to reject). No! he was not mistaken. The holy lives of these Thessalonian saints, and their missionary spirit and zeal and activity and success show us that they were not mistaken. The low standard of Christian life to-day and the fictitious standards of missionary effort show us that there is a *mistake* somewhere. But it was not in the model church of Thessalonica; it is in the churches of the present day, with all their worldliness, and, their unspirituality of life and walk.

To turn, now, to the second half of this great member *"u"* (v. 1-

---

104. Professor George H. Gilbert, D.D., Chicago Theological Seminary, on "The Apostle's Creed revised by the teaching of Jesus, in the *Biblical World,* Sept., 1898.

105. It is this popular belief that makes many teachers inclined to take up and dabble with Spiritism. It is thus a dangerous snare, and a ready door to many other errors, such as "Prayers for the dead," the "larger hope," the worship of the Virgin Mary, &c., &c. All these doors are closed if *Resurrection* be the one great and only hope; as it is, at the coming of Christ.

11). We have seen that it corresponds exactly to "u'" (iv. 13-18) which we have just been considering.

From this, too, we learn certain important truths.

1. That while there was one thing as to which the Thessalonian saints were ignorant, and needed instruction ("a," iv. 13): there was another as to which there was no need for him to write ("a," v. i).

2. This was concerning the great appointed time,[106] "the day of the Lord." "Times and seasons" may, and do, concern the world, and its coming judgment in that day: but these saints had the blessed hope (iv. 13-18) of being gathered to meet and be with the Lord before that day should burst upon an ungodly world (2 Thess. ii. 1).

This was the *first* reason why there was no need for the Church of God to trouble itself about "times and seasons."

3. We learn also that there is a vital difference between the Church and the world (*"b,"* v. 2-6). Note the interchange of the pronouns in this member "they," "ye" and "us." We "are not in darkness," because we have the prophetic word, which is the only light in this dark place (2 Pet. i. 19). But the world is in darkness; and will be talking of "peace and safety" up to the very moment when the "sudden destruction" shall come upon them.

4. The *second* reason is (*"g,"* v. 7, 8) that they that sleep, sleep in the night: but we are of the day: let us therefore be sober, etc.

5. The *third* reason is (*"d,"* v. 9, 10), because God hath not appointed us to wrath, but to obtain a full and final salvation, which will be completed only by resurrection at he coming of the Lord.

6. Therefore we are not to sleep as others do, but to watch. Nevertheless, whether we watch or sleep, we shall live together with Him. There is a great contrast between the two words used for "sleep" in "u," iv. 13-18, and *"u,"* v.1-11. They are quite different. In "u," iv. 13-18, the word is κοιμάομαι *(koimaomai*[107]*), to*

---

106. The plural being used by the figure *Heterosis* for the singular, in order to emphasise it.

107. It is from this that we have our word *cemetery*, a sleeping place for the dead.

fall asleep involuntarily: hence used (in nearly every place) of death; but only of saints. It occurs eighteen[108] times, and its occurrences will enable any one to test the point.

They are as follows:–

Matt.	xxvii.	52.	many bodies. . . . *slept.*
"	xxviii.	13.	and stole him away while we *slept.*
Luke xxii.		45.	he found them *sleeping* for sorrow.
John	xi.	11.	our friend Lazarus *sleepeth.*
"	"	12.	Lord, if he *sleep, he* shall do well.
Acts vii.		60.	when he had said this, he fell *asleep.*
Acts xii.		6.	Peter was *sleeping* between.
"	xiii	36.	fell on *sleep,* and was laid.
1 Cor. vii.		39.	but if her husband be *dead.*
"	xi.	30.	sickly among you, and many *sleep.*
"	xv	6.	but some are fallen *asleep.*
"	"	18.	then they also which are *fallen asleep.*
"	"	20.	the firstfruits of them that *slept.*
"	"	51.	we shall not all *sleep.*
I Thess. iv.		13.	concerning them which are *asleep.*
"	"	14.	them also which *sleep* in Jesus.
"	"	15.	shall not prevent them which are *asleep.*
2 Pet. iii.		4.	since the fathers *fell asleep.*

In *"u,"* v. 1-11, the word is καθεύδω *(katheudō), to go to sleep* voluntarily, or prepare one's self for sleep; hence, not used of death, but either of taking rest in sleep, or of being unwatchful.

The twenty-two occurrences will decide the meaning.

They are as follows:–

Matt. viii.		24.	but He was *asleep.*
"	ix.	24.	the maid is not dead, but *sleepeth.*
"	xiii.	25.	But while men *slept.* .

---

108. 3 x 6, marking the end of man.

"	xxv.	5.	they all clambered and *slept*.
"	xxvi.	40.	and findeth them *asleep*.
"	"	43.	came and found them *asleep* again.
"	"	45.	*Sleep* on now, and take your rest.
Mark iv.		27.	and should *sleep*, and rise night and day.
"	"	38.	*asleep* on a pillow.
"	v	39.	the damsel is not dead, but *sleepeth*.
"	xiii.	36.	he find you *sleeping*.
"	xiv.	37.	and findeth them *sleeping*, and saith unto Peter, Simon, *sleepest* thou?
"	"	40.	He found them *asleep* again.
"	"	41.	*Sleep* on now, and take your rest.
Luke viii.		52.	she is not dead, but *sleepeth*.
"	xxii.	46.	Why *sleep* ye? rise and pray.
Eph. v.		14.	Awake, thou that *sleepest*.
1 Thess.v.		6.	let us not *sleep*, as do others.
"	"	7.	for they that *sleep*, *sleep* in the night.
"	"	10.	whether we wake or *sleep*.

This scope of this passage is further established by the word rendered "watch" (ch. v. 6) and "wake" (ch. v. 10). It occurs twenty-three times, and is twenty times rendered *watch*, except Rev. iii. 2 *(watchful)*, 1 Pet. v. 8 *(be vigilant)*, and here, in 1 Thess. v. 10 *(wake)*, where it means *to keep awake*. See Neh. vii. 3.

This surely settles for us the scope and meaning of the whole passage; which is in correspondence and contrast with iv. 13-18. It ends, appropriately with the same injunction, "Wherefore comfort yourselves together" (ch. v. 11), as does the former passage (iv. 18), "Wherefore comfort one another with these words."

This latter doctrinal half concludes with a prayer (ch. v. 23, 24), as does the former half (iii. 11-13); and, it is the prayer that "**the God of peace Himself** (who brought again from the dead the Lord Jesus, Heb. xiii. 20; for the title used here connects it with this thought) **may sanctify you wholly**[109]; **and that your spirit and soul**

---

109. ὁλοτελεῖς *(holoteleis)*.

and body as one whole[110] (or entire), **without blemish, at** (so R.V., not "unto" as A.V.) **the coming** (the Parousia) **of our Lord Jesus Christ may be preserved.**"

The whole man (not a part of him) transformed, glorified, immortalized; and preserved entire, and presented faultless, in the Father's presence with exceeding joy (Jude 24).

This is to be in that day, and not before. Not till then will this prayer receive its full and eternal answer for all who are Christ's. Well may it be added:–"Faithful is he that calleth you, who will also perform (all that He has promised)."

---

110. ὀλόκληρον *(holokleeron).*

The Epistles to the Thessalonians.
IV. THE SECOND EPISTLE.
CHAPTER 1.

In directing our studies to the Second Epistle to the Thessalonians, we commence at once with its structure, in order to discover its scope.

The Structure of the Epistle as a Whole (In brief.)

A | i, 2. Epistolary. Introduction (shorter) "grace"and "peace."

    B | a | 3-10. Thanksgiving (longer).

        b | 11, 12. Prayer (shorter).

          c | ii. 1-12. Admonition (longer, prophetic, general).

    B | a | ii. 13-15. Thanksgiving (shorter)

        b | 16—iii.5. Prayer (longer).

          c | 6-15. Admonition (shorter, practical, personal particular).

} Doctrine

A | iii. 16-18. Epistolary. Conclusion (longer) "peace" and "grace."

We are struck at once with its simplicity and beauty also with its obvious design—the longer members being contrasted with the shorter in each case. The introversion of "A" and "*A*" being:—

```
A | x |  grace        }    i. 1, 2.
  |   | z | peace     }
A |   | z | peace     }   iii. 16-18.
  | x |  grace        }
```

Each of the longer members, "B" and *"B, "* has its own internal structure, and may be expanded.

For example, we may compare the two *Thanksgivings* "a" (i. 3-10), and *"a "* (ii. 13-15); the first longer and the second shorter:—

The Two Thanksgivings.
THE EXPANSION OF "a," (i. 3-10), and "a, " (ii. 13-15).
The First Thanksgiving.

a | d | i. 3-. Obligation. "We are bound to thank God always for you, brethren," &c.

    e | -3-5. Reason. "Because" of their faith, and love, and patience.

    f | 6-10. The enjoyment of "rest" at the Apocalypse of Christ.

The Second Thanksgiving.

a | *d* | ii. 13-. Obligation. "We are bound to thank God always for you, brethren," &c.

    e | -13. Reason. "Because God had from the beginning chosen you to salvation."

    f | 14, 15. The obtaining of the "glory" at the coming of Christ "in that day" before His Apocalypse.

There are two important passages in this epistle which call for our closest attention. The *Doctrine* here ("B" i. 3—ii. 12) is mixed in "a" (chap. i.) with *Thanksgiving,* and in "c" ii. 1-12 with *Admonition.*

These are the two which will therefore require our study viz.: "f," (i. 6-10 above), and "c," (ii. 1-12). See structure above. We may, however, in passing, notice the two prayers "b" (i. 11, 12), and "b" (ii. 16—iii. 5).

The Two Prayers.
THE EXPANSION OF "b" (i. 11, 12), and *"b"* (ii. 16—iii. 57).
The First Prayer.
b | g | i. 11. "We pray always for you."
     h | 12-. "That the name of out Lord Jesus Christ may be glorified in you."
     i | -12. And that ye may be glorified "in Him."

The Second Prayer.
b | g | ii. 16—iii. 1-. "Brethren, pray for us"
     h | -1-4. "That the word of the Lord may have free course, and be glorified, even it is with you," &c.
     i | 5. And that ye may be directed into God's love, and Christ's patient waiting.

Taking the former passage, "f" (i. 6-10), first, we shall have again to give its own structure, and then a translation in full"—

THE EXPANSION OF "f" (i. 6-10).
The being at Rest at Christ's Apocalypse.
f | s | 6. Tribulation recompensed to the troublers.
     t | u | 7-. Rest for the troubled believers.
         v | -7. When: "At the revelation of the Lord Jesus."
     s | 8, 9. Vengeance rendered (R.V.) to the enemies.
     t | v | 10-. "When He shall have come."
         u | -10. Glory for the troubled believers.

Ver. 6. **It is a just thing with** (*i.e.*, in His esteem of) **God to requite to those who trouble you, tribulation.**
     Ver. 7. **And to you who are troubled, rest with us, at the revelation of the Lord Jesus from heaven with his mighty angels** (with emphasis on mighty, by the figure *Heterosis).*
     Vers. 8, 9. **In fiery flame, inflicting punishment on those that know not God (Gentiles), and on those that obey not the Gospel of our Lord Jesus (Jews), who will suffer the penalty of eternal destruction** (driven out) **from the presence of the Lord, and from**

210

the (manifestation of the) **glory of His power** (in the glorification of His Saints).

Ver. 10. **When He shall have come,** 2nd Aor. Subj. See below. This *coming* is in contrast with the *revelation* which is the subject of "v" *v.* -7 (*i.e.*, before that revelation in judgment, He shall have come), **in that day, to be glorified in His saints, and to be marvelled at in all them that believed,**[111] (believed, I say), **because our testimony** (brought), **unto you was believed.**

From this we learn certain important truths.

1. First, that there *is* a way to endure suffering which shall glorify God, and manifest His gifts of patience and faith. Whatever that way was, it is clear from verse 4 that these Thessalonian saints knew it; and it was another evidence of their high standard of Christian character.

2. They knew, as we learn from verse 5, what God's purpose was in thus calling them through suffering to His glorious kingdom. Their willingness thus to enter that kingdom shows that they knew its value, and counted all else but dross.

3. Tribulation was not peculiar to them (nor is it to us). Their enemies also knew what trouble was, but *they* knew not how to glory in it. To the saints it was a threshing (as the word means), a separating of the precious from the vile, the wheat from the chaff. To the others it was a "just recompense of reward." And

4. Verses 6 and 7 show us that this is a "righteous" and just thing; and not a cruel thing, as many suppose.

5. Then we are told of the promised "rest" which all the troubled ones are to have *together* ("with us"). There is a time appointed when they shall enter into it. It will not be entered at different times and in different manners. It is a "rest" definite and real, both as to its nature, its state, and its time. It is a rest to be

---

111. G. L. T. Tr. A. WH. and R.V. read πιστεύσασιν *(pisteusasin)*, *believed* (Aor. participle), instead of πιστεύουσιν *(pisteuousin), who believe* (pres. part).

entered into all at one time. "Rest with us."[112] The Lord's own appointed time.

6. And He has told when this is to be in 1 Thess. iv. 13-18: viz.: at the coming forth of the Lord Himself, to receive us to Himself, and take us up to meet Him in the air, and so to be for ever with Him. Having definitely revealed this hope by the Holy Spirit and "by the word of the Lord" in the first epistle, he is not here unsaying that and teaching a different way of entering on the enjoyment of that Rest. But, pausing for a moment, he contrasts our "rest" with the terrible judgment of the ungodly, and assures us that when that comes upon them, we shall be already at rest; for that judgment will not break forth until *"He shall have come to be glorified in His saints"* (2 Thess. ii. 10), *i.e.*, after it and not before it. The Lord will be first glorified in His saints; and this will take place before that judgment shall be revealed. For it will not be revealed until He *"shall have come"* to receive them to Himself, according to His promise in 1 Thess. iv. 16, 17.

There is no forcing of words here. Words are used in order to reveal and interpret unknown truths to us, and to make known facts of which we should otherwise be "ignorant." There is a reason, therefore, why the word here used is ἔλθῃ *(elthē)*, *he shall have come.*

It is the subjunctive mood and second aorist tense, and must have this meaning and no other. Sometimes the translators observe it, and sometimes they do not; and where they do not it is perfectly clear that they ought to have so rendered it: if only on the ground of consistency and uniformity of rendering.

This is not a matter of argument or opinion; it is a question of fact. Anyone with common sense is able to form his own judgment if we give the following few examples: —

---

112. The word here (ἄνεσις *anesis)* is not the same as is rendered "rest" in Heb. iv. 9. There it is σαββατισμός *(sabbatismos), sabbath-keeping,*. Here it is rather *relaxation* from all labour and trouble and care. It occurs elsewhere only in Acts xxiv. 23 and 2 Cor. ii. 13 *(rest* in spirit, ease in mind); vii. 5 *(rest* to flesh, bodily ease) viii. 13 *(rest* from contributing, rest of purse).

212

Matt. xxi. 40.— "When the lord therefore of the vineyard *cometh i.e., shall have come.*

Luke xvii. 10.— "So likewise ye, when ye *shall have done* all these things." (Here the A.V. so renders it).

Mark viii. 38.— "Of him also shall the Son of Man be ashamed when *he cometh:*" *i.e., when he shall have come.*

John iv. 25.— "When He *is come (i.e., shall have come),* He will tell us all things."

Rom. xi. 27.— "This is my covenant unto them, when *I shall take (i.e., when I shall have taken)* away their sins."

Acts xxiii. 35.— "I will hear thee, said he, when thine accusers *are* also *come;*" *i.e., shall have come.*

John xvi. 13.— "When the Spirit of Truth *is come:*" *i.e., shall have come.*

1 Cor. xv. 24, 25.— "When *He shall have* delivered up the kingdom to God, even the Father ; when He *shall have* put down all rule and authority and power, for he must reign until. he bath put *(i.e., shall have put)* all enemies under His feet."' Here the A.V. twice translates it correctly, and then the third time in the same context renders it differently.

From these passages it is perfectly clear that when the judgment on the ungodly is revealed, the Lord *shall have* (already and previously) come to be glorified in His saints, "in that day," and have given them the promised "rest," of which he had already told them in the former epistle, and reminded them in this chapter (verse 7).

As we are thus definitely told when and how this "rest"is to be entered upon, all other modes and times of entering it are shut out. That is to say, it will not be in this life not at death; but when the Lord shall come to be glorified in His saints "in that day" which He hath appointed and promised: *i.e.,* the day of our "gathering together unto Him."

The words "in that day" are put (by the figure *Hyperbaton)* out of their place, right at the very end of the sentence, in order to attract our attention and to show us that they are the emphatic words of the sentence. If therefore we fail to give them the weighty meaning which they are intended to have, we shall miss the very point of the whole passage.

"In that day" refers to that glorious day of which he had spoken so fully in 1 Thess. iv., not the day of 2 Thess. i. 8, 9, the day of the revelation of the Lord Jesus in judgment; but that day when He shall have previously given them "rest" and gathered them to Himself.

Present tribulation therefore is the proof to us that Christ has not yet thus gathered and glorified His saints; for, when "that day" comes, it will find the Church of God at "rest": and then will be revealed tribulation for the troublers.

All hope of rest, reward, and glory is deferred, to be consummated in "that day" of glorification.

Towards "that day" His finger ever points, and their eyes ever turn.

How could they be *idle,* with "that day" ever before them—"that day" which would end every opportunity for service?

How could they be *sinful,* with the word ever on their lips, "Even so come, Lord Jesus"?

How could they be *worldly,* when at any moment the assembling shout of the Lord Himself might be heard, and draw forth from their hearts the joyful exclamation:

"The voice of my Beloved,
Behold, He cometh"?

If this Church of the Thessalonians be a typical Church, Do we know of any other Church, Ancient, Mediæval, or Modern, which has exhibited such characteristics as these?

Oh! that we might profit by the instruction conveyed to us in these epistles; and possess the secret which produced such wondrous results.

The Epistles to the Thessalonians.
V.—THE SECOND EPISTLE (ii. 1-12).

It would seem as though this second Epistle to the Thessalonians was written soon after the first, and were called forth and sent in order to repair for them, and for us, the mischief caused by false teachers.

This mischief appears to have marred their "hope" for while in the first Epistle (i. 3) their "faith" and "love" and "hope" were causes of thanksgiving to God, in this second Epistle no mention is made of *hope*. Faith and love are mentioned as abounding, but their hope had suffered. The great object of this Second Epistle is to recover the hope they had lost and it was written in the interests of the blessed hope of "our gathering together unto Him," so that they might wait for God's Son from heaven as they had done in former days.

The first chapter contained general comfort and teaching concerning the "rest" which remained for the saints, and the retribution which awaited their enemies, and the assurance that before that retribution came the Lord "*shall have come* to be glorified in His saints."

The second chapter carries on the same teaching, in which further details are given concerning this same great fact; showing the difference between the two events: *viz.*,

(1) The *Parousia* of our Lord Jesus Christ and our gathering together unto Him, and

(2) *The Day of the Lord*, and of His judgment.

This further instruction concerning the former is given in *the interest of* the former; for this is the meaning of the Greek ὑπὲρ *(hyper)*, which is much more than "by" (as in the A.V.) and stronger that "concerning." The R.V. has *"touching,"* which is much better.

215

The true meaning is *in the interest of,* or, *on its behalf.*

We will now give the structure of the member "c," ii. 1-12 (see page 208), which is Prophetic and Admonitory:—

THE EXPANSION OF "c," ii. 1-12.
Admonition (longer, prophetic).

c | j | ii. 1-3-. Exhortation *not* to believe what the Apostle did *not* say (neg.).

    k | -3, 4. Reason. "For," &c.

  j | 5, 6. Exhortation to believe what the Apostle *did* say (pos.).

    k | 7-12. Reason. "For," &c.

This may be exhibited more fully by expanding "k" -3, 4) and "k" (7-12), setting out the *Reason* with more detail:-

c | j | ii. 1-3-. Exhortation, &c. (negative).

    k | l | -3-. The Apostacy (open).

        m | -3. The Revelation of "the Man of Sin." (The beast from the sea. Rev. xiii. 1-10). ⎫
           n | 4. The character of his acts (see Rev. xiii. 6-8). ⎬ Reason

j | 5, 6. Exhortation, &c. (positive).

    k | *l* | 7. The mystery (secret working) of Lawlessness. ⎫
        m | 8. The Revelation of "the Lawless one." (The beast from the *earth.* Rev. xiii. 11-18). ⎬ Reason
           n | 9-12. The character of his acts (see Rev. xiii. 13-15). ⎭

Having now the scope of the whole passage before us, we have the light which it sheds on the words of which it is composed; enabling us better to discover and understand their design and interpretation.

If we now give the passage (ii. 1-12) in full, we shall have the words before us as we endeavour to discover their meaning. The reason for our translations we shall give below.

(j). Chap. ii. 1-3-. **Now we entreat you, brethren, in the interests of** (our blessed hope, of which I have spoken to you and written fully in the first Epistle, *viz.,*) **the Coming** *(Parousia)* **of our Lord Jesus Christ, and of our gathering together unto Him, that ye be not quickly** (or lightly, with little reason) **shaken in mind, nor yet troubled, either by spirit** (by anyone appearing to have a spiritual gift of prophecy), **nor by word** (of mouth), **nor by epistle** (purporting to have been written) **as by us, to the effect that (as if) the Day of the Lord is set in.** Let not anyone deceive you (emphatic) **in any way whatever,**

(1). Ver. -3-. **Because** (that day will not come) **unless the apostacy shall have first come,**

(m). Ver. -3-. **And the man of sin**[113] **shall hays been revealed, the son of perdition.**

(n). Ver. 4. **He that** (or the one that) **opposes and exaltath himself above all that is called God or that is worshipped, so that he himself within the shrine** *(ὁ ναός,* the Holy Place of the Temple) **of God sitteth down, showing himself forth** (or exhibiting the proof) **that he is God.**

(*j*). Vers. 5, 6. **Do ye not remember, that while I was yet with you I said these things to you? And what holdeth** (him) **fast now, ye know, to the end that he should be revealed in his own** (appointed) **time***(καιρός, season).*

(*l*) Ver. 7. **For the secret** (counsel) **of lawlessness is, already working: only, there is one** (Satan) **who at present holdeth fast** (to his possessions in the heavenlies) **until he be cast out** (into the earth, Rev. xii. 9-12, and stand upon the sand of the sea, Rev. xiii. 1, R.V.)

(*m*). Ver. 8. **And then shall be revealed that lawless one, whom the Lord Jesus will consume with the breath of His mouth, and destroy with the brightness of His coming** (Is. xi. 4).

---

113. L.T. Tr. W.H. and R.V. marg. read *lawlessness.*

(n). Vers. 9- 12. (Even him) **whose coming is according to the working (the energy) of Satan, with every form of power, and with signs (miracles),and with lying marvels, and with every form of deceit of unrighteousness for them that perish:** (Why?) **because they did not receive the love of the truth that they might be saved. And on account of this God will send to them a working** (an energy, as Satan will. See verse 9) **of error, that they should believe the lie** (which the secret counsel of iniquity is working among them now, verse 7): **that they all might be condemned that did not believe the truth, but had pleasure in iniquity.**

In this new revelation made here by the Holy Spirit concerning "things to come," as prophesied and promised in John xvi. 13, there are several important subjects which must be carefully considered in order. The questions are raised and practically stated in the translation given above.

1. They were in trouble again here, as they had been in 1 Thess. iv.; and this is written for the express purpose of removing it. Their trouble was this. They had been taught by the Holy Spirit through Paul that before "the Day of the Lord" should come, they would be caught up to meet the Lord in the air, to be for ever with the Lord. They had been taught that the Lord would come *for* them, and receive them unto Himself, before that great and terrible Day should set in. They had been taught concerning their "gathering-together unto Him" at His coming forth into the air; and therefore had no need to be instructed as to the times and seasons connected with their coming in judgment unto the earth *with* Him (1 Thess. v. 1). The former depended on no time or season; the latter did.

If therefore the Day of the Lord were really set in,[114] and they had not been "gathered together unto Him," then they had every reason to be troubled. If that Day of the Lord had opened, and they had not been "caught up to meet the Lord in the air," then they might well be troubled. If the Lord Jesus was indeed about to be

---

114. This is the meaning of *ἐνίοτημι (enistēmi), to stand in, to set in,* or *to be present.* (See page 219).

revealed in judgment on His enemies, and He had not previously come "to be glorified in His saints" (2 Thess. i. 10), then their faith was vain, their hope was vain, their teachers had deceived them, and all that they had taught them was false. No wonder their hope had waned.

Well might they then have been troubled, until they received this complete explanation. Some person or persons had shaken their minds by a false statement and report as to what the Apostle bad said. He now writes to correct the matter, and to put things straight.

2. As to the expressions used, they compel this interpretation:

(a) "The day of Christ" in verse 2 must be read "the Day of the Lord," as in the Revised Version, which is in harmony with all the Textual Critics (Griesbach, Lachmann, Tischendorf, Tregelles, Alford, and Westcott and Hort). There is all the difference between the two. The "day of Christ" is the day referred to in this new revelation when we shall be "gathered together unto Him" (Phil. i. 6; ii. 16): "the day of the Lord" is the day of the Old Testament prophecy, long foretold and well known, connected with His coming judgment on the world.

(b) "At hand." The word ἐνίστημι (enistemi) is nowhere else so translated. It means, as we have already said, *to set in*, or *to be present*, and is generally so translated. These are all its seven occurrences—

Rom. viii. 38.   nor things *present*, nor things to come.

Gal. i. 4.   that he might deliver us out of this *present* evil world.

1 Cor. iii. 22.   things *present*, or things to come all are yours.

1 Cor. vii. 26.   this is good for the *present* distress.

Heb. ix. 9.   which was a figure for the time then *present*.

219

2 Tim. iii. 1.   perilous times shall come *(i.e., be present)*.

On what principle are we to take this seventh occurrence in 2 Thess. ii. 2, differently from all the other six?

On the other hand the English expression "at hand" occurs twenty times, but is never the rendering of this word *enistēmi*!

3. Verse 3 gives the all-conclusive reason why the Day of the Lord cannot set in, or open, until the Church of God shall have been "caught up to meet the Lord," and has been "gathered together unto Him": and until He has been "glorified in His saints" (2 Thess. i. 10). For,

If the Day of the Lord had set in, then the last great apostasy must have taken place: Antichrist must have been revealed (for he is to be destroyed by the brightness of that coming); and all that Daniel had prophesied concerning his career must have taken place. What can be more express than the Spirit's word: "Let no man deceive YOU in any way whatever."

But the great mass of professing Christians to-day *are deceived,* in spite of all this solemn warning.

The Church to-day puts off that Coming for a very different reason.

The Holy Spirit says, "That day shall not come till the apostasy shall have first come." Popular theology says, "That day shall not come till the world's conversion shall have come"! (slightly different!)

The Holy Spirit's teaching was the world was not yet bad enough. Modern teaching is that the world is not yet good enough (some difference here!)

Well! the Thessalonian saints believed their teachers; and the churches to-day believe theirs!

The one lived according to its faith, and was a model for all time for its holiness of life and missionary zeal; while the churches of to-day live according to their faith, and all men see their works; while even the world cries out that Christianity is a failure"! The placards and notices exhibited at the doors of churches and chapels show plainly that those within have lost faith in apostolic teaching, which proclaimed that "the Gospel is the power of God unto salvation unto every one that believeth"; and are quick to adopt the newest methods and the latest fashions in order to "get the people in."

But all this is surely leading up to the very apostacy which is here foretold. It does not need a keen eye to see that the whole tendency of "religious" activity and teaching is in this direction. It is preparing the way for the revelation of Antichrist under the very name of Christ for the churches are rejecting what the Spirit is teaching through Paul's epistles, on the very plea of going back to "the teaching of Jesus"!

4. As to the apostacy itself, whatever there may be in the Roman Catholic Church (which is not merely a religion, but a State) in a partial or historical foreshadowing of it, or preparation for it, there is only one interpretation of "THE APOSTACY," and that is, the open renunciation of God and of Christ.

Individuals may apostatize. Churches may become corrupt: but THE Apostacy will be marked by the features described in this chapter, viz.: the open rejection of all that God has revealed concerning Himself, whether as the God of Revelation, or as the God of Creation.

We see these two great foundations of the coming Apostacy in the secret workings of this lawlessness to-day, and this not in the Church of Rome merely, but in the Protestant Churches!

Time was when the advocacy of this was confined to the platforms of infidelity; but now, from multitudes of pulpits, of churches and chapels alike, Divine Revelation is being replaced by Reason, and Creation is being rejected for Evolution. Revelation is being demolished and set aside by the Higher Criticism, and Creation is spoken of as "an unphilosophical thought."

And this, mark, not by the open enemies of God and His Christ, but by His professed followers, from high Ecclesiastics of the Church of England to the ministry of the "Free Churches"; whose teachings and writings are more dangerous than those of Bolingbroke and Voltaire, because those who utter these blasphemies (which are of the very essence of this coming Apostacy)

221

and those who are betraying the Church are not only not rejected by Society or ejected from the Church, but are the very ones who are singled out for advancement and promotion and are cherished and honoured by Society, both in the Church and in the State.

All this is far worse thin Romish error. That is defect and excess in matters of doctrine; but this is leading to the rejection of all doctrine, and to destroying it at its very fountain head. Romish error is propagated by men who at least are consistent: we know our foes, and can meet them like enemies in the open. But this essence of Apostacy is proclaimed by the very men who are paid to oppose it; while the poor sheep are actually handed over to the wolves by the very shepherds themselves! These false shepherds spend one part of their time in destroying the pastures of the sheep, and the other part in amusing the goats!

If this is not Apostacy, what is? If these be not the secret (counsels) of iniquity or lawlessness, where are we to look for them? For lawlessness it is. Lawlessness is and will be the great and necessary outcome of the teaching of these false shepherds. "The spirit of the times," which rejects the teachings of "the Spirit of God" in having thrown off the restraints of God and His Word, is not going to endure "the restraints of man!" The two are inseparably linked together, as cause is to effect.

A careful study of Dan. vii., viii., and ix., with Rev. xiii., will show us exactly what this Apostacy will be.

5. The structure of this passage shows us that there are two periods contrasted (verse 7), The *secret* period of its working, and the *open* period of its revelation. We have made this quite clear in the structure and in the translation.

A day is coming, an appointed time, when Antichrist will be revealed, and no longer secretly work, but openly take his seat in, "the Temple of God" (for the reception of divine honours, exhibiting the proofs that he is God, with all the power and authority given to him by Satan. And, because God does not then and there strike him dead on the spot, the multitude, with all the greater readiness, being penally deluded, believe the lie.

Those who believe the lie do so not from simple ignorance, but because they "love the lie, and have pleasure in iniquity." They are men who will not hear the voice of God, but listen to resisters like Jannes and Jambres: men who seek out and give heed to lying spirits, and reject the Spirit of Truth: men who will not believe "all that the prophets have spoken," but incontinently swallow the monstrous assertions and lies of "The False Prophet."

These are the multitudes who will come under this judgment and "believe THE Lie."

6. The revelation of this lawless one, and the change from the secret to the open phase of his working, will be in its own appointed season.

The popular belief about a *restraining* power which hinders it, and that this power is the Holy Spirit in the church, arises from a misapprehension as to the meaning of the word κατέχω *(katecho)* here used. That the church of God is the salt of the earth, and that, while the Holy Spirit abides in it the revelation of Antichrist cannot take place, *is perfectly true,* because the church will be removed before that day can come, as verse 2 clearly states. But that is not necessarily the subject of verses 6 and 7.

Translators and interpreters fail to remember that the word κατέχω *(katechō),* which is rendered "withhold" in verse 6 and *"let"* in verse 7 (and in R.V. *"restrain"* in both verses), being transitive, must have an *object or* accusative case after it; and, as it is omitted by *Ellipsis* it has therefore to be supplied in the translation.

The verb κατέχω *(katechō)* means *to have and holdfast.* The preposition κατά *(kata),* in composition, does not *necessarily* preserve its meaning of *down,* to hold down; but it may be *intensive,* and mean *to hold firmly, to hold, fast,* to hold in secure possession. This is proved by its usage; which clearly shows that restraining or withholding is no necessary part of its meaning. It occurs nineteen times, and is nowhere else so rendered. On the other hand there are four or five other words which might have been better used had "restrain" been the thought in this passage.

Indeed, its true meaning is fixed by its use in these epistles. In 1 Thess. v. 21 we read *"hold fast* that which is good," not restrain it, or "withhold" that which is good! But the idea is of keeping, and retaining, and holding on fast to, that which is proved to be good. So it is in all the passages where the word occurs.[115]

This fixes for us the meaning of the verb κατέχω, for it cannot be that, in the first Epistle (1 Thess. v. 21) it means to "hold fast" something ("that which is good,") and that in the second Epistle it means something quite different! But WHAT is it that thus holds fast "the man of sin"? and WHO is it that holds fast something which is not mentioned, and which has therefore to be supplied? For, in verse 6, *that* which holds fast is neuter, τὸ κατέχον *(to katechon)*, while in verse 7 it is masculine, ὁ κατέχων *(ho katechōn)*: so that in verse 6 it is some*thing* (neuter) which holds the man of sin fast, while in verse 7 some*one* is holding fast to something.

According to verse 6, it is some place out of which he ascends (Rev. ix. 1, 2 and xi, 7), and in which he is now held fast in sure possession until the season arrive when he is to be openly revealed: meanwhile, his secret counsels and plans are already working,

---

115.	Matt. xxi. 38.	*Let us seize on* his inheritance.
	Luke iv. 42.	*And stayed* him, that he should not.
	Luke viii. 15.	Having heard the word, *keep* it.
	Luke xiv. 9.	Thou begin with shame *to take* the lowest room..
	John v. 4.	Of whatsoever disease *he had (i.e.,* was held).
	Acts xxvii. 40.	And *made* toward shore (*i.e.,* they *held* their course, or *kept* going for the shore).
	Rom. i. 18.	*Who hold* the truth in unrighteousness.
	Rom. vii. 6.	Being dead to that wherein we were held (margin and R.V.).
	1 Cor. vii. 30.	As though they *possessed not.*
	1 Cor. xi. 2.	And *keep* the ordinances.
	1 Cor. xv. 2.	If ye *keep in memory* what I preached.
	2 Cor. vi. 10.	And yet *possessing* all things.
	1 Thess. v. 21.	*Hold fast* that which is good.
	Philem. 13.	Whom I would have *retained* with me.
	Heb. iii. 6.	If *we hold fast* the confidence.
	Heb. x. 23.	*Let us hold fast* the profession.

preparing the way for his revelation.

The whole subject of the context is the revelation of two personages (not of one), viz., "the man of sin" (verse 3) and "the lawless one" (verse 8). These correspond with the two beasts of Rev. xiii.[116]

Thus we have here two subjects: (1) "The Man of Sin" (the beast from the sea, Rev. xiii. 1-10), and the open apostacy which precedes and marks his revelation; (2) "The Lawless one" (the beast from the earth, Rev. xiii. 11-18), and the working of his secret counsels which precedes his revelation; and the ejection of the Devil from the heavens brings it about.

An attempt has been made to translate the words ἐκ μέσου γένηται *(ek mesou genē tai) be taken out of the way,* as meaning, "arise out of the midst." But this translates an idiomatic expression literally; which cannot be done without introducing error. ἐκ μέσου γένηται is an idiom for *being gone away,* or *being absent* or *away.*

This is clear from the other places where the idiomatic expression occurs.[117]

---

116. See the structure of Rev. xiii. in the expository notes, to follow.

117. In Matt. xiii. 49, the wicked are severed *"from among* the just" (*i.e.,* taken away). In Acts xvii. 33, "Paul departed *from among* them" (*i.e.,* went away). In xxiii. 10, he was taken "by force *from among* them" (*i.e.,* taken out of the way). 1 Cor. v. 2 is very clear, where he complains that they had not mourned that "he that hath done this thing might be taken away *from among* you." In 2 Cor. vi. 17, we are commanded, "Wherefore come *out from among them* and be ye separate." In Col. ii. 14 we read of the handwriting of ordinances which was against us ; Christ "took it *out of the way. "* We have the same in the Septuagint in Isa. lii.11: "Depart ye. . . go ye *out of the midst* of her," and Isa. lvii. 1: "the righteous is taken *away from* the evil to come."

The same usage is seen in Classical writers—Plutarch (*Timol* p. 238, 3) : "He determined to live by himself, having *got himself out of the way, "* i.e., apart from the public; Herodotus (3, 83; and 8, 22): The speaker exhorts some to "be on our side; but, if this is impossible, then sit down *out of the way,"* i.e., leave the coast clear, as we should say, keep neutral and stand aside. The same idiom is seen in Latin—Terence *(Phorm.* v. 8, 30) She is dead, she is gone *from among us"* (*e medio abiit).* The opposite expression shows the same thing. In Xenophon *(Cyr.* 5, 2, 26), one asks, "What *stands in the way* of your joining us?"(ἐν μέσῳ εἶναι).

225

Thus the lawless one is, at present, being held fast in a pit (while his secret counsels are at work); and the Devil is holding on to his position in the heavenlies (Eph. ii. 2; vi. 12). But presently there will be "war in heaven" (Rev. xii. 7), and Satan will be cast out into the earth. Then in Rev. xiii. 1, we read, "and he (Satan) stood upon the sand of the sea" (R.V.) Then it is that he will call up the lawless one, whom John immediately sees rising up out of the sea to run his brief career, and be destroyed by the glory of the Lord's appearing.

7. With this terrible doom of the ungodly before them, the Holy Spirit leads the writers of this Epistle to turn with joyfulness to the saints in Thessalonica; and to all who, like them, know their standing, and blessed hope, in Christ: But we are bound to give thanks alway to God for you, brethren beloved of the Lord, because God hath from the beginning chosen you to salvation through sanctification (or setting apart) of the Spirit and belief of the truth whereunto He called you by our Gospel, to the obtaining of the glory of our Lord Jesus Christ. Therefore, brethren, stand fast, and hold the traditions which ye have been taught, whether by word, or our Epistle" (verses 13-15).

And finally, they pray (iii. 5), "and the Lord (the Holy Spirit) direct your hearts into the love of God (the Father) and into the patient waiting of Christ."

He is waiting now and "from henceforth expecting" (Heb. x. 12, 13), and we too are waiting. "As He is, so are we in this world."

With a few admonitions, the Epistle now closes.[118]

---

118. In order to complete the structure, we give in a note
THE EXPANSION OF "c," iii. 6-15 (see page 208).
Admonition (shorter, general).

c	o	iii. 6.	Command concerning separation.
		p	7-9. The example of Paul and his brethren.
	o	10.	Command as to non-workers.
		p	11. The example of non-workers, those referred to in "c" (ii. 2).
	w	12, 13.	Command as to work.
		π	14, 15. The examples to be shunned.

226

We have thus come to the end of our studies, to the end of these Epistles addressed by the Holy Spirit to churches, through Paul. We have learned the lessons (or some of them) which he has written for the express purpose of our education as Christians.

We have seen the effect of this teaching in the education and formation of this typical model church. All leads up to and centres in Christ.

"He shall glorify ME" was the Lord's own prophecy and promise concerning the Holy Spirit; and, wherever He teaches and works, that is the one result.

Christ is glorified in this teaching in these seven Epistles. He is our all. The saved sinner is shown the depths of the pit and the miry clay out of which he is taken (Rom. i). Then he is shown how, according to "God's Gospel," he is justified and saved by God's sovereign grace. Then the standing in Christ which God has given him, by the same free grace, is revealed to him; and he learns that he died with Christ, and has risen with Christ; that, though the flesh is in him, he is "not in the flesh," but seated in the heavenlies in Christ. And now his one blessed hope is to be with Christ and like Christ for ever. This will be only when Christ comes for him. And now, whether he fall asleep, or be alive and remain to that coming, Christ is his hope: he is shut up to Christ. Apart from a Risen Christ, he has not even the hope of rising again (1 Cor. xv. 18). Things may get worse and worse here: but God has called him "to the obtaining of the glory of our Lord Jesus Christ"; and therefore he waits for God's Son from heaven.

This is our blessed hope, to be caught up and taken away from "the evil to come," before it comes.

Not a word does the Holy Spirit say in this Epistle about man's being under probation. He is not under probation. He once was; but now he is a ruin, a total wreck; and it is just here that "God's gospel" meets him, with the message of the grace of God.

Not a word is said about the world's being in its infancy or, of its improvement or reformation; for the sentence of its condemnation has been passed, and it only waits now for execution to be put in.

Not a word is said about the world's conversion, or any outpouring of the Spirit on the church. Not a word about an

227

intervening golden age between man's day (1 Cor. iv. 3) and the day of the Lord.

Not a word about all these "fables" of the nineteenth century to which men have "turned their ears" (2 Tim. iv. 4).

There is *no* time or season which hinders our being caught up and gathered together unto Christ (1 Thess. v. 1). There *is* a time and season before "the day of the Lord" can come to this world in judgment. But the reason of its delay is that the cup of its iniquity is not yet full. There lacks yet the Apostacy, the revelation of the Man of Sin, and the Lawless one, to complete the moral transgression and rebellion of the world.

The Thessalonian saints knew all this. Why then should they call in question the doctrine of the Resurrection (Cor.), when that was the very thing for which they looked and waited as the fruition of all their hope?

Why should they turn again to the weak and beggarly elements of this world (Gal.), when the glories of the world to come filled their vision?

Why should they "mind earthly things" (Phil.), when they were thus occupied with heavenly things?

Why should they be spoiled by the teachings of vain and deceitful philosophy (Col.), when they looked for glorious facts and blessed realities?

No divisions had to be reproved; for they were "one body in Christ," and walked in recognition of this truth, with one faith and one hope.

No errors had to be combatted; for they were too zealous in serving the living and true God, and in true missionary activity, to be "striving about words to no profit."

They were no dreamers, no mere enthusiasts. But the truth in which they had been brought up kept them sound in doctrine and diligent in service.

If the same soundness and the same diligence is the great need of the church in the present day, then the one abiding lesson of these Epistles to the Church of Thessalonica is this—that holy living and missionary zeal must be the spontaneous working out of that truth which God Himself must have first worked in us (Phil. ii. 13).

The Other Pauline Epistles.
(NOT ADDRESSED TO CHURCHES).

Having seen and considered the Epistles addressed to churches by the Holy Spirit through Paul, it remains now only to say a few words on the other Pauline Epistles.

What place do they occupy?

What mission do they discharge ?

The answer is that they are remarkable, not so much for what they contain, as for what they do *not* contain.

When the Church shall have been caught up and gathered to the Lord, the seven Church Epistles will be only of historical interest and use to those who are left on the earth to go through or come out of the Great Tribulation; just as the historical books of the Old Testament are of use and interest to us now. Whatever there may be in them then by way of *application,* the *interpretation* will necessarily go with the Church for whose special instruction they were given.

This, then, is the gap to be filled by the other nonchurch epistles, especially that to the Hebrews.

There will be those on the earth who will "learn righteousness," and be saved, though not to the position which the Church will occupy. There are "many mansions" in the Father's house; and the position occupied by the Church will be occupied by none other.

There will be those who come out of Great Tribulation (Rev. vii.). There will be the 144,000 of Rev. vii. and xiv. These will need the Word of God. These will need truth which they may not only *apply to,* but *interpret of,* themselves.

This is where the other New Testament writings will come in; especially John's Gospel, the Epistle to the Hebrews, and the Epistles to the Seven Assemblies in Rev. ii. and iii. While there is every truth in them that they will need, there is nothing that will interfere with their standing in the slightest degree. That is why (we believe) there is no reference to the Mystery, and no mention of the Church of God, or the Body of Christ, in those writings, and no Church truth or teaching as such. Nothing about the members of the Body having died or risen with Christ (for we shall have actually then risen). Nothing about being seated by faith in the heavenlies in Christ (for we shall be actually seated there with and in Christ). Nothing about Jews and Gentiles being "one body" in Christ, "one new man"; (for the Church, composed of both, will be in heaven; and the Jews, as such, on the earth).

Hence it is that in the Gospel of John there is so little in common with the other three Gospels. Nothing recorded in them is repeated in John which would have interfered in any way with the teaching that will then be required; nothing to mar that teaching, or make it difficult.

So with Hebrews. Paul's name is specially associated with the seven church epistles. He was the chosen vessel by which the Spirit would instruct the Church of God; and make known the revelation of the Mystery, and the truth concerning the one Body of Christ. This, we believe, is the reason why Paul's name is omitted from that epistle; and, though it was written by him, he is thus, personally, dissociated from it.

But let no one wilfully or ignorantly mistake our meaning.

The whole of John and Hebrews is *for* us, for the Church here and now; all is needed by us: but, while they do not contain ALL the teaching that we need, so neither do they contain ANY that will not be needed after the Church has gone.

That is why we said that those writings are remarkable and noticeable, *not for what they contain, but for what they omit.*

Why is it that Heb. vi. and x. are the constant perplexity of uninstructed Christians?

Why is it that what is true in Heb. vi. 1-8 and x. 26-31, of those to whom they are to be interpreted, is used to upset what is equally true of us in Rom. viii., which is to be interpreted only of the standing of those who are members of the Body of Christ? Both Scriptures are true if we thus rightly divide them, and interpret them of those to whom they are respectively spoken.

We will speak of this more fully in our next number, which will be on the special place and teaching of the Epistle to the Hebrews.

Any other explanation of the difficulty (for difficulty it is, and is felt to be by thousands of Christians,) is at the expense of truth. Either Heb. vi. and x. and John xv. 6 are apt to get explained away, and the awful warning made of none effect: or Rom. viii. is explained away; and then we are robbed of the eternal security and preservation of those who are in Christ.

How much better and easier to accept this explanation which is in obedience to 2 Tim. ii. 15; in harmony with the teaching of the other epistles and leaves the truth of each untouched and untarnished, to have all its blessed effect and wondrous power?

It is an explanation, which rightly divides the word of truth (or at any rate attempts and strives to do so); leaves each truth in the full possession of those of whom it is to be interpreted; yet robs neither party of one truth, or any fraction of truth, which properly and correctly belongs to it.

The Three Pastoral Epistles are needed and useful as revealing the corruption which was so soon to follow the revelation of the Mystery.

In the Epistle to Timothy the Church of God is seen for a few brief moments in its *rule;* while in the second Epistle it is seen in its *ruin.* The Mystery is the good deposit which was committed to Timothy (2 Tim. i. 12, 14, R.V., margin); but no sooner is it mentioned by name in 1 Tim. iii. 16 than the Mystery of Iniquity is revealed in the next chapter.

The Second Epistle to Timothy completes the picture of the *ruin,* and exhibits the four downward steps which lead to judgment:—

1. In 2 Tim. i. 15, we have the departure from the Pauline teaching.
2. In 2 Tim. ii. 17, we have the mischievous working of those who "err concerning the truth."
3. In 2 Tim. iii. 8, we have the opposition of those who "resist the truth."

231

4. In 2 Tim. iv. 4, we have the apostasy of those who "turn away their ears from the truth and shall be turned unto fables" (*lit.*, myths).

This fills up the details of the picture, and contains the substance of all Ecclesiastical history. It is Divine Church history in brief.

One other point has to be carefully borne in mind: and that is, that none of these seven churches, and certainly not that of Thessalonica, ever possessed the four Gospels as we have them. Not one of them, not even the Apostle Paul himself, ever saw John's Gospel!

And yet they were perfect churches. The church of the Thessalonians, as we have seen, remarkably so. A model church indeed., Specifically called a τύπον *(typon) type, i.e.,* a typical church (1 Thess. i. 7). So that it was, and of course is, possible to have a perfect model church without having the four Gospels before its members! This could not have been if the newly-invented cry of the present race of teachers be correct. On every hand we are told we must go back to "the teaching of Jesus"! These churches could not do that! There was no record of it extant to which they could go back! And yet they flourished.

The Ascended Christ, the Head of the Body, *at once* "gave gifts unto men" (Eph. iv. 11. 1 Cor. xii. 28, &c.), and these were for the express purpose of edifying or building up the Body; while the Holy Spirit used those gifts, and imparted all the instruction needed by the newly-planted churches.

And yet to-day the four "gospels" are looked on as specially containing "the gospel of God." But this is far from being the case. The Gospels are the completion of the Old Testament history as well as the beginning of the New. The King and the Kingdom had been prophesied and promised all through the ages. At last He came. "He came unto His own (possession), but His own (people) received Him not" (John i. 11). Indeed, they rejected both Him and His kingdom, and put Him to death. This is not good news, but terrible in the extreme. Then, after His ascension, the King and the Kingdom were again proclaimed as ready to be revealed on the repentance of the nation (Acts iii. 20, 21), and He was again rejected, His messengers being persecuted and killed!

Then, after all that, and in spite of all that, we open the first Epistle—the Epistle to the Romans, and hear the special message delivered to the churches:—

> "Paul, a servant of Jesus Christ,
> By Divine calling—an Apostle,
> Separated unto THE GOSPEL OF GOD."

Here is the declaration of the grace of God: showing how He could and would save sinners in spite of all; and how He could be "just, and the justifier of him that believeth in Jesus."

And yet, the gospel is seldom preached from this Epistle, where it is all contained! It is more often preached from incidents in the gospel history: though, of course, it is even then impossible to preach it properly without referring more or less to the epistle to the Romans. Here we have Ruin, Redemption, and Regeneration in all their fulness laid open to our view, and impressed upon our hearts.

Thus the four Gospels and the Epistle to Hebrews are shown to have their own proper place and *interpretation;* and though we may and ought to *apply* every word in them so far as it is in accord with our own Church Epistles, specially written, not only *for* us, but *about* us, we must leave the *interpretation* to those to whom it belongs; and neither rob them of what is their own, nor use what is true of them to destroy that which is equally true of us.

233

The Epistle to the Hebrews

We have already indicated what we believe to be the dispensational place and position of the Epistle to the Hebrews. But it is necessary to speak of this more fully, inasmuch as the failure to notice this is the cause of great trouble to many of the children of God.

The number of questions put to us with regard to the falling away mentioned in Heb. vi. 3-8, and the "no more sacrifice for sins," &c., in Heb. x. 26-35, shows the seriousness of the difficulty which is created through not seeing the scope of the Epistle and not "rightly dividing the word of truth."

That there is a difficulty is certain; and it is a great one. But it is entirely of our own creation. There is no difficulty whatever in the Epistle itself. It arises only because of our wilful, selfish persistence in reading "The Church" into every part of the word of God. Many, while repudiating the title of "Churchmen" with reference to the Historic church, are most devout "Churchmen" with regard to the Bible. Hence the difficulty.

"What God hath joined together, let not man put asunder" (Mark x. 9). These words are true: and they express an eternal principle, which reaches in its application far beyond the interpretation which confines them to the marriage tie.

But the converse is, and must be, equally true: *That which God hath put asunder, let not man join together.*

This eternal truth cannot be violated without loss and disaster; whether it be in our practical life, or in our reading and interpretation of the Word of God.

God has "put asunder," for example, the Epistle to the Romans and the Epistle to the Hebrews. He might have connected or incorporated the two in some way, if it had pleased Him to do so: but He has put them entirely "asunder," in fact and in form. And it is by

234

joining them together we suffer harm and loss, and fall into the fatal snare of using one truth to upset another truth.

A statement may be perfectly true of the persons addressed, and of the time and occasion, &c., to which it specially refers. Another statement, elsewhere, may also be perfectly true in the same way. But, if we join them together, and interpret them of the same persons, and of the same circumstances, all truth vanishes, and we have a great difficulty at once created, if not a direct contradiction.

Take an example from Deut. vi. 25. "It shall be our righteousness, if we observe to do all these commandments before the LORD our God, as he hath commanded us." These words are perfectly true as spoken to certain persons and at a certain time. But we read in Gal. ii. 16, "By the works of the law shall no flesh be justified." These words also are perfectly true under another dispensation. Deut. vi. 25 is true of those under the covenant of *works*, and Gal. ii. 16 is equally true of those who are under the covenant of *grace*. If they are thus put and kept "asunder" all is perfectly clear; but if they are joined together, then the saint may well be perplexed, and the enemy of God's Word has a weapon put into his hand to use against all truth.

We may take another illustration, which will bring us at once to the point before us.

I may have a letter put into my hands, which I *assume* is written *to me*. I read on, and find much that is intensely interesting, and exceedingly profitable for me. But I find also references to matters which do not concern me. Things are said about my position which do not quite describe it. There may be a reference to a debt which I do not owe, or to an order which I do not remember having given. Persons and events are mentioned: but, not knowing exactly to whom or to what they refer, there is much that puzzles and perplexes me.

But all the difficulty is removed when I discover, and understand, that though the letter is put into my hand on purpose FOR me to read and learn, it was not actually addressed TO me.

Then it is all clear. I quite see how I may profit by much of the instruction that is contained in the letter; and I am no longer troubled by that which seemed so different from another letter which the same writer had previously addressed directly *to me,* and which was all ABOUT me.

Now this is exactly the case with the Epistle to the Hebrews. It is written "FOR our learning," but it is not addressed TO us.

It is addressed to Hebrews at a particular time, under certain circumstances, and in a certain condition of mind. *The interpretation* therefore belongs exclusively to them; while the *application* belongs to all Christians in all time.

These Hebrews and their spiritual condition we find described in Acts xxi. 20-26. They are the thousands who believed on and after the day of Pentecost.

Of course, with those that believe that the day of Pentecost was the birthday of the Church, we shall have another difficulty.

It is only a belief of certain good men, whose traditions are handed down, firmly believed as an article of faith, and stoutly defended by those who demand in all other questions a "thus saith the LORD." No such statement is found in the Acts of the Apostles. On the contrary, we find Peter exercising his ministry to the *nation,* and using "the keys of the kingdom" to open it to his own People, and to the Gentiles.

The nation is dealt with as such; and the one condition of national repentance is preached as the condition for the reception of national blessing. Acts iii. 12-26 is clear as to this. It is the "men of Israel" who are addressed. It is the rulers and representatives of the nation who are dealt with (Acts iv. 1, 5, 6; v. 17, 18, 27, 33, 34; vi. 15, &c.).

It is not the formation of the Church of God which is being described in those chapters; but another presentation of the King and the Kingdom. These had been rejected when presented by Christ in the Gospels. And now they are rejected again, when presented by the Holy Ghost in the Acts of the Apostles.

It was not until after all this that the secret or Mystery concerning the Church or Body of Christ was revealed to the Apostle Paul, and through him to the Church at large.

Those Pentecostal believers, who are the ideal of many Gentile Christians to-day, were Hebrews who received the Lord Jesus as the Messiah, while many doubtless knew but little of Him as their

236

Saviour. It may be the same with much of the Mission work among the Jews to-day. But, whatever may be the case now, we are not left in ignorance as to the Pentecostal believers.

When Paul reached Jerusalem, in Acts xxi. 17, he met the Apostles and Elders in council, and they uttered these weighty, memorable words to Paul: *"Thou seest, brother, how many thousands of Jews there are which believe;[119] and they are all zealous of the Law"* (Acts xxi. 20).

We need not quote the whole passage (20-33), as it is not our object to refer to the Apostle Paul. We are concerned with the Pentecostal Jewish believers and it is clear that they were so "zealous of the Law" that they had not forsaken Moses, nor given up circumcision, but walked after the customs. Moreover, they offered sacrifices (verse 26), and were prepared to kill Paul for his contrary teaching. "All the city was moved, and the people ran together." There were many thousands, remember; and the Holy Spirit in this history has not said a word to distinguish them from those who carried out the assault on the apostle Paul,

It was exactly what James "and all the Elders" foresaw. It was this very thing they desired to prevent. They feared and dreaded this outbreak on the very ground of religion; because of Paul's teaching concerning the Church of God versus the Law of Moses.

Now, if we remember all this, we see at once that the Epistle to the Hebrews was written to these "many thousands of Jews who believed"; and yet, at the same time, were "ALL zealous of the

---

119. We must note that this is literally *have believed.* It is the perfect participle of πιστεύειν *(pisteuein).* The perfect of this verb occurs only sixteen times in the New Testament. One sense of the perfect seems to be *have all along* as in 2 Cor. ii. 13. "I have all along had no ease," &c. And from this the sense of *professing to be* or *do* anything. Observe, it does not say what or to what extent they had believed; or what was the character of their belief. As there were *myriads (μυριάδες)* of them, it is hardly likely on the face of it that it was a sound or saving faith in each case. With many, doubtless, it was only their belief as Jews in the Lord Jesus *as the Messiah,* and not as sinners a faith in Him *as their Saviour.* The same may be the case with many Jewish believers to-day, as the Lord is too generally preached as the Messiah and not as the Saviour, on the lines of Romans' teaching.

237

Law," *i.e.*, they observed the law very zealously.

To such the Epistle to the Hebrews would come with all its truth and power. Even we ourselves can understand it better if we look at the Epistle in this light. We can see exactly why the various arguments are used, and why all the many references to the Law are made. We can distinguish what is written FOR us: and not confound it with what is written TO us in the Epistle to the Romans.

There we learn our position as having died with Christ, been buried with Christ, and risen with Christ. There we learn how there is "therefore no condemnation to them that are in Christ" (Rom. viii. 1), and no separation from the love of God which is in Christ.

And, learning all this, as a blessed fact written to and of ourselves, we shall never again be upset at what is written to others; or use what is truth, as written to them, to upset what is equally truth, as written to us. In other words, we shall not use one truth to upset another truth.

If any of our readers are "Jews . . . zealous of the Law," then Heb. vi. and x. are meant and are true for you, and the sooner you take those scriptures to heart the better! But, for you who are in "Christ," and know your standing "in Him," we exhort you to rejoice in all that is written to you as to your completeness and perfection in Christ Jesus our Lord.

Thus, then, we have the place, position and scope of the Epistle to the Hebrews. It was written by Paul, as is clear from a comparison of 1 Pet. i. 1. 2 Pet. iii. 1, 15. But his name is omitted, so that Jews might not be prejudiced against its teaching; and that the churches might not confuse it with the other Pauline Epistles addressed to them.

"WITHOUT THE CAMP."

So far, we have looked only at the negative aspect of the Epistle to the Hebrews; but, without going into the Epistle as a whole, it will be well to add a few words, and look at it in its positive aspect, and see the scope of it, and its teaching, as it stands in relation to the other Pauline Epistles.

It is addressed, as we have seen, to Jews who believed, and were yet "all zealous of the law." Knowing, therefore, the condition of those to whom it was written, we are better able to understand it, and to see how wonderfully it is adapted to meet the case of those who were still bound up to a Jewish ritual.

It is "God" Himself who addresses them. No human name is allowed to appear as the writer; least of all, that of Paul. All Paul's other Epistles (without exception) commenced with his name: but not this one. This was not to be open to any prejudice which might be caused by the presence of that offensive name.

It was, moreover, quite in accordance with the Divine manner of addressing His People Israel. It was no new thing with them to be addressed by the voice of God. "At sundry times" He had spoken directly to their fathers. They were perfectly familiar with that Divine mode of communication. And the "many thousands of Jews who believed" all bowed to the truth that God had "spoken unto US by His Son."

But, believing this, they had not apprehended the value of Christ's death as the one sin-offering, making obsolete all sacrifices and all ordinances. They still clung to their rites and ceremonies; they were "zealous of the law" (Acts xxi. 20.); they walked after the customs *(v.* 21), and they made "vows" *(v.* 23) ; they used divers "baptisms" (Heb. vi. 2), and continued to offer sacrifices (Acts xxi. 26).

The object of the Epistle to these Hebrews is, therefore, to show that all these things were done away by the one offering once offered, and all made of none effect: they were a "shadow of things to come"; but we now have the substance of all in the Person and work of the Lord Jesus.

God had spoken in time past to the fathers by the prophets; but now He had spoken by His Son.

The whole of the first two chapters is taken up with the statement of these two great truths:—the Divine speaking, and the Divine Son of God.

The structure of these two chapters brings this out very beautifully.

A| i. 1, 2-. God speaking by His Son.
  B| -2-14. The Son. God: "better than the angels."
A | ii. 1-4. God speaking by His Son.
  B | 5-18. The Son. Man: lower than the angels."

Here, we see at once the alternation of the two themes and the contrast in the corresponding members.

The second member is seen to be parenthetical with regard to the first and third. And in like manner the third member is parenthetical with regard to the second and fourth.

The third member reads on from the end of the first; thus:

   i.   1, 2-. God, who at sundry times and in divers manners, spake in time past unto the fathers by the prophets, hath in these last days spoken unto us by His Son. . .

   ii.   1, &c. wherefore we ought to give the more earnest heed to the things which we have heard, &c.

In like manner the fourth member reads on from the end of the second; thus:

   i.   14. Are they not all ministering spirits sent forth to minister for them who shall be heirs of salvation? . . .

   ii.   5. for unto the angels hath he not put into subjection the world to come, &c.

The Son of God, therefore, is the great subject in this Epistle; and its object is to show how He has superseded the Law and its ordinances; and summed up and combined all in Himself. It is to show that the "rest" promised to the People of Israel was not obtained at their entrance into the Land with Joshua (iv. 8, 9); and to lead the saints into the rest obtained through the priesthood of Christ, and the perfection of His person in His death as an offering to God.

Chapter i. proclaims the Divine personality of the Lord Jesus; and the four distinct aspects of His relation to the Father as the Son of God, and, therefore, "better than the angels."

Chapter ii. declares Him as Man; made "a little lower than the angels for the suffering of death." This death had four distinct objects in view:

The bringing of many sons to glory (v. 10).
The presenting to God a sanctified people, His brethren (v. 11).

The deliverance from the devil, who had the power of death (v. 14); and

The making propitiation for the sins of the People as a merciful and faithful High priest (v. 17, 18).

For these purposes the Son of God took part in flesh and blood of the "seed of Abraham." It behoved him in all things to be made like unto His brethren; that, having suffered, being tempted, He might be able to succour them that are tempted.

Hence the key-note of the Epistle is "better" and Hebrew believers are shown how that "in Christ" they have everything "better" than under the Law of which they were so "zealous."
They had

A better covenant (vii. 22).
Better promises (viii. 6).
Better substance (x.. 34).
A better hope (vii. 19).
A better sacrifice (ix. 23).
A better country (xi. 16).
A better resurrection (xi. 35).
A better thing (xi. 40).

Not only is the *word* "better" used, but Christ is shown to be

Better than angels (i).
Better than Moses (iii).
Better than Joshua (iv).
Better than Aaron (vii).

241

Better than the Law (x).

Another word which characterises this Epistle is the word "once"; *i.e., once for all.* (See vi. 4 vii. 27; ix. 7, 12, 26, 27, 28; x. 2, 10; xii. 26, 27.)

The Epistle is written to those who knew the Law. Hence they are exhorted in various ways:—

"Let us" fear (iv. 1); labour (iv. 11); hold fast (iii. 6 iv. 14; x. 23); come boldly (iv. 16); go on (vi. 1) draw near (x. 22); consider (x. 24); lay aside (xii. 1) run (xii. 1); have grace (xii. 28); go forth (xiii. 13); offer (xiii. 15).

The great design is to get them to break away from the traditional teaching to which they clung with such religious zeal. It had waxed old, and was about to vanish away(viii. 13). The Levitical Law and all its ordinances were among the "things that are shaken. . . that those things which cannot be shaken may remain" (xii. 26-28).

All had failed. The Law: "for the Law made nothing perfect" (vii. 19). It was characterised by "weakness and unprofitableness" (vii. 18).

According to chap. vi. 1, 2, all these things were "dead works." It was necessary to "go on unto perfection" (vi. 1, *maturity* would express the Greek better); and to those who were minded thus to "go on" it is said, "Beloved, we are persuaded better things of YOU" (vi. 9).

Christ is the one object for faith in this Epistle. He supersedes all else. To look for Him (ix. 28) and to look *to* Him (xii. 2) is the substance of which all beside was only shadow.

To cling to tradition or to religion, as such, is to give up both these positions.

It is this that gives all its importance to the climax which is reached in chap. xiii., which is the great lesson of

THE CAMP.

It is stated in verses 11-14:

"The bodies of those beasts, whose blood is brought into the sanctuary by the High Priest for sin, art burned without the camp. Wherefore Jesus also, that he might sanctify the People with his own blood, suffered without the gate. Let us go forth therefore unto him without the camp, bearing his reproach. For here have we no continuing city, but we seek one to come."

This scripture evidently refers to the camp of the People of Israel in the wilderness; and the important question, for the right application to Christian position and practice to-day is,

WHAT IS THE CAMP?

The Camp cannot be the world, for the Camp consisted of the people whom God had, by the covenant of circumcision, separated from the world unto Himself. The Camp was characterised by the presence of God, as it is written: "The LORD thy God walketh in the midst of thy camp, to deliver thee, and to give up thy enemies before thee; therefore shall thy camp be holy" (Deut. xxiii. 14).

That which distinguished the Camp was the visible presence of God in the cloud, which was their shelter by day and their light by night. In the camp everything was arranged by Divine authority, and everything was sustained by Divine power, in a wilderness where there was neither food to eat nor water to drink. Yet it is from this place of manifest blessing that the saints are called out, in Heb. xiii. 13, into that which is, in the world's esteem, the most despicable; to the place outside, where the ashes were poured out, and where the sin-offering was consumed, to have fellowship with the Lord Jesus there. The reason given is this—*"For here have we no continuing city."*

Jerusalem is left for judgment: the fig tree has proved itself to be incapable of bringing forth fruit meet for repentance; and the sentence is gone forth to "cut it down."

From the day of Pentecost to the end of Paul's ministry in the synagogues, at Ephesus (Acts xix.), the presence of God the Holy

Spirit was manifest, in the signs that accompanied the ministry of the apostles, preaching "the kingdom of God," in association with Jerusalem as the city concerning which the Lord Jesus had told them to tarry in it (Acts i. 4). The word rendered "tarry" implies more *fixed residence* than our English tarry.

The Camp, the antitype of Israel in the wilderness, began on the day of Pentecost; the presence of God was then first manifest with the apostles at Jerusalem ; the Holy Spirit and the signs whereby His presence was manifested answered to the type of the cloud whereby the Lord led His People out of Egypt and through the wilderness. Power from on high accompanied the preaching of the kingdom of God, "to the Jew first and also to the Greek," in the synagogues until that preaching ended at Ephesus (Acts xix.). "The Acts of the Apostles" is the history of what was the antitype of the Camp of Israel in the wilderness.

This is proved by the third and fourth chapters of this Epistle: the People are addressed as equivalent to those who came out of Egypt by Moses, and are exhorted to labour to enter into the rest set before them, "lest any man fall after the same example of unbelief." That which this Epistle sets before the People of God is a Sabbath of rest, when "he that is entered into his rest, hath also ceased from his own works, as God did from His." It declares the priesthood of Christ, and the perfection of His One Offering, "who through the Eternal Spirit offered Himself without spot to God," so perfecting for ever them that are sanctified, in that one offering, through faith in Him; and having entered into His rest, and sat down at the right hand of God, has brought all His People into the same rest from all the carnal ordinances belonging to a worldly sanctuary: thus causing them to cease from their own works as God did from His; and to rest in His presence in the Holy place, "having hearts sprinkled from an evil conscience, and a body washed with pure water."

Paul, in the epistle to the church of God at Corinth, shews also that the church up to that time was the antitype of the Camp in the wilderness: for in 1 Cor. x. he says, "I would not that ye should be ignorant how that all our fathers were under the cloud, and all passed through the sea; and were all baptized unto Moses in the cloud and in the sea;" then, speaking of their overthrow in the

wilderness, says, "Now these things were our types;" and again, in
v. 11, "Now all these things happened unto them for types."

So Scripture teaches us in the plainest language possible that the
Camp spoken of in Heb. xiii. 13 is not Israel as a nation, but the
company of believers in the apostles' day, as seen in the "Acts of the
Apostles," in association with Jerusalem and endued with visible
power from on high.

The object of God's presence in the camp of Israel was "to
deliver thee, and to give up thy enemies before thee." This was as
evident with the Camp during "the Acts" as with Israel in the
wilderness. The deliverance of Peter, first from the high priest, and
afterwards from Herod, with the death of Herod, and the deliverance
of Paul at Philippi, shew that the believers were one Camp, whether
at Jerusalem or among the Gentiles, wherever any were gathered to
the name of the Lord Jesus, so long as the patience of God lingered
over Jerusalem and the things that pertained to the kingdom of God
were the subject of the apostles' preaching. While this continued the
Gentiles were brought into the Camp by the ceremonial purification,
the washing of the flesh in water, when God had purified their hearts
through faith (Acts x. 47 and xv. 9).

But, when the rulers at Jerusalem and in the synagogues among
the Gentiles persisted in rejecting the testimony of the Holy Spirit
through the apostles concerning Jesus as the seed of David, the
Lord's anointed, then Jerusalem was left to its desolation and Israel
ceased to be a nation.

Then it could be written "we have no city remaining." Israel had
lost its earthly centre. The worldly sanctuary and all that pertained
to it disappeared, and have never been replaced. In the immediate
prospect of this the Epistle to the Hebrews was written: proclaiming
the Lord Jesus a Priest after the order of Melchizedek, so ending the
Levitical priesthood ; and His One offering as fulfilling and ending
all the sacrifices, all the sprinklings of blood, and all the washings
with water that hitherto had been in use. The one sacrifice of the
Son of God took the place of all the offerings; and the presence of
the Holy Spirit in the believer took the place of all the ordinances
upon the flesh.

Their separation from Jerusalem entirely altered the position of the saints, and the character of the Hebrew believers; with no city on earth, and no priest but in the heavens, they ceased to be characterised by authority and power. They were henceforth to be identified with the altar and the sacrifice of Him who "suffered without the gate"; the rejected of His own People, but the Beloved and Accepted of God.

The ashes without the camp are the figure of the true position and character of the saints of God to-day. In the world's esteem most despicable, as Paul says (1 Cor. iv. 13): "We are made as the filth of the world, the offscouring of all things unto this day"; but, in the sight of God, most precious, the result of the perfect obedience of His Beloved Son, the burnt-offering voluntarily laid upon the altar of His Father's will and wholly consumed as a sweet-smelling savour, the perfection of spiritual worship. On the other hand, the ashes without the camp proved the perfect putting away of sin by the One sin-offering burned without the camp. The value of the sin-offering and the value of the burnt-offering were seen together in the clean place "without the Camp;" and to this place the saints are called out to bear the reproach of Him who suffered there, where the ashes were poured out (Lev. iv. 12. Num. xix. 9).

The Camp is represented to-day by any company of men who profess to have *succeeded to the authority or the power* given by the Lord to the Twelve Apostles once manifested in association with Jerusalem. "For here we have no continuing city."

Hence, this Epistle has a very powerful *application* to thousands of professed "believers" in the present day; an application as powerful as its *interpretation,* which came to those thousands of Jews who were "all zealous of the law." All who now are merely religious; holding by tradition; relying on ordinances; depending on rites and ceremonies, priests and sacraments, all these need the special lesson of this Epistle to-day; and to all such its *application* comes with overwhelming force, as powerfully as its *interpretation* came at the first to those of the Jewish believers who were zealous of the law.

But those who have gone forth "without the camp" know their completeness in Christ, read their standing in the Epistle to the Romans, and know that in Him there is "no condemnation," and from Him there can be no separation.

The Cause of "the Present Distress."

Departure from the teaching of the Pauline Epistles was the beginning of apostasy in the Church—the commencement of the dark ages. The Reformation was an awakening to a sense of this disobedience, but it was only "in part" and the condition of the Protestant Evangelical Churches to-day exhibits as sad a condition, from another point of view, as the Church before the Reformation, and needs another Reformation, as great, though of another kind and in a different direction.

To see the root causes of this confusion we shall have to go back to the beginning, and see what Paul's ministry really was, and was intended to be. It is recorded in Acts xiii.-xxviii. It is not taken up until after the record of Peter's ministry is closed.

Paul (Acts xiii.-xxviii.) proclaims to Jews and Gentiles alike, perfection, *apart from all ordinances,* in union with Christ, in whom dwells all the fulness of the Godhead bodily. He preaches Christ as the Head of His body, the Church. He declares "all the council of God (Acts xx. 27). He "fully preaches the word of God" (Col. i. 25, margin). Paul's ministry completes the testimony which thus, in connection with the Parable of the Great Supper, ends in *grace;* while the ministry of Peter and the Twelve, in connection with the Parable of the Dinner, ends in *judgment,* see Matt. xxii. 7, where we have the significant words: "He sent forth his armies, and destroyed those murderers: and burned up their city."

This refers to the destruction or Jerusalem, while the Third ministry (begun by Paul) to the Gentiles is carried on after that destruction, during the National rejection, and while Jerusalem lies desolate. No words could more distinctly express the present dispensation of Grace to the Gentiles given to the apostle Paul.

After speaking the Parable of the Great Supper, the Lord first lays down the great truth that those who receive Him must be prepared to give up all connected with Judaism (Luke xiv. 26, 27), as exemplified by Paul in Phil. iii., where all that he once counted as "gain," he counted as dross and loss for Christ's sake.

This is followed by three solemn illustrations as to this coming change in the dispensation, ending with the words (v. 35), "he that hath ears to hear, let him hear." They are the "Tower," the "King," and the "Salt." These are given after the rejection of Israel had been spoken of in verse 24. Three solemn warnings are conveyed by these as to the folly of claiming the apostolic commission and *authority* when not possessing apostolic *power*: the warning which Christendom did not heed, and the error into which it has fallen.

THE BUILDING OF THE TOWER.
(Luke xiv. 28-30).

The Lord gave *authority* and *power* to His apostles to gather a people to His great supper (Luke ix. 1; Mark xvi. 15-18; Luke xxiv. 47-49; Acts ii- 38, and xv. 14)This was connected first of all with Jerusalem (Acts i. 4), and with Himself as the King of Israel and Lord of all. *This authority and power ceased with the apostles to whom they were given, and they never were and never could be transmitted by them to others.*

The apostles exercised this authority and power. They baptized; and, by the laying on of hands, they conferred miraculous gifts; but *they could not transmit to those recipients the authority and Power to give those gifts and signs to others.* And when the ministry of the kingdom ended, Paul's ministry of "the gospel of the grace of God was to be continued and carried on among Jews and Gentiles alike, calling out the members of Christ's Spiritual Body until that Body should be complete.

By this illustration of the "Tower" the Lord warns us not to claim this apostolic *authority,* unless we have the *power* to complete the work by the laying-on-of-hands, and the bestowal of miraculous gifts, which were the inseparable signs of that power and that authority.

In other words we are not to begin to "build", unless we are able to "finish."

Instead of this, men soon began to *build the Church upon the foundations of the Kingdom;* they began to build this Tower, and they went to war with the great enemy. They assumed to act in "apostolic succession," but were destitute of its *authority* and *power.* The result of this attempt to build the Tower is another Babel (Gen. xi.), and it will now soon end in another Babylon (Rev. xvii.). That which claims to be the continuation of the ministry committed to the twelve apostles becomes "Babylon, the mother of harlots and abominations of the earth."

The Lord Jesus sent forth His apostles to proclaim the Kingdom of God, with power and authority over all devils (Luke ix. 1). This was the proof that the Kingdom of God was come to Israel (Luke xi. 20). The Lord warns men not to proclaim the King or the Kingdom unless they have power to cast out Satan, the great king who is opposed to them. If they have not this power, their true course is to act as ambassadors, seeking the peace of those who are afar off.

The parable teaches plainly the change in the character of the gospel as sent to the Gentiles by Paul from its character as addressed by Peter and the Twelve to Israel. To Israel it proclaimed the Lord Jesus as the King, by His apostles as the heralds of His authority and power; but now to the Gentiles, afar off, the ministers of the Gospel are ambassadors of Christ, desiring His enemies to be reconciled to God.

Those, therefore, who *in any sense* lay claim to the figment of "Apostolic Succession," and those also who, while they reject it, yet ignorantly assume the continuation of the apostolic ministry (after the authority, and power, and sign-gifts have alike ceased), are trying to build this Tower, but are unable to finish it. Nay, worse, far worse than this, this building results in another tower of Babel—for *confusion* is the meaning of its name, and confusion is what we see everywhere around us. They are unable to cope with the great king with whom they contend: they "forsake" not those things that they have (*v.* 33), and they cannot be, the Lord Jesus says, "My disciples." They may pretend to be the Apostles' successors, but are not Christ's disciples.

The great lesson for us lies in the fact that *the apostasy of Christendom began in the departure from the teaching committed to Paul* concerning "The Mystery," or the great Secret concerning the Church of God as the Body of Christ, "the pillar and ground" of all Church truth.

ORDINANCES ARE THE TEST!

Paul's "teaching" declares that Christ is made of God the Head of the Church, which is His Body, and that true believers are the "members of Christ," indwelt by the "one Spirit," wherewith, by the "one baptism," they have been baptized by the "one Lord," in to the "one Body" (Eph. iv.); that these members of Christ are sanctified in Christ; and are called by God into fellowship with His Son; that they are one Spirit with Him, and are "the temple of the living God."

For these, "Christ hath abolished in his flesh, the law of commandments contained in ordinances." Col. ii. gives us their true standing. They are "complete in Him" (v. 10). Hence, their circumcision is that which is "made without hands," being "the circumcision of Christ" (v. 11); and if their circumcision is effected without hands, then, of necessity their baptism must be of the same character. Their baptism is Christ's burial (v.12): for them, ordinances are "blotted out" and "taken out of the way" (v. 14), and they are asked Why, if they died with Christ from the rudiments (i.e. religious ordinances) of the world, Why are they "subject to ordinances after the commandments and doctrines of men?" (v. 20, 22). Thank God, there are those who thus know *their completeness and perfection* in Christ.

But there are thousands who have not this wondrous knowledge. The eyes of their understanding are not enlightened (Eph. i. 18). They are led by those who claim to be successors of the Apostles, and who claim to continue—not *Paul's ministry, but that of the Twelve!*

And what was

"THE TEACHING OF THE TWELVE APOSTLES"?

In 1883 there was published, under this title, a MS., then recently discovered in the library of the Patriarch of Jerusalem, at Constantinople. The date of the MS. was June 13th, 1056: but all scholars are agreed that it is a copy of a work which was originally written in the last quarter of the first century. Its existence had long been known, for it had been quoted by the Sub-Apostolic Fathers, Barnabas (A.D. 71), and Hermas (A.D. 100), and by Clement of Alexandria (A.D. 192). Eusebius (H.E. iii. 2), A.D. 330-340, mentions it as well-known in his day, and classes it among the "controverted books"of the Canon.[120]

The work consists entirely of moral precepts, and rules as to prayer, fasting, baptism, and the Eucharist, and ends with a solemn reference to the coming of the Lord and the resurrection of the dead.

We cannot, of course, believe that this was the *actual* teaching of the Twelve. But this is what it had degenerated into before the close of the first century. We can well understand why all Sacramentarians should hail the appearance of this ancient writing: and, instead of seeing in it the corruption of Christianity, and the commencement of the Apostasy, should welcome it, and make it the ground of their own "teaching." But it shows a lack of discernment indeed for others to speak of this *Didache,* or "Teaching of the Twelve," with approbation, and to see in it a model for the present day, instead of a departure from Primitive Christianity.

Alas! the teaching of Paul was soon apostatised from! and even the teaching of the Twelve "was corrupted"! That corrupted teaching may be summed up in two words,

MORALITY AND ORDINANCES.

Is not this exactly what we see around us on every hand to-day? Holding fast to these two, the other two have been abandoned and practically lost, viz., (1) the coming of the Lord, and (2) resurrection as the hope of the Church!

This was the cause, the beginning, of the apostasy of Christendom: this it was that led up to and brought on "the dark ages": and this is the secret cause of "the present distress in the churches.

The ministry of Paul is rejected, and *the ministry of the Twelve* is still carried on by those who, though destitute of the Apostles'

---

120. Two or three reproductions of it have been published in English, with notes, &c.

authority and *power,* impose on their hearers "the commandments and doctrines of men," and put them in subjection to "ordinances": and, worse than that, they *add* "commandments" . . . "touch not, taste not, handle not"!

Christianity, to-day, has woefully degenerated. *Ordinances*, have become more and more positive in their character; *preaching* is everywhere being set aside, while even *morality* itself becomes more and more negative. For the most part it consists in abstinence from this or that; and in vows and pledges and badges. It is "touch NOT, taste NOT, handle NOT": but "all are to perish with the using"; and all are characteristic of the ministry which is now being everywhere exercised.

[THE END.]

APPENDIXES.

I.

The dates when the Church Epistles were written, according to Lightfoot, *Biblical Essays* (p. 222): —

1 Thess.	A.D. 52	from Corinth.
2 Thess.	A.D. 53	from Corinth.
1 Cor.	A.D. 57	from Ephesus (Spring)
2 Cor.	A.D. 57	from Ephesus (Autumn)
Galations	A.D. 57	from Corinth (Winter or early Spring of 58).
Romans	A.D. 58	from Corinth (Spring)
Philippians	A.D. 62	from prison in Rome after his shipwreck.
Colossians	A.D. 62	(In the Autumn).
Ephesians	A.D. 62	

II.

The dates of the other Pauline Epistles: —

1 Tim.	A.D. 67	from Corinth.
Titus	A.D. 67	from Corinth.
2 Tim.	A.D. 68	from Rome (Spring), last imprisonment.
Hebrews	A.D. 68	Spring.

Martyrdom in the Summer of 68, the 14th year of Nero's reign.

III.
THE ACTS OF THE APOSTLES

may be thus connected with the Epistles, if, against the respective passages, we put the names of the Epistles written at that time and place.

Acts xviii. 1, 2	1 Thess. and 2 Thess.
Acts xix. 1	1 Cor.
Acts xx. 1	2 Cor.
Acts xx. 3	3 Galations and Romans.
Acts xxviii. 16-30	Philemon, Philippians, Collossians, and Ephesians.
at end	1 Tim., Titus, 2 Tim., Hebrews

I. — INDEX OF SUBJECTS

II. — INDEX OF NEW TRANSLATIONS

III. — INDEX OF TEXTS EXPLAINED.

IV.—INDEX OF GREEK WORDS EXPLAINED.

261

COSIMO is a specialty publisher of books and publications that inspire, inform and engage readers. Our mission is to offer unique books to niche audiences around the world.

COSIMO CLASSICS offers a collection of distinctive titles by the great authors and thinkers throughout the ages. At **COSIMO CLASSICS** timeless classics find a new life as affordable books, covering a variety of subjects including: *Biographies, Business, History, Mythology, Personal Development, Philosophy, Religion and Spirituality,* and much more!

COSIMO-on-DEMAND publishes books and publications for innovative authors, non-profit organizations and businesses. **COSIMO-on-DEMAND** specializes in bringing books back into print, publishing new books quickly and effectively, and making these publications available to readers around the world.

COSIMO REPORTS publishes public reports that affect your world: from global trends to the economy, and from health to geo-politics.

FOR MORE INFORMATION CONTACT US AT
INFO@COSIMOBOOKS.COM

❋ If you are a book-lover interested in our current catalog of books.

❋ If you are an author who wants to get published

❋ If you represent an organization or business seeking to reach your members, donors or customers with your own books and publications

COSIMO BOOKS ARE ALWAYS AVAILABLE AT ONLINE BOOKSTORES

———— VISIT COSIMOBOOKS.COM ————
BE INSPIRED, BE INFORMED

Lightning Source UK Ltd.
Milton Keynes UK
UKOW03f1338161014

240194UK00001B/71/P